USING TECHNOLOGY
in Mental Health
Practice

USING TECHNOLOGY
in Mental Health
Practice

EDITED BY
Jeffrey J. Magnavita

AMERICAN PSYCHOLOGICAL ASSOCIATION
Washington, DC

Published by
American Psychological Association
750 First Street, NE
Washington, DC 20002
www.apa.org

APA Order Department
P.O. Box 92984
Washington, DC 20090-2984
Phone: (800) 374-2721; Direct: (202) 336-5510
Fax: (202) 336-5502; TDD/TTY: (202) 336-6123
Online: http://www.apa.org/pubs/books
E-mail: order@apa.org

In the U.K., Europe, Africa, and the Middle East, copies may be ordered from
Eurospan Group
c/o Turpin Distribution
Pegasus Drive
Stratton Business Park
Biggleswade Bedfordshire
SG18 8TQ United Kingdom
Phone: +44 (0) 1767 604972
Fax: +44 (0) 1767 601640
Online: https://www.eurospanbookstore.com/apa
E-mail: eurospan@turpin-distribution.com

Typeset in Meridien by Circle Graphics, Inc., Columbia, MD

Printer: Sheridan Books, Chelsea, MI
Cover Designer: Beth Schlenoff, Bethesda, MD

Library of Congress Cataloging-in-Publication Data

Names: Magnavita, Jeffrey J., editor.
Title: Using technology in mental health practice / edited by Jeffrey J.
  Magnavita.
Description: Washington, DC : American Psychological Association, [2018] |
  Includes bibliographical references and index.
Identifiers: LCCN 2017049012| ISBN 9781433829062 (hardcover) |
  ISBN 1433829061 (hardcover)
Subjects: LCSH: Mental health services—Technical innovations. |
  Communication in medicine—Methodology. | Medical informatics.
Classification: LCC RA790.5 .U85 2018 | DDC 362.20285—dc23 LC record available at
https://lccn.loc.gov/2017049012

British Library Cataloguing-in-Publication Data
A CIP record is available from the British Library.

Printed in the United States of America
First Edition

http://dx.doi.org/10.1037/0000085-000

10 9 8 7 6 5 4 3 2 1

Contents

III

Professional Development   143

Contributors

Allan Abbass, MD, Dalhousie University, Halifax, Nova Scotia, Canada

Jasen Elliott, PhD, Private Practice, Calgary, Alberta, Canada

Devika Fiorillo, PhD, Private Practice, Tysons, VA

Jon Frederickson, MSW, Washington School of Psychiatry, Washington, DC

Richard Gevirtz, PhD, Alliant International University, San Diego, CA

Ed Hamlin, PhD, Institute for Applied Neuroscience, Asheville, NC

Daniel L. Kirsch, PhD, Electromedical Products International Inc., Mineral Wells, TX

Michael J. Lambert, PhD, Brigham Young University, Provo, UT

Paul M. Lehrer, PhD, Robert Wood Johnson Medical School, Piscataway, NJ

Laura Loucks, PhD, Emory University School of Medicine, Atlanta, GA

David D. Luxton, PhD, University of Washington School of Medicine, Seattle

Jeffrey J. Magnavita, PhD, ABPP, Private Practice, Glastonbury, CT

Jeffrey A. Marksberry, MD, Electromedical Products International Inc., Mineral Wells, TX

Tony Rousmaniere, PsyD, Private Practice, Seattle, WA

John M. Santopietro, MD, Silver Hill Hospital, New Canaan, CT

Thomas L. Sexton, PhD, ABPP, Professor Emeritus, Indiana University, Bloomington

Steven A. Sobelman, PhD, Private Practice, Baltimore, MD

Carolyn L. Turvey, PhD, University of Iowa Carver College of Medicine, Iowa City

Marat V. Zanov, PhD, Madigan Army Medical Center, Tacoma, WA

Jeffrey Zimmerman, PhD, Private Practice, Cheshire, NY

Liza C. Zwiebach, PhD, Emory University, Atlanta, GA

Thomas L. Sexton

Foreword

I remember as a graduate student getting my first personal computer. A very big metal box with plastic clips opened to reveal a keyboard, a space-like black screen, and two big slots for 5.4-inch floppy disks (one containing the "program," the other the "data"). When you plugged the device in and switched it on, the screen turned green and displayed small white letters with very odd characters at the end of each line. It connected to e-mail through a dial-up modem that made a scratchy sound as it dinged into its connections. I felt pretty special and "high tech." It was magic. I was intrigued not only by the technology of the machine but also by questions about how this tool might be used in what I was learning every day in school. In fact, my first peer-reviewed professional publication was "Computer Applications in Private Practice,"[1] in which I imagined a world where computers might help psychologists with many of the mundane aspects of the profession (notes, billing, test scoring and interpretation, among others). To me it seemed that if we could get those tasks done more easily, we could spend more time applying our trade—focusing on clients and treatment. At that time, a world in which these tasks could be done automatically was hard to imagine.

In the ensuing decades, the world of psychological practice has changed dramatically. We have more refined and evidence-based treatment models, an expansive scientific foundation of research, and specialty practices with unique perspectives working with the complex problems of individuals, couples, families, and communities. Technology now has an enormous impact on the ways in which we communicate, consume information, and manage our professional lives. The impact of technology now stretches well beyond office and client management to include clinical tasks such as scoring tests, implementing online assessments, and even engaging in "telehealth" as a means of delivering psychological services.

---

[1]Sexton, T. L. (1988). Computer applications in private practice. *Psychotherapy in Private Practice*, 5(4), 27–40.

But it is not the technology itself that is most impressive. In fact, we should not get distracted by the shiny new devices and other "tools" of technology (like my first computer or the newest phone). Technology is advancing and will continue to advance far faster than we will ever be able to keep up with. What we do today with our smartphones will quite quickly seem obsolete in the near future. Instead, it is the innovation in psychological science and practice that comes about as a result of the doors opened by technology that is most important. *Innovation* is defined as the development of solutions that meet new needs, unarticulated needs, or old customer and market needs in new ways. Innovation is not just improving or doing something better—it implies doing something different (Latin *innovare* "to change"). As a result, innovations allow us as a profession to tackle some of the most universal questions we face, such as: What is good research? What is good practice? How can we make it better? How can we extend our work to those in need? Consider the major challenges we can take on with the innovations offered by technology:[2,3]

- Improve clinical research and reduce the research practice gap by providing access to more ecologically valid "data" on how problems and change work within individuals, couples, and/or families. For example, technology makes it possible to easily access the newest research findings on improving communication. It enhances our ability to test and measure new concepts and ideas in practical situations through more comprehensive and less invasive data collection about even the most nuanced elements of our work. Technology allows for community-based research collaboratives, in which practitioners combine data to give a view into a particular type of client, problem, or treatment. Technology allows every clinician to be a local scientist.
- Improve treatment outcomes by enhancing clinical assessment, the application and implementation of clinical practices, and the ongoing measurement of clinical progress. Technology has the potential to increase psychologists' ability to identify, prioritize, and target the most important needs of clients and their relationships. Technology can now assess mood and emotion from machine learning (ML)–and artificial intelligence (AI)–developed algorithms. Technology now makes it possible for every practitioner to examine the effect of treatment session by session, visualize change at the individual and systemic levels, assess how each family member or partner is responding to treatment, and compare their experiences of the family and couple relationships. Clinicians can now study their own outcomes, demonstrate areas in which they have particular strengths or need additional training, and participate in research–practice collectives that bundle their data to provide insight into broader trends of practice.

---

[2]Sexton, T. L., & Fisher, A. R. (2016). Integrating ongoing measurement into the clinical decision-making process with measurement feedback systems. In J. J. Magnavita (Ed.), *Clinical decision making in mental health practice*. Washington, DC: American Psychological Association.

[3]Sexton, T. L., Patterson, T., & Datchi, C. D. (2012). Technological innovations of systematic measurement and clinical feedback: A virtual leap into the future of couple and family psychology. *Couple and Family Psychology: Research and Practice, 1,* 285–293. http://dx.doi.org/10.1037/cfp0000001

▪ Improve the reach and access of mental health treatments. Telehealth and other video conferencing tools bring new avenues for the delivery of treatment. Improved reach through technology means more people may be impacted by the profession's research and knowledge. Improved access allows us to open doors to treatment that have never been opened before.

With all innovation come ethical and professional questions. That is the nature of a developing and evolving field. Yet, as noted in this volume, we need to remain vigilant to the limits of confidentiality, privacy, and communication in this digital age. We need to stay aware of the limits we know and the limits we have yet to even see.

In this volume, Jeffrey J. Magnavita has amassed an impressive list of authors who are using technology in different ways, across diverse areas of psychological practice. The chapters illustrate the ways in which technology is now taking the qualitative experiences of clients and putting them into a digital form. In each case, the chapters illustrate how digital technology can help any aspect of psychological practice by facilitating data analysis, synthesizing assessment, and increasing accessibility. In each chapter, we see how technology enables psychologists in everyday practice to make better assessments and interventions, and to more comprehensively evaluate their practice.

Innovation can be complex. On one hand, it opens doors to areas we have never even imagined. I never could have imagined where technology was headed when I published what I thought was a comprehensive view on technology in private practice.[4] On the other hand, the innovations presented in this volume also challenge us all. The opened doors mean new ways of thinking and new ways of working. Just like our clients, this step can be a difficult one. The question is much like that faced by our clients—will we take the step and embrace something new?

---

[4]Sexton, T. L. (1988). Computer applications in private practice. *Psychotherapy in Private Practice, 5*(4), 27–40.

Preface

It seems that every day there is a new announcement about technology—breakthroughs such as deciphering the human genome, having monkeys use their thoughts to manipulate the limbs of avatar images, and advances in artificial intelligence allowing machines to speak like humans. The technologies are breathtaking in their novelty, power, scope, and ability to advance humanity. At the same time, inventions like the Amazon Echo, which "listens" to aggregate users' personal data for more efficient performance as a virtual assistant,[1] help to illustrate the dark side of technology. While such devices have myriad positive applications, they can potentially be misused. Unwanted surveillance makes our information vulnerable to identity theft and other disruptions that affect our institutions and us as individuals.

During my more than 3 decades of mental and behavioral health practice, there have been dramatic advancements in the technological applications available to clinicians. My own journey as a psychologist, author, teacher, theorist, and psychotherapist has been made possible and immensely more efficient by the use of technology. Writing books, for example, was an onerous task before the development of word processing and the Internet. When I first started my writing career, I spent endless hours in libraries searching for the sources I needed. Now, thanks to digitization of content, institutional site licenses for journal subscriptions, and search algorithms, I am able to access all the scholarly resources from my laptop from just about anywhere in the world. I am also able to communicate with other researchers and scholars from around the world in real-time. I have enjoyed rich collaborations with many innovators across the country and around the world. I have been able to expand my reach internationally using teleconferencing. I have been able to receive and offer supervision using online video services. I have also been able to attend educational events virtually, when it was not possible to attend in person. Listservs—although they may seem creaky next to the newer live networking interfaces—have provided me with professional communities to counter

---

[1]O'Brien, A. (2017, January 16). Ask Alexa? No, hear this Alexa. *The New York Times*, p. A21.

the isolation of clinical practice. Administrative software programs for booking, record keeping, billing, and clinical communications have increased the efficiency of my clinical practice, allowing me to devote more time to writing and teaching. Along with these diverse activities, I have been able to serve in leadership capacities in professional organizations and serve as a consultant for a number of mental and behavioral health technology startup ventures. Technology has made all of this possible and continues to expand my professional opportunities, creating and developing new mental health ventures. More recently, I launched a new company called Strategic Psychotherapeutics, with the aim of optimizing behavioral and mental health care combining science, expertise, and technology, to enhance practitioners' efficacy via online learning and consultation.

When I ran for president of the American Psychological Association in 2015, one campaign item that I was interested in launching was to develop *psych-incubators*,[2] where new ideas about potential startup companies using psychological science and psychotherapeutics could be presented and nourished. It remains a hope of mine that like-minded mental health professionals will partner with investors and those with business experience to develop incubators, where new innovative ideas that can solve the challenges of our field and serve as vital and profitable ventures can be hatched and given legs. The mental health system needs innovation and disruptive new developments that capitalize on advances in technology and clinical science, altering the way we operate.

According to Canton,[3] "the sheer velocity of change offers a mixed bag of opportunity and risk" (p. 2). In his book *Future Smart*, he wrote, "Digital health smartphone apps are sensing, watching, monitoring, and analyzing our personal health status and will eventually become predictive, able to forecast our health, with accuracy" (p. xii). I find such developments exciting, and I hope that you share in my eagerness to try out new tech tools as adjuncts to our professional services, or at the very least, to make us more efficient in our work. Unfortunately, not everyone feels this way. Change is not easy. What is familiar to us is comfortable and feels secure, but the disruptive nature of change is unavoidable. Rather than fearing that our work will be subsumed by technology, we need to be adaptive and open to new ways of providing care. Our work is still relevant. The future of behavioral and mental health care will be a synthesis of technology, consumer-oriented services, and access to the best evidence. This volume has afforded me the opportunity to glimpse what the future holds. It has been my pleasure to bring together many leading innovators in technology and mental health. I hope that you enjoy reading and learning about these topics as much as I did while serving as editor for this cutting-edge group of contributors.

---

[2]Magnavita, J. J. (2016). Psych-incubator. *Journal of Unified Psychotherapy and Clinical Science, 4*, 85–87.
[3]Canton, J. (2015). *Future smart: Managing the game-changing trends that will transform the world*. Boston, MA: Da Capo Press.

USING TECHNOLOGY

in Mental Health
Practice

Jeffrey J. Magnavita

Introduction
How Can Technology Advance Mental Health Treatment?

This volume presents some of the exciting new developments and evolving technologies in the field of mental and behavioral health. Specifically, my coauthors and I discuss ways that technology fosters (a) better access to care and a higher degree of patient-centered care; (b) development of improved treatments, including alternatives and helpful adjuncts to pharmacological treatments and psychotherapy; and (c) development of our abilities as professionals, in terms of refining the quality of our work and extending our leadership from research and practice into business and innovation. Our purpose is to help readers use technology to advance these goals in their professional psychology practice.

How Can Technology Move Mental Health Forward?

We are in a revolutionary time, with change driven in large part by technology. Opportunities now exist to address important issues in health care as aided by these developments (National Institute of Mental Health, 2016). One looming challenge facing psychology professionals is to provide mental

http://dx.doi.org/10.1037/0000085-001
Using Technology in Mental Health Practice, J. J. Magnavita (Editor)

health services to those in need who do not have access to care; there is a huge gap between the need for mental health services and their availability (Rabbitt, Kazdin, & Scassellati, 2015). For example, it is estimated that approximately 70% of those suffering from adult depression who need services will not receive them (Olfson, Blanco, & Marcus, 2016). This presents a major public health challenge, one that requires innovation, for which technology is essential.

One answer to the problem of access is *telehealth*—also known in our field as *telepsychotherapy, telepsychology*, and *telemental health*. The Agency for Healthcare Research and Quality and the National Institute of Mental Health (Mohr, Burns, Schueller, Clarke, & Kinkman, 2013) initiated a review of mental health behavioral intervention technologies by an expert panel. Their conclusion was that "videoconferencing and standard telephone technologies to deliver psychotherapy have been well validated. Web-based interventions have shown efficacy across a broad range of mental health outcomes" (Mohr et al., 2013, p. 1). Video technology has become so inexpensive that it is now included in most computers. This is providing options, not only for telehealth but also for remote supervision that brings expert consultants directly into our offices.

Rapid advancements are also taking place in the development of sensors and devices used to measure biometric data. Embedded in a smartwatch or other wearable device, biosensors can measure heart rate, posture, stress data, blood alcohol level, and activity level. If you wear the device to bed you can also monitor sleep patterns. All these data can be fed into smartphone apps. Using an app in conjunction with your smartphone's built-in audio input, you can also analyze mood from voice tone and word patterns (Kraft, 2017).

Apps for secure communication and other types of data exchange are also on the rise. Electronic health record apps connect patients to doctors, monitor drug distributions, and in many ways increase the reach of health clinics. Innovators of all kinds—startups, nonprofits, scientist–clinicians acting as consultants—are tackling a huge array of problems with technology-first solutions (Schmidt & Cohen, 2013).

Hand-in-hand with apps, other treatment technologies are emerging as alternatives and as adjuncts to traditional treatments such as pharmaceuticals and psychotherapy. Their increased affordability enhances their potential to move clinical research forward. Treatment technologies include virtual reality, biofeedback devices, neurofeedback devices, transcranial magnetic stimulation, electrocranial therapy, and others. These devices can also be used to assess and monitor the biological and emotional components of various states.

While it has been slower on the uptake than medicine, the field of behavioral and mental health is now fully entering the world of technology-enhanced services. Moreover, these advances and trends are being embraced and expected by the public. A recent article in *Forbes* reported that "emerging trends in recent years have the potential to completely change the health care environment for those struggling with mental health conditions" (Utley, 2016, p.1). *Forbes* editors selected four technologies for investors and consumers to watch: a mobile app (Pacifica) for anxiety; a mobile app (WEconnect) for addictions that track mind, body, and spiritual activity levels and keep the person connected to support systems; a wearable device (Spire) that monitors physiological states and can detect emotions, triggering a notification that is sent to your phone when you need to improve your mood; and a neurostimulation device (Fisher Wallace Stimulator) that stimulates the brain to release dopamine and serotonin and is thus useful for improving mood. These advances in technology are offering the field of mental health abundant entrepreneurial opportunities for those who embrace these changes, enjoy innovation, and want to find new ways to resolve the challenges facing the field.

Clinical decision making is fundamental for effective clinical practice and requires access to high-quality information (Magnavita, 2016). Technology allows access to the most up-to-date information instantly. In a previous publication, *Clinical Decision Making in Mental Health Practice*, the authors highlighted the importance of understanding how bias in decision making can be reduced using technology. Decision making requires expertise, high-quality information, and analytics: how to weigh factors and predict probabilities in an unbiased fashion. Technology provides many aids to improve and enhance the process of informed clinical decision making. Caspar, Berger, and Frei (2016) discussed various aids to clinical decision making, including (a) knowledge databases, (b) Internet-accessible information on mental health problems and treatments, (c) web-based platforms providing psychoeducation about treatment options, (d) computer-assisted and Internet-based questionnaires and tests, (e) assessment of biological states, (f) feedback systems, (g) videorecordings of patients for supervision and peer consulting, (h) actuarial/statistical decision making using algorithms, (i) use of videoconferencing among clinicians, and (j) webinars capitalizing on the wisdom of specialists (pp. 149–157). Many of these methods are being improved as we accumulate more health-related information in large data sets called "big data." In this volume, we examine patient feedback systems as one mechanism for improving clinical decision making. These are systems that are designed to gather patients' views about how treatment is going, feedback that providers can use to improve treatment and, hopefully, improve outcomes.

Audience for This Book

This book is largely for mental health practitioners who already use technology for personal or professional purposes. Most chapters forge into the *why* and *how* without spending too much time on the *what*; the authors assume readers are familiar with certain terminology, such as hardware, software, operating system, Internet, browser, search engine, cloud storage, network, app, webinar, video calling, media streaming, e-mail, text, and encryption.

Our target audience includes scholars and practitioners who wish to become entrepreneurs. This could mean starting a company; it might also include partnering as a business collaborator or advisor to other entrepreneurs whose product or service impacts mental and behavioral health care in some way. Psychology is behind the curve in generating the interdisciplinary collaborations and business enterprises (e.g., startup companies) that we see in other scientific disciplines. The field of psychology can start to catch up by marrying technology, psychological science, and business. As already noted, there are many innovative developments that are shaping the nature and scope of mental health practice. Kraft (2017) referred to the shift this way:

> [We are moving] from the "Quantified Self" era, where the data has generally remained siloed on the devices and apps of the individual and not integrated into clinical care, to the emergence of "Quantified Health," where the data from common consumers' wearables, scales, BP cuffs, glucometers and even home lab data, will flow through consumer's smart phones . . . into the electronic medical records . . . (EMRs) of the clinician. (p. 46)

These emerging areas offer interesting opportunities for those with entrepreneurial drive, whether they work inside or outside the support structures of major research institutions.

Having said this, we think there is much here for both digital natives and digital immigrants. Prensky (2001) distinguished between digital natives and digital immigrants, noting that the immigrants learn to adapt to their environments, while to some degree retaining a "foot in the past" or having an "accent" (p. 2). A type of socialization has to occur among those of us who didn't grow up with digital technology. Becoming familiar with technology is like learning a new language. By contrast, the digital natives "are used to receiving information really fast, often in relatively short bytes. . . . They like parallel process and multi-tasking," and further, their brains may actually be different in structure than the brains of digital immigrants (Prensky, 2001, p. 2). Most of those born after the year 2000 are fundamentally different from those born before, in that they grew up with technology and were almost always digitally connected. While it is more difficult for the digital immigrants to assimilate new approaches, they often find it gratifying to master new technologies and experience how they can improve and enhance professional functions once a basic level of proficiency is achieved.

There are many versions of what a technology-based or technology-assisted practice might look like. In this book, we do not take the stance that all practitioners should incorporate all or even most of the technologies described herein. Instead, we expect that readers already conduct periodic needs assessments to help them determine the changes to their practice that will best align with their goals. For example, in the coming year, do you want to focus on increasing administrative efficiency? Will doing so allow you to spend more time examining your treatment decisions? Might that, in turn, optimize patient outcomes? Readers who will get the most out of this book are those who have a realistic view of what their practice needs to thrive and/or expand. They also have the capacity to purchase new tools, train users, and take concrete steps to ensure protection of clients' personal health information.

Organization of This Volume

In Chapter 1, Steven A. Sobelman and John M. Santopietro review the HIPAA and HITECH laws, ethical principles and enforceable ethics standards, and practice guidelines that are essential to successfully incorporating and managing the technologies available.

Chapters 2 and 3 cover technologies whose main benefit is increasing access to mental health care. Comer and Barlow (2014) proposed that specialty care in mental health could be efficiently delivered using video technology, so that those in underserved areas could have access to high-quality care. And, in fact, as Carolyn L. Turvey demonstrates in Chapter 2, the telemental health movement is well underway, although it is not without pitfalls. In her chapter, Turvey emphasizes client safety and confidentiality in situations where the clinician is treating a client at a remote location, such as the client's home, where there is no staff member to manage either logistics or the care-receiving environment.

Chapter 3, by David D. Luxton, introduces several classes of apps that are designed to complement or in other ways integrate with traditional mental health care. According to the National Institute of Mental Health (2016): "Mobile devices like cell phones, smartphones, and tablets are giving the public, doctors, and researchers new ways to access help, monitor progress, and increase understanding of mental wellbeing" (p. 1). Luxton's chapter illustrates these and other functions of apps, highlighting throughout their value for enhancing access, affordability, and client-centered care.

Chapters 4 through 7 focus on specific technology-based treatments. The cost of purchasing most technological products declines as time passes. For example, when I first started a group practice over 3 decades ago, neurofeedback equipment cost thousands of dollars—out of reach for most practitioners. Yet today, as you will read, many therapeutic devices are proving to be a valuable, inexpensive resource for practitioners to use with those patients suffering from trauma and anxiety disorders, where retraining brain states is beneficial. In Chapter 4, Liza C. Zwiebach, Laura Loucks, Devika Fiorillo, and Marat V. Zanov show how virtual reality therapy can be used in outpatient and inpatient settings to enhance treatment response by controlling exposure to traumatic events in a realistic format.

In Chapter 5, Jeffrey A. Marksberry and Daniel L. Kirsch present a noninvasive approach for using electrical stimulation to the brain to alter brain states. This technology is widely applicable to many settings and has a fairly short learning curve for the interested clinician. Many patients purchase or rent home-use versions of these devices and find them quite useful to down-regulate anxiety between sessions.

In Chapter 6, Ed Hamlin informs us how neurofeedback evolved and how it is proving to be a valuable resource for those interested in teaching patients how to alter their brain states, which has important implications for a variety of clinical syndromes seen in clinical settings. Portable EEG devices, which have become very inexpensive, are now being used in a variety of ways to enhance and augment psychological treatment.

In Chapter 7, Paul M. Lehrer and Richard Gevirtz provide a concise overview of heart rate variability (HRV) biofeedback for those interested in understanding its benefits or incorporating it into clinical practice. As other iterations of biofeedback, HRV "is mainly used as an intervention in which the effective factor is information a patient receives about physiological states that can otherwise not be validly monitored by the patient him- or herself" (Caspar, Berger, & Frei, 2016, p. 152). This general approach has been criticized by some as being reverse logic. In short, the criticism goes, just because one's brain generates a certain type of activity or frequency wave while the person is in a desired state (e.g., a calm or focused state) does not necessarily mean that training oneself to produce the targeted brain activity translates into an ability to attain the desired mental state. The approach toward biofeedback we take in this volume is two-fold: (a) we share the evidence base supporting the clinical use of biofeedback, and (b) we encourage practitioners to explore its possibilities. Now that the technology is affordable, it makes sense to continue testing and validating it to further uncover the relationships between body and mind.

Chapters 8 through 11 move into applications of technology for professional development. In Chapter 8, Michael J. Lambert, one of the pioneers in the area of patient feedback systems, describes how collecting and interpreting data with such systems can lead to better outcomes by keeping practitioners informed of the progress that is being made and allowing us to address threats to treatment.

Chapter 9, by Jasen Elliott, Allan Abbass, and Tony Rousmaniere, shows how using video technology can enhance an iterative process of deliberate practice as we strive to become more effective therapists. In Chapter 10, Jon Frederickson and Tony Rousmaniere show us how to use technology to advance your training, often without having to leave your office.

In Chapter 11, Steven A. Sobelman and I explore the topic of how technology creates new possibilities for entrepreneurship, offering a vehicle for innovation in mental health and opportunities for new business ventures to solve the problems the field faces. Understanding entrepreneurship and the potential benefit of marrying technology, psychological science, and psychotherapeutics can provide alternative career options for innovators.

And in the final chapter, Jeffrey Zimmerman and I present a thought process practitioners can use when developing or expanding the scope of their practice via technology.

I use or have used most of the technological advances presented in this volume. While there are additional advances that might have been included in this volume, I chose those that I, and many of my colleagues, have found to be most beneficial and relatively inexpensive. The chapter authors and I hope that by the time you finish reading this book, we will have helped you answer most, if not all, of the following questions:

- How can I ensure that my practice's technology use is HIPAA-compliant?
- How do I evaluate the technology available to me for fit with my goals, current skills, and practice culture?
- How can technology help me refine the treatments I deliver for better patient outcomes?
- How can I use technology to expand my practice offerings?
- How can I use technology to share my knowledge with others?
- How can I leverage my research and/or practice experience to create useful products?
- How can I ensure that sound psychological science is guiding the development of new technology being developed to serve the mental and behavioral health sector?

Behavioral and mental health care is beginning to experience an explosion in technology-based trends. This technological revolution is radically altering the delivery of health care. By 2020, it is predicted that most of heath care will experience a digitalization and be predictive and preventive, based on real time data from wearable devices and biosensors, and the deciphering of big data from electronic medical records and other sources (Deloitte LLP, 2014). New products are being introduced with promises to improve mental health and many more opportunities for development and innovation will be possible. New business enterprises to meet the needs of this expanding technology-based era will be available for those who have entrepreneurial interest and skills.

With these rapid developments in technology and the provision of mental health care, there will be a need for ethical guidelines that are responsive to this changing terrain. In the next chapter, we will look at the laws, ethics codes, practice standards, and clinical guidelines you will need to understand as you implement or refine your professional use of technology.

References

Caspar, F., Berger, T., & Frei, L. (2016). Using technology to enhance decision making. In J. J. Magnavita (Ed.), *Clinical decision making in mental health practice* (pp. 147–174). Washington, DC: American Psychological Association. http://dx.doi.org/10.1037/14711-006

Comer, J. S., & Barlow, D. H. (2014). The occasional case against broad dissemination and implementation: Retaining a role for specialty care in the delivery of psychological treatments. *American Psychologist, 69*, 1–18. http://dx.doi.org/10.1037/a0033582

Deloitte LLP. (2014). *Healthcare and life sciences predictions 2020: A bold future?* London, England: Deloitte Centre for Health Solutions.

Kraft, D. (2017, March). Quantified self to quantified health: How tech helps doctors fill gaps in patient records. *Wired.* Retrieved from http://www.wired.co.uk/article/hospital-prescribing-tech

Magnavita, J. J. (Ed.). (2016). *Clinical decision making in mental health practice.* Washington, DC: American Psychological Association. http://dx.doi.org/10.1037/14711-000

Mohr, D. C., Burns, M. N., Schueller, S. M., Clarke, G., & Kinkman, M. (2013). Behavioral intervention technologies: Evidence review and recommendations for future research in mental health. *General Hospital Psychiatry, 35*, 332–338. Retrieved from https://www.ncbi.nlm.nih.gov/pubmed/23664503

National Institute of Mental Health. (2016). *Technology and the future of mental health treatment.* Retrieved from https://www.nimh.nih.gov/health/topics/technology-and-the-future-of-mental-health-treatment/index.shtml

Olfson, M., Blanco, C., & Marcus, S. C. (2016). Treatment of adult depression in the United States. *JAMA Internal Medicine, 176*, 1482–1491. http://dx.doi.org/10.1001/jamainternmed.2016.5057

Prensky, M. (2001). Digital natives, digital immigrants Part 1. *On the Horizon, 9*(5), 1–6. https://dx.doi.org/10.1108/10748120110424816

Rabbitt, S. M., Kazdin, A. E., & Scassellati, B. (2015). Integrating socially assistive robotics into mental healthcare interventions: Applications and recommendations for expanded use. *Clinical Psychology Review, 35*, 35–46. http://dx.doi.org/10.1016/j.cpr.2014.07.001

Schmidt, E., & Cohen, J. (2013). *The new digital age: Reshaping the future of people, nations and business.* New York, NY: Alfred A. Knopf.

Utley, T. (2016, January 25). 4 technologies innovating mental health in 2016. *Forbes.* Retrieved from http://www.forbes.com/sites/toriutley/2016/01/25/4-technologies-innovating-mental-health-in-2016/#1935d0d6bb3c

EXPANDING ACCESS TO CARE

Steven A. Sobelman and John M. Santopietro

Managing Risk
Aligning Technology Use With the Law, Ethics Codes, and Practice Standards

1

isk management may be derived from law, professional standards and the individual institution's mission, and public relations strategies and is expressed through institutional policies and practices (Brock & Mastroianni, 2013). When it comes to running a technologically and ethically sound practice, psychologists, psychiatrists and other mental health professionals must do some homework. They must have an up-to-date understanding of (a) statutes such as the Health Insurance Portability and Accountability Act of 1996 (HIPAA); (b) codes of ethics and professional guidelines that define the clinical standard of care, as well as how to manage risk; and (c) the specific vulnerabilities associated with all types of eHealth technology used in the practice, from record-keeping to technology-assisted interventions. This chapter provides an overview of some of the fundamental issues to consider when incorporating technology into a mental health practice. Some specific legal issues, such as licensing in multiple jurisdictions, are discussed in Chapter 2, which also contains illustrations of how to maintain privacy and a safe environment in the clinic.

http://dx.doi.org/10.1037/0000085-002
Using Technology in Mental Health Practice, J. J. Magnavita (Editor)

The Challenge of Ethical Practice in the Information Age

Many mental health professionals, especially those trained before the millennium, have often had a head-in-the-sand response to technology, either avoidance or a tendency to accept only minimal responsibility for the risks associated with technology use. Although paper records and simple security measures (e.g., locked file cabinets) may work for some, there is a steady march toward more inclusion of technology in our work. For those who have ventured into such advances, the accompanying security risks and concerns are ever more complex. We know that increased use of information technologies has created risks to the privacy of individuals (Drummond, Cromarty, & Battersby, 2015). This also applies to the privacy of patients in a mental health care setting. While it's true that new technologies are always emerging and new vulnerabilities are always being created—and that specific references in this chapter will likely be dated within a year of publication—the approach we recommend to "stay current" provides a steady frame to address a constantly changing ethical and regulatory landscape.

FALSE SENSE OF SECURITY

It is easy to get lulled into a false sense of security when it comes to using electronic devices or the Internet for your practice. As software interfaces become better designed and more intuitive, what used to be a steep learning curve has flattened out. Faster Internet speeds and broader bandwidth allow us to effortlessly upload video, eligibility requests, et cetera to the cloud, where data can live until we call it up. Our computers don't "blue screen" often, like they did decades ago; wireless connections work fine most of the time. Thus, we are lulled into thinking that hacks will happen to others and not to us. Some other poor therapist or health system will have to notify the government about the breach affecting their patients' Protected Health Information (PHI; United States Department of Health and Human Services, 2013), but we are covered. After all, we had our IT pro install antivirus software when she set up our new system 5 years ago. All we have to do is set it up and forget it, right? Wrong!

Mental health practitioners are increasingly using electronic means for communicating, recording, and storing data. Data breaches should be of concern to all practitioners, especially mental health clinicians who deal with highly confidential and potentially very damaging information. Many health providers, including those who specialize in mental health, keep patient e-mails and text messages, contact information, billing records, and schedules in an environment that is rife for hacking ("Largest Healthcare Data Breaches of 2016," 2017).

Are you guilty of this too? Before we get to specifics of the law, ethics, and practice standards, let's spend a few minutes going over three basic types of security measures that all professional therapists need to put in place for their practice and monitor on a regular schedule. In information security these are known as *physical*, *administrative,* and *technical* controls. Within each category there are also preventive, detective, and corrective methods of control.

Physical Controls

Physical security controls are the most basic of security systems and include the locked file cabinet example above. They are what we use to control availability and physical access to sensitive information, ensuring that

> unauthorized persons are excluded from physical spaces and assets where their presence represents a potential threat. All types of computers, computing devices and associated communications facilities must be considered as sensitive assets and spaces and be protected accordingly. Examples of physical security controls are physical access systems including guards and receptionists, door access controls, restricted areas, closed-circuit television (CCTV), automatic door controls and human traps, physical intrusion detection systems, and physical protection systems. Administrative and technical controls depend on proper physical security controls being in place. (Yau, 2013)

Although it is not likely that the costs of extreme measures such as "human traps" would outweigh the benefits at a typical mental health private practice, many of the other controls listed above are just good common sense.

Administrative Controls

Administrative controls are the practices and procedures around all work that is performed in an office or virtual environment. Some examples include having clear operating hours and after-hours response systems in place for service continuity, an ongoing training and education schedule for all employees, and basic "good housekeeping" such as having clear sign-on procedures, backing up data on a nightly basis, and keeping equipment in working order. Phones should be password protected and any patient names stored in the device's built-in system should be limited (e.g., to first names and a last-name initial). Examples also include having emergency management plans in place, and screening and alert systems that trigger further assessment (e.g., for suicide risk) or reporting (e.g., mandatory reporting of suspected abuse). Administrative controls additionally spell out expectations for all employees regarding the maintenance of their own health and their daily preparedness to work in a patient care environment. Finally, "administrative controls are the process of developing and ensuring compliance with policy and procedures. They tend to be things that employees may do, or must always do, or cannot do" (Northcutt, 2013, para. 3).

For the most part, administrative controls are intended to limit the effects of human error on ethical practice. Human error represents the most likely cause of data breaches and computer virus propagation. Many of us have heard stories of laptops or USB drives with sensitive data being lost or stolen. Sending a fax or an e-mail to the wrong address, clicking on a phishing link, and other mistakes can lead to data breaches, with potentially harmful results. Avoiding these types of errors requires education and awareness about the potential mistakes that can be made with various devices and software. To minimize mistakes, you might, for example, implement a system for error interception, such as a buffering system so that there is a delay before information is sent. When an employee is terminated, there should be a clear list of steps that are routinely followed: "disable their account, change the server password, and so forth" (Dulaney, 2014, para. 10). All communications should include a statement of the communication's confidential nature and limits of privacy, which should discourage data breaches that might occur due to a patient's failure to use secure channels. Although some errors cannot be corrected, practitioners still have an obligation to track them to see where there may be faults in the system that need correction.

Technical Controls

Technical controls are those controls implemented through technology, such as firewalls, intrusion detection and prevention systems (e.g., antivirus, antimalware programs), and encryption. These are the controls that protect Social Security numbers and credit card data. They also protect computer systems from spyware, which allows hackers to access personal information covertly online. In case of device theft, remote wiping technology can be employed to delete sensitive information and/or disable the device altogether. The best security against malicious acts is to employ device encryption, as well as end-to-end encryption for e-mails and messaging systems. One should also carefully evaluate services that help ensure HIPAA compliance when considering apps, videoconferencing services, and cloud storage.

Mining data for patterns is a potential source for a data breach. The Federal Trade Commission (2012) noted that "consumers face a landscape of virtually ubiquitous collection of their data. Whether such collection occurs online or offline does not alter the consumer's privacy interest in her or her data" (p. 18). Summary data can be extracted and inferences made without our knowledge. The Winston Law Firm website http://www.stopdatamining.me reminds us that "collecting, analyzing and selling every aspect of your life for marketing purposes is perfectly legal. Indeed, it's worth billions of dollars of business. Data brokers acquire and rate trillions of transactions per day and their databases contain updated information" on every market transaction that takes place nationwide. Mental health providers should know that

> it is therefore relatively easy for those with access to metadata to infer that a private citizen who has regular contact (data) with the professional e-mail address of a mental health professional may be in therapy for some form of mental health issue. (Drummond et al., 2015, p. 231)

To prevent mining of confidential data, we recommend the judicious use of standalone (i.e., non-Internet connected) systems where feasible. To minimize the effects of data mining online, consider using browser extensions that block data tracking cookies and actively opting out of data broker and direct marketing activities.

HEALTH INSURANCE PORTABILITY AND ACCOUNTABILITY ACT OF 1996 (HIPAA)

Now that we've covered some basics, we can go into more depth about why issues of confidentiality around patient information are a critical aspect to consider in this new technological era. The first reason is simple: It's the law. HIPAA has become a fixture both in parlance and practice throughout health care and has been at times confusing and misunderstood. The United States legislation that provides data privacy and security provisions for safeguarding medical information, both the HIPAA Privacy Rule and Security Rules are triggered when a health care provider (or an entity such as a billing service acting on behalf of the health care provider) transmits health information in electronic form about any designated standard transactions. The American Psychological Association (APA; 2013) in a publication designed to address HIPAA concerns states,

> for most mental health and health practitioners, triggering the need to comply with HIPAA and the Privacy Rule occurs when they do all the following: Electronically transmit Protected Health Information (PHI) in connection with insurance claims or other third-party reimbursement. (p. 2)

This APA publication continues:

> the most common form of electronic transmission for practitioners is via the Internet (for example, sending e-mail to a patient or an insurance carrier or making transactions on an insurance company website). Electronic transmission also includes transmitting electronic information: to cloud storage, from a mobile device, such as a smart phone or tablet, via Wi-Fi networks and flash drives, as well as via websites where patients submit PHI. (p. 3)

It is important to note that PHI includes any past, present, and future information that is generated or received by a health care provider, an employer, a school, a life insurance policy, or a health insurance company.

The HIPAA Privacy Rule ensures that all covered entities keep patients' PHI secure and properly educate their patients about their rights under HIPAA. Proper education involves providing patients with a written statement that describes how health care providers and other covered entities can use or share their PHI. This should be included in the initial consultation both verbally and in a written format. The HIPAA Security Rule details the steps health care providers must take to keep patients' electronic PHI secure. Providers are required to continually assess the security of their electronic health record systems and then put specific physical, administrative, and technical safeguards in place (as described above) to protect against the risks that were revealed during the assessment.

It is very important to note that

> the Privacy Rule specifically does not preempt a narrow range of state laws, such as laws giving or denying parents access to their children's records, regardless of how stringent they are. The result of the complicated preemption analysis is that the law you must follow is a mixture of Privacy Rule and state privacy law provisions. (APA, 2013, p. 4)

As HIPAA became more engrained in the everyday practices of health care providers, in 2009 the U.S. Congress passed the Health Information Technology for Economic and Clinical Health (HITECH) Act. With the initiation of HITECH, regulations and guidelines were enacted and directed toward protecting PHI in the digital age. This act was the start of "a major shift in the enforcement strategy of the Office of the National Coordinator for Health Information Technology (ONC). Because of the HITECH Act, non-compliance resulted in financial and professional standing losses for businesses" ("What is Protected Health Information?", 2017, para. 12).

> In January, 2013, the HITECH-HIPAA final rule was announced, which implemented all the HIPAA modifications mentioned in the HITECH Act. One notable change was the direct application of HIPAA to business associates, which were previously governed by their contract with a covered entity. However, after the modifications from the HITECH Act, business associates became subject to HIPAA sanctions as well as enforcement. ("What is Protected Health Information?", 2017, para. 13)

Business associates are entities that extend a practitioner's ability to use patient data in an efficient way. They may perform a variety of functions, such as processing or administration, data analysis, utilization review, quality assurance, billing, benefit management, practice management, and repricing. Business associate services include legal, actuarial, accounting, consulting, data aggregation, management, administrative, accreditation, and financial services. Examples of business associates can be found online (https://www.hhs.gov/hipaa/for-professionals/privacy/guidance/business-associates/index.html). As of 2013, it was business associates that caused more than 20% of all security breaches reported to the HHS; such breaches affect approximately 12 million patients each year (Solove, 2013).

Numerous resources are available from the APA Practice Organization (http://www.apapractice.org; and http://www.apapracticecentral.org/business/hipaa/hippa-privacy-primer.pdf, which offers more specifics on HITECH-HIPAA).

Professional Ethics Codes

Although professional organizations have always provided guidance and guidelines on technology, change is so rapid that it becomes a challenge for them to keep the guidelines current. Thus, part of the burden of risk management falls to ethical decision making on the part of practitioners, extending to the training they provide their staff (Sobelman & Younggren, 2016). Unfortunately, simply using new technologies can sometimes expose underlying vulnerabilities or misuses, such that a new guideline is required; however, the goal thus far has been to write guidelines more broadly and in such a way as to enable them to be applied to multiple, even unforeseen, circumstances. The APA's *Ethical Principles of Psychologists and Code of Conduct* (2017; hereinafter, APA Ethics Code) states the following:

4.01 Maintaining Confidentiality

Psychologists have a primary obligation and take reasonable precautions to protect confidential information obtained through or stored in any medium, recognizing that the extent and limits of confidentiality may be regulated by law or established by institutional rules or professional or scientific relationship.

4.02c Discussing the Limits of Confidentiality

Psychologists who offer services, products or information via electronic transmission inform clients/patients of the risks to privacy and limits of confidentiality.

The more recent *APA Guidelines for the Practice of Telepsychology* (American Psychological Association, Joint Task Force for the Development of Telepsychology Guidelines for Psychologists, 2013) recommend that psychologists become knowledgeable and competent "in the use of the telecommunication technologies being utilized" and make sure that client/patients are made aware of the "increased risks to loss of security and confidentiality when using telecommunication technologies" (pp. 791–799).

Sometimes ethical guidelines can even sound like an alert and strike a cautionary tone, as in the following from the American Psychiatric Association (2013): "Growing concern regarding the civil rights of patients and the possible adverse effects of computerization, duplication equipment, and data banks makes the dissemination of confidential information an increasing hazard" (p. 6). Additionally, the American Psychiatric Association (2016) recently warned that "the advent and expansion of the use of electronic medical records and the increasing use of care coordinators and integration of medical care present challenges to traditional notions of patient confidentiality" (p. 4). An abundance of caution is appropriate, given the weight of the U.S. Health and Human Services mission to "ensure that people have equal access and opportunities to participate in certain health care and human services programs without unlawful discrimination" (see https://www.hhs.gov/ocr/).

In other words, it is incumbent upon us as practitioners to understand that we are responsible for the security and confidentiality of our client and patient records, no matter what method or technology we use. Compliance with the law and with the enforceable ethics codes of our professional associations resides with us, and we cannot pass the buck to office managers or our IT support staff. It is we who must inform our patients of the limitations. A thorough informed consent process, including documentation thereof, should be a standard part of practice. Specific risks spelled out in informed consent forms may include e-mail and text messaging risks.

In the APA Ethics Code, the General Principles, as opposed to Ethical Standards, are *aspirational* in nature. As noted in the text,

> Their intent is to guide and inspire psychologists toward the very highest ethical ideals of the profession. General Principles, in contrast to Ethical Standards, do not represent obligations and should not form the basis for imposing sanctions. Relying upon General Principles for either of these reasons distorts both their meaning and purpose.

The APA Ethics Code Task Force attempted to address a possible conflict between law and ethics by allowing psychologists to adhere to a legal obligation in the face of a competing ethical obligation, by stating the following:

> 1.02 Conflicts Between Ethics and Law, Regulations, or Other Governing Legal Authority
>
> If psychologists' ethical responsibilities conflict with law, regulations, or other governing legal authority, psychologists clarify the nature of the conflict, make known their commitment to the Ethics Code and take reasonable steps to resolve the conflict consistent with the General Principles and Ethical Standards of the Ethics Code. Under no circumstances may this standard be used to justify or defend violating human rights.

In the next section, we offer a technology-infused mental health care scenario that presents various low-level and higher level risk management challenges. As you read, reflect on the ethical principles and laws cited above, as well as the information security control examples presented. For each technology-related action in the case study, try to identify specific ways the practitioner can manage risk while still offering direct benefits to the patient in terms of access to care and treatment that meets high standards, and/or indirect benefits to the patient in the form of professional development for the clinician.

Case Study

A young man is concerned about how much he is worrying about starting graduate school. Worrying is starting to pervade his mind to the point where he is having trouble sleeping and even remembering to eat. He decides to look up his symptoms on the Internet. He types some key words about his symptoms into a search engine and discovers a mental health informational site that provides a symptom checklist. After he completes a brief symptom checklist, the site returns a result that suggests that he might be suffering from an anxiety disorder. The site provides psychoeducation—information about various anxiety disorders, possible causes, and evidence-based treatment approaches, as well as some stress reduction suggestions. He tries some of the stress reduction exercises and experiences a degree of relief in the fact that he is experiencing symptoms that are not uncommon. Still, his symptoms trouble him.

He returns to the informational site and clicks on a link that brings him to a mental health clinician referral site, and then to a therapist locator site providing listings for mental health professionals. He searches through a number of profiles and decides on a professional nearby that he believes is qualified. He is able to click on a link to a professional website and the clinician's Facebook page and Twitter account, and after reviewing the therapist's credentials decides to proceed with scheduling an initial session. Through the therapist's website, he is able to review the practice policies and insurances accepted. He completes a comprehensive intake questionnaire and symptom description online. He schedules an appointment online too.

The practitioner is notified of the new patient and is able to review the intake form and symptom checklist to derive an initial sense of the clinical issues and patient characteristics. The pretreatment data are automatically uploaded and stored in an encrypted database to be used to monitor progress and serve as baseline criteria to measure outcomes. All of this is done with the patient's informed consent.

After the patient's first office visit, the intake information, pretreatment data, and initial clinical evaluation are used to formulate an initial treatment plan. The clinician accesses the Internet and uses a search engine for the latest clinical practice guidelines (Hollon, 2016) to determine the recommended evidence-based treatments and to keep abreast of the most current findings. At this time, any needed information can be discovered using PICOT (Patient/population, Intervention, Comparison intervention, Outcome, Time frame) questions which are formulated to help clinicians discover the most current evidence (New York University Libraries, 2017). Based on the evaluation and pretreatment data, a diagnostic formulation is made. Clinician and patient discuss various treatment options by phone and agree on an approach to try, starting with the patient's next appointment. The patient is invited to use his smartphone to download some apps he can use to keep track of mood and anxiety, so that a better picture of the triggers can be identified. Another app using biometric sensors via his smartphone is used to gather some physiological concomitants of his anxiety, such as heart rate variability and patterns of movement. These data can be uploaded from the patient's smartphone to the clinician's portal site, where she is able to monitor trends and also utilize the physiological parameters to assess treatment response. The patient is also provided with links to various sites that offer supportive and accessible adjunctive psychoeducation.

In another office in her suite, the clinician has a room devoted to helping patients learn how to make state changes—represented by optimal balance between the sympathetic and parasympathetic nervous systems, called *coherence*. For our patient, in this example, the clinician prescribes adjunctive heart rate variability biofeedback, which is overseen by a technician. For other patients, other treatments are considered, such as neurofeedback, virtual reality therapy, electrocranial therapy, and transcranial magnetic stimulation (TMS). While she does not have the resources for TMS in her practice, when appropriate, she refers to another clinician who does.

During the course of treatment, the patient arrives 5 minutes early for each session and is asked to complete a scale on a tablet that links to the clinician's computer. A summary of the treatment alliance and patient progress is available to the clinician before she meets with her patient. During the session, the patient reports that he will be unable to attend face-to-face sessions for a month, and after discussing the advantages and limitations of teletherapy, and providing informed consent, the patient and clinician decide that during this period they will conduct teletherapy sessions. These sessions prove to be a relief to the patient as a break in treatment seemed untimely.

As part of the clinician's continuing professional development, she has signed up for some online webinars on the latest evidence-based strategies for working with anxiety disorders. During the webinar she hears of additional training, including an online supervision group that she decides to join. As part of the training, she is required to have videotape supervision of her patients. She asks her patient if he would allow his sessions to be videotaped for this purpose. He agrees, and she uses a digital video camera and saves the video on a password-protected site. Using an encrypted video communication service, she meets virtually with her supervisor, and together they are able to view the videotape of her patients providing shared clinical material as opposed to self-report.

As you read this case study, did any red flags present themselves? Maybe you identified some areas where you would like more detailed information on both the benefits and risks—social media policies, for example (for a list of articles for clinicians about social media, see http://drkkolmes.com/clinician-articles/). Or maybe you were able to articulate some questions to ask your staff or business associates about how best to safeguard patient data and take calculated risks with technology. Additionally, you might ask the following:

- In which parts of the scenario does the clinician's responsibility to comply with HIPAA/HITECH come into play?
- Was informed consent obtained at every juncture when it is needed?
- What physical, administrative, and/or technical vulnerabilities has the clinician accounted for, and how might those controls be reinforced?
- Aside from specific security vulnerabilities, what boundary challenges need to be considered? (Kolmes & Taube, 2014)

Conclusion

Online mental health programs have a strong evidence base. APA defined *evidence-based* as "the integration of the best available research with clinical expertise in the context of patient characteristics, culture and preference" (APA Presidential Task Force on Evidence-Based Practice, 2006, p. 273). Their role in population health strategies needs further exploration, including the most effective use of limited clinical staff resources. Turvey and Roberts (2015) reminded us that patient portals and personal health records serve to enhance mental health treatment also, though concerns specific to mental health must be addressed to support broader adoption of portals. User-friendly, well-designed, patient-centered health information technology may integrate many functions (connecting patient records or e-mails or treatment enhanced technologies) to promote a holistic approach to care plans and overall wellness. The security needs of using this technology will require that providers and patients be well informed about how best to use these technologies to support behavioral health interventions (Turvey & Roberts, 2015).

It is an intimidating and possibly consuming task to stay up-to-date with all the advances in technology in the mental health field. And with the changes in the technology landscape, mental health practitioners will continually need to adhere to high standards of care. Therefore, it should be abundantly clear that keeping data secure must be of paramount importance. But even encryption companies have been hacked, as in the case of TrueCrypt (Constantin, 2015). So, what are we supposed to do if even those systems that meet the highest industry standards can be compromised by hackers? Let's be clear: There will never be a perfect security and privacy solution to any electronic medical record, health-related electronic communication, telehealth program, or mobile health app. On some level, our efforts to follow HIPAA standards, professional standards, and ethical standards, and to maintain a risk-managed practice setting, will always be aspirational. The best we can do is to accept and own our responsibilities as professionals and adopt practices that help us to stay current.

References

American Psychiatric Association. (2013). *The principles of medical ethics with annotations especially applicable to psychiatry.* Retrieved from https://www.psychiatry.org/File%20Library/Psychiatrists/Practice/Ethics/principles-medical-ethics.pdf

American Psychiatric Association. (2016). *APA commentary on ethics in practice.* Retrieved from https://www.psychiatry.org/File%20Library/Psychiatrists/Practice/Ethics/APA-Commentary-on-Ethics-in-Practice.pdf

American Psychological Association. (2013). *The privacy rule: A primer for psychologists.* Retrieved from http://www.apapracticecentral.org/business/hipaa/hippa-privacy-primer.pdf

American Psychological Association. (2017). *Ethical principles of psychologists and code of conduct* (2002, Amended June 1, 2010 and January 1, 2017). Retrieved from http://www.apa.org/ethics/code/index.aspx

American Psychological Association, Joint Task Force for the Development of Telepsychology Guidelines for Psychologists. (2013). Guidelines for the practice of telepsychology. *American Psychologist, 68,* 791–800. http://dx.doi.org/10.1037/a0035001

APA Presidential Task Force on Evidence-Based Practice. (2006). Evidence-based practice in psychology. *American Psychologist, 61,* 271–285. http://dx.doi.org/10.1037/0003-066X.61.4.271

Brock, L. V., & Mastroianni, A. (2013). *Ethics in medicine: Clinical ethics and law.* Retrieved from the University of Washington School of Medicine website: http://depts.washington.edu/bioethx/topics/law.html

Constantin, L. (2015). *Newly found TrueCrypt flaw allows full system compromise.* Retrieved from https://www.csoonline.com/article/2987148/data-protection/newly-found-truecrypt-flaw-allows-full-system-compromise.html

Drummond, A., Cromarty, P., & Battersby, M. (2015). Privacy in the digital age: Implications for clinical practice. *Clinical Psychology: Science and Practice, 22,* 227–237. http://dx.doi.org/10.1111/cpsp.12105

Dulaney, E. (2014). Picture this: A visual guide to security controls [Web log post]. *Certification Magazine.* Retrieved from http://certmag.com/picture-this-visual-guide-security-controls/

Federal Trade Commission. (2012, March). *Protecting consumer privacy in an era of rapid change: Recommendations for businesses and policymakers.* Retrieved from https://www.ftc.gov/reports/protecting-consumer-privacy-era-rapid-change-recommendations-businesses-policymakers

Health Insurance Portability and Accountability Act of 1996, Pub. L. No. 104-191-110 (1996).

Hollon, S. D. (2016). Developing clinical practice guidelines to enhance clinical decision making. In J. J. Magnavita (Ed.), *Clinical decision making in mental health practice* (pp. 125–146). Washington, DC: American Psychological Association. http://dx.doi.org/10.1037/14711-005

Kolmes, K., & Taube, D. O. (2014). Seeking and finding our clients on the Internet: Boundary considerations in cyberspace. *Professional Psychology: Research and Practice, 45*, 3–10. http://dx.doi.org/10.1037/a0029958

Largest Healthcare Data Breaches of 2016. (2017). *HIPAA Journal.* Retrieved from https://www.hipaajournal.com/largest-healthcare-data-breaches-of-2016-8631/

New York University Libraries. (2017). *Framing the research question: PICO(T).* Retrieved from https://guides.nyu.edu/c.php?g=276561&p=1847897#1733240

Northcutt, S. (2013). *Security controls.* Retrieved from https://www.sans.edu/cyber-research/security-laboratory/article/security-controls

Sobelman, S. A., & Younggren, J. N. (2016). Clinical decision making and risk management. In J. J. Magnavita (Ed.), *Clinical decision making in mental health practice* (pp. 245–271). Washington, DC: American Psychological Association. http://dx.doi.org/10.1037/14711-010

Solove, D. J. (2013). HIPAA turns 10: Analyzing the past, present and future impact. *Journal of AHIMA, 84*(4), 22–28. http://library.ahima.org/doc?oid=106325#.WgB8R1tSzIV

Turvey, C. L., & Roberts, L. J. (2015). Recent developments in the use of online resources and mobile technologies to support mental health care. *International Review of Psychiatry, 27*, 547–557. http://dx.doi.org/10.3109/09540261.2015.1087975

United States Department of Health and Human Services. (2013). *Breach notification rule.* Retrieved from https://www.hhs.gov/hipaa/for-professionals/breach-notification/index.html

What is protected health information? (2017). Retrieved from the USF Health website: https://www.usfhealthonline.com/resources/key-concepts/what-is-protected-health-information-or-phi/

Yau, H. K. (2013). Information security controls. *Advances in Robotics & Automation, 3*:e118. http://dx.doi.org/10.4172/2168-9695.1000e118

Carolyn L. Turvey

Telemental Health Care Delivery
Evidence Base and Practical Considerations

2

atients can receive mental and behavioral health care services in their home, at their office, or anywhere else using high-quality, reliable, videoconferencing software on a personal computer, laptop, or mobile device. As more providers begin offering telemental health care, patients can choose from an ever-broader range of providers and types of treatments. Services in high demand, such as pediatric mental health or marital and family counseling, can be accessed more easily as geography does not determine the availability of a service (Choi, Hegel, et al., 2014; Choi, Wilson, Sirrianni, Marinucci, & Hegel, 2014; Lindgren et al., 2016; Nelson & Bui, 2010). Specialty services, such as mental health care conducted in non-dominant languages (e.g., Spanish or American Sign Language; Lopez et al., 2004; Moreno, Chong, Dumbauld, Humke, & Byreddy, 2012; Shim, Ye, & Yun, 2012; Shore et al., 2008; Ye et al., 2012; Yellowlees et al., 2013), are also accessed more easily through telemental health.

This expanded choice for receiving care is already practiced by some, but it has yet to become a part of mainstream mental health care. Adoption is slow, but accelerating, with innovations in service delivery models, reimbursement models, and underlying technology that are attracting new

http://dx.doi.org/10.1037/0000085-003
Using Technology in Mental Health Practice, J. J. Magnavita (Editor)

providers, payers, and consumers. However, adoption is almost always preceded by three key questions that need to be explored for telemental health:

1. Are mental health treatments that use the Internet to connect to patient's homes or other private spaces as effective as same-room care?
2. Does providing mental health care via the Internet address concerns of privacy? Is it HIPAA compliant?
3. Is providing care to patients using the Internet in home settings safe?

Predictably, the answer to each of these key questions is "It depends." When conducted properly, telemental health services are as effective, private, and safe as same-room care. Patients can have a broad choice of services tailored to their preferences and needs. However, the full specification of optimal care has yet to be determined and is part of an ongoing national and international discussion.

This chapter addresses key issues regarding telemental health delivered through online videoconferencing technologies and elucidates some of the conditions under which telemental health is practiced optimally. The scope of this chapter includes the provision of mental health services provided by a licensed health care professional when using real-time videoconferencing services transmitted via the Internet. This chapter pertains to telemental health services when the initiating, receiving, or both provider and client are using a personal computer with a webcam or a mobile communications device (e.g., smartphone, laptop, tablet) with two-way camera capability. This chapter does not address communications between professionals and clients via testing, e-mail, chatting, social network sites, online "coaching," or other non–mental health services.

Although the scope of this chapter is defined by the communication technology used—Internet-based psychotherapy—the more important focus is the implications of this technical advance for how mental health care is delivered. Use of the Internet for high-quality and reliable videoconferencing on commonly available technologies such as laptops, tablets, and smartphones means patients can access care when located in a wide range of settings. Prior to this, the most common form of telehealth was clinic-to-clinic videoconferencing, where patients received care in the structure of a health care setting comparable to that of same-room care. In this form of care, a private room designated for the visit is used. Health care professionals are readily available to assist in both management of the appointment and also for emergency management. In this context, telemental health is almost identical to same-room care, but for the use of videoconferencing technology.

Definitions and Background

Internet-based telemental health, when delivered to less formal nonclinical settings, such as the home or a patient's work space, has a broad range of clinical, administrative, and ethical implications. Careful consideration of the implications of providing care to patients in nonclinical settings is essential to providing ethical high-quality Internet-based telemental health. Internet-based telemental health delivered to nonclinical settings requires the use of some general protocols. However, in addition to these protocols, providers need to use their clinical judgment about each individual patient to determine the wisdom of providing care without the usual supports of same-room care.

For the purposes of this chapter, the term *nonclinical setting* refers to settings where trained clinical staff are not readily available at the patient site; where the patient is not located in a physical structure that is a clinical setting; and where the patient is primarily responsible for the conduct of the session. Obviously, if care is provided by a professional, online telemental health can be characterized in some respects as "a clinical setting." Prior discussions of this distinction have referred to this setting as "where clinical staff are not readily available" (Luxton, Sirotin, & Mishkind, 2010; Tuerk & Shore, 2015). Although technically this is accurate, I prefer to call this a nonclinical setting because it connotes more readily the novel use cases for Internet-based telemental health—telemental health delivered to patients in their homes and other private settings.

My experience with telemental health, particularly conducted via the Internet, is based primarily on experience implementing new practice models in research and quality improvement programs within an academic medical center. I was responsible for building and continue to manage a telemental health clinic between the mental health service line of the Iowa City Veterans Affairs (VA) Health Care System and Western Illinois University (WIU), which is located in a rural Illinois town with a large veteran population. WIU has a large veteran population because it has excellent law enforcement and emergency management training programs—degree programs sought after by many veterans after leaving the service. However, the university is located in a rural area that is approximately 2 hours driving distance from the Iowa City VA Medical Center. During the establishment of this clinic, the author was introduced to issues of conducting telemental health across jurisdictional medical practice lines, providing care to nonclinical settings, and maintaining privacy for patients when collaborating closely with nonmedical organizations.

I also have experience conducting telepsychology, both phone-based and video-teleconferencing, from an academic medical center to homebound older patients with depression and chronic illness. This gave me direct experience providing care to patients directly in their homes, with its related clinical and privacy issues.

Finally, since 2004, I have been an active member of the American Telemedicine Association, which has a strong commitment to promoting telemedicine in a way consistent with best clinical standards. In this context, I was the chair of a committee responsible for developing guidelines for optimal practice of online telemental health (Turvey et al., 2013). This rounded my experiences by providing the opportunity to work with colleagues who have thought in depth about the many issues pertaining to this new model of providing psychiatric and psychological care.

As this chapter proceeds though a discussion of the key aspects of responsible online mental health care, I use examples from these experiences to illustrate how they are not abstract, nitpicky issues but critical points that clinicians must reflect upon and decide on *before* embarking on telemental health practice using online technologies for videoconferencing.

Evidence Base for Online Telemental Health

There is a large amount of sophisticated research literature demonstrating the comparability of mental health care provided through videoconferencing to that provided in a same-room environment (Chakrabarti, 2015; Grady et al., 2011; Hilty et al., 2013). The bulk of this research occurred before Internet-based videoconferencing became widespread and is based primarily on clinic-to-clinic systems using older codec technologies. Telemental health—be it psychiatric evaluations, psychotherapy, or psychological testing—when conducted properly is as effective as same-room care for patients with mood disorders (Carlbring et al., 2011; Choi, Hegel, et al., 2014; Christensen, Griffiths, Mackinnon, & Brittliffe, 2006; Fortney et al., 2007; Mohr et al., 2013; O'Reilly et al., 2007), anxiety (Fortney et al., 2015; Frueh et al., 2007; Knaevelsrud, Brand, Lange, Ruwaard, & Wagner, 2015), eating disorders (Mitchell et al., 2008), and substance abuse disorders (Cucciare, Weingardt, & Humphreys, 2009; Day & Schneider, 2002; Gainsbury & Blaszczynski, 2011). With adequate assistance at the remote site, telemental health is effective for young children (Lindgren et al., 2016; Myers, Palmer, & Geyer, 2011; Myers, Vander Stoep, Zhou, McCarty, & Katon, 2015; Nelson & Bui, 2010; Wacker et al., 2013), as well as older individuals, even some with dementia (Holden & Dew, 2008; Rabinowitz et al., 2010).

Condition-specific studies debunked commonly held myths, such as that psychotic patients cannot use telemental health because it will exacerbate their delusions of references regarding television (Sharp, Kobak, & Osman, 2011). The studies found that patients with schizophrenia benefitted greatly from telemental health, with reduced hospitalization and no increase in psychotic symptoms. Older adults, and presumably technophobes, have also benefitted from telemental health, even when there is evidence of cognitive impairment (Holden & Dew, 2008; Rabinowitz et al., 2010). To this day, stakeholders new to telemental health convey concerns that it is lower quality care, yet there is no research base to support this skepticism. Additionally, several excellent reviews of this evidence base are available and updated regularly (Andersson & Cuijpers, 2009; Chakrabarti, 2015; Grady et al., 2011; Hilty et al., 2013; K. M. Myers & Turvey, 2012).

The question remains as to whether this evidence base stemming primarily from clinic-to-clinic telemental health will generalize to Internet-based telemental health. Fortunately, a small but growing research literature on Internet-based telemental health, often provided directly to consumers in their homes, concurs with earlier findings and suggests that the effectiveness of this new delivery model is as robust as clinic-to-clinic consultation. It is interesting that some of the earliest work has focused on providing direct-to-home care to developmentally delayed children where travel to an office can be quite burdensome to the family, and to homebound elders who, despite their lack of familiarity with technology, are able to make use of the user-friendly designs of current Internet-based videoconferencing technologies.

Wacker et al. (2013), at the University of Iowa, have implemented applied behavior analysis (ABA), a state-of-the-art treatment for challenging behavior in autism. In ABA, mental health specialists train families of autistic children to identify the "function" that maintains challenging behavior in an autistic child. Then, with clinician guidance, the parent works with the child to develop more adaptive and effective communication strategies. Wacker et al. reported on a pilot randomized controlled trial that compared the effectiveness of in-home ABA therapy, clinic-based telehealth, and home-based telehealth. Each condition experienced over 90% reduction in problem behavior with no difference between treatment arms, meaning home-based telehealth was as effective as sending a clinician directly into the child's home. In fact, the results revealed that when the clinician went to the child's home, it actually required more visits when compared to clinic-based or in-home telehealth. In addition, there was not a significantly larger response rate for the home-based online treatments compared with clinic-based telehealth. Wacker et al. speculated that delivering the care directly to the home via teleconference makes it easier to generalize treatment effects to where problem behaviors most often occur.

Wacker et al.'s (2013) work is perfectly suited for telehealth because functional analysis of problematic behavior will be more accurate when observed in naturalistic settings—that of the home. However, resources needed for home-based care would be prohibitive but for the potential of videoconferencing. Moreover, home-based telehealth for family therapies use full participation of the family, and issues of privacy related to some household members (described below) is less of a concern.

At the other end of the age spectrum, Choi and colleagues at the University of Texas at Austin (Choi, Hegel, et al., 2014; Choi, Marti, et al., 2014; Choi, Wilson, et al., 2014), provided problem-solving therapy (PST) to 121 depressed, low-income, homebound adults aged 65 and older. This three-arm pilot randomized controlled trial compared in-person PST, to tele-PST, to supportive phone calls. Participants were provided a laptop computer with built-in microphones and video and videoconferencing software. Despite their age and presumed unfamiliarity with technology, acceptance was high on a multidimensional treatment evaluation assessment, and there were no differences between groups on this measure. Tele-PST and in-person PST were equally effective with a slightly larger improvement on the nine-item Patient Health Questionnaire (PHQ-9) for the Tele-PST group (mean effect size = 0.77) than for the in-person PST group (mean effect size = 0.70).

These two use cases illustrate the best of telemental health in providing effective patient-centered care. Although the clinical effectiveness may be comparable to same-room care, there are enormous added benefits to patients and their families. The travel burden is greatly reduced, which is particularly meaningful to low-income patients. Clinicians gain critical information about how patients function in their own home with their family members. There are dire provider shortages for both pediatric and geriatric mental health, particularly in rural areas. Telemental health helps to overcome these barriers.

These additional benefits of online telemental health need to be measured more systematically to accurately capture the value of this service. Rabinowitz et al. (2010) calculated reduced travel burden in telemental health, including total travel cost, gasoline cost, and time savings for both patients and providers. Fortney et al. (2015) found that the positive impact of cognitive processing therapy delivered via telemedicine was fully mediated by attendance at eight or more sessions, which was greater in the group receiving telehealth. Treatment completion, patient satisfaction, reduced loss of work or child care time are all powerful benefits to patients and providers alike, particularly in the care of patients with special needs. These benefits deserve more systematic exploration in the research of care delivered directly to patients in their homes.

So, is online telemental health effective? Yes! There is an enormous evidence base for comparable technologies and a small but growing base for Internet-based care that suggests comparable effectiveness and superior patient satisfaction and compliance outcomes.

Best Practices in Online Telemental Health

The research literature demonstrating the effectiveness of online telemental health provides scant guidance on how to go about providing care in this venue. However, the mental health field has been grappling with proper conduct of telemental health for decades, and telemental health is one of the most common applications of telemedicine. There are several resources available to provide guidance on how to set up a telemental health practice. First, mental health professional organizations publish regular guidelines for ethical care, such as the *Guidelines for the Practice of Telepsychology* (American Psychological Association, 2013), the *Standards for Technology and Social Work Practice* (National Association of Social Workers & Association of Social Work Boards, 2005), the *Guidelines for Providing Psychological Services and Products Using the Internet and Telecommunications Technologies* (Australian Psychological Society, 2011) and, of course, the American Telemedicine Association's *ATA Practice Guidelines for Video-Based Online Mental Health Services* (Turvey et al., 2013). These guidelines vary by the amount of detail or specific guidance they provide, but reading them is the required first step for any professional interested in conducting online therapy—particularly if they are a member of the profession targeted.

In addition to these guidelines, several texts and websites provide more hands-on guidance from experienced professionals, and most of these are of high quality. A list of these websites and some of the texts is provided at the end of this chapter.

As these guidelines, texts, and websites provide detailed guidance about the conduct of telemental health, the remainder of the chapter will focus on key areas that still need further explanation, emphasis, or discussion. As proponents of telemental health, we are often in the role of cheerleader or salesperson in trying to convince health care professionals of the benefits of telemental health. However, this practice warrants further development and discussion to ensure that we are providing both the best care and care alternatives to our patients.

BEGINNING THE TREATMENT: INFORMED CONSENT

Starting therapy when using online-based videoconferencing is largely similar to that of same-room care. The therapist is responsible for setting the framework for the therapy, managing expectations about roles and structure, and informing the patient about any potential risks. Informed consent, including aspects related to using Internet-based videoconferencing, is standard. The references and guidelines cited earlier provide a comprehensive list of all topics therapists may want to review in the consent process when embarking on online therapy. However, the therapist needs to address these larger issues in light of the fact that communication will be occurring via videotechnology.

At the start of the therapy, it is helpful to review with the patient some of the basic aspects of videoconferencing. Discussions may include the importance of positioning vis-à-vis the camera and lighting, how to manage eye contact, and the potential for fluctuations in quality of the video transmission. In addition, discussion of what will happen if the technology fails is needed (most providers establish telephone backup should the Internet connection fail, so that sessions are not disrupted). Most current videoconferencing packages available for purchase or available online without fee include features that help diagnose connection problems, including the presentation of the transmission quality at each site. Clinicians and patients may want to review this before starting a session and troubleshooting any remediable connection problems before beginning the session.

Emergency management, discussed in detail below, should also be addressed, with the therapist obtaining the appropriate emergency contact information and establishing a clear protocol. The therapist may explain how emergency management differs greatly from same-room care and requires more of the patient. The patient is then aware of their need to collaborate with the provider should concerns arise.

A frank discussion of privacy at the start of therapy is also critical. This topic is also discussed in more detail below, but the therapist must discuss how the patient's health information is being stored, as well as the privacy of the technology being used for videoconferencing. Conditions under which privacy may be breached should also be discussed.

There is no strict regulation about whether informed consent must be written and signed. States vary on their regulations about this. Regardless, the clinician must review and inform the patient about the specific aspects of conducting mental health treatment using online videoconferencing technologies and document this discussion in the medical record.

ASSESSING APPROPRIATENESS AND RISKS OF TELEMENTAL HEALTH FOR EACH PATIENT

Clinicians unfamiliar with telemental health often question its appropriateness for certain patients. Often people fear that use of videoconferencing will exacerbate paranoid delusions of reference. To date, there has been no research supporting the notion that telemental health is contraindicated for specific patient groups. Older individuals with cognitive impairments, people with psychotic disorders, and children with autism have all benefited from telemental health.

Concerns also pertain to high-risk patients—particularly those at risk for harming themselves or others. Many of the safety protocols established for same-room care cannot be executed in online telemental health. A mental health provider cannot signal a code when providing care directly to a patient located in his home. In contrast to other health specialties, mental health providers cannot always rely on patients to cooperate fully in an emergency context. For example, one would expect a cardiac patient experiencing severe chest pain to call 911 or arrange to be taken to an emergency room. In contrast, a patient intent on self-harm may not cooperate and go for an evaluation, particularly if the patient does not want to be admitted to a hospital.

Several providers, particularly those working within the Department of Veterans Affairs (VA), have developed a protocol for managing the safety of telemental health patients who receive care in nonclinical settings (Luxton, Sirotin, & Mishkind, 2010; Tuerk & Shore, 2015). The main recommendation is to know the local first responders' contact information and, in addition, ask the patient to identify a community support person who will be available to assist the therapist and the patient should an emergency situation arise. The therapist would have direct contact information for this person readily available, and the therapist, patient, and community support person would discuss what might be expected of him or her in case of an emergency. Therefore, the therapist can call upon both formal and informal supports to assist in case of an emergency. Identifying a community support person provides a supportive alternative to relying solely on local first responders and may allow resolution of the emergency with minimal escalation. In the long run, this will preserve the therapeutic alliance.

The use of communication technologies to remotely manage patients who may become violent and/or self-harm is not new. Many clinicians have had the experience of speaking with a patient on the telephone who reveals that he or she is suicidal. Managing this risk through videoconferencing is similar, and the establishment of protocols only strengthens the ability of clinicians to manage the situation safely. The main difference introduced by Internet-supported treatments is the greater likelihood that providers will deliver care to patients in communities that are unfamiliar to the clinician, which has several implications for emergency management.

CASE EXAMPLES: EMERGENCY PROTOCOLS

For the telemental health clinic between the Iowa City VA Medical Center and the rural university campus in an adjoining state, I needed to take several steps towards establishing an emergency management protocol. Although the clinicians would be providing care across jurisdictional boundaries, within the VA system, providers licensed in one state are able to provide care to patients in other states, provided the patients go to a VA facility to receive remote care. However, when discussing this with the head of our mental health service line, she was by no means glib about this. Illinois has different commitment and duty-to-warn laws with which all providers conducting telemedicine through this clinic and others in Illinois had to become familiar. In addition, I spoke with local mental health clinicians, both psychiatrists and psychologists, about their experiences in emergency management. They had several insights into how both the local law enforcement and local emergency room staff manage psychiatric emergencies, and these insights informed how I designed my protocol. Once developed, I then met with all stakeholders to communicate this protocol. These meetings need to be repeated on a regular basis. Local variability in how psychiatric emergencies are handled is likely more the rule than the exception, so clinicians providing care to remote unfamiliar sites need to do some investigating before providing care.

In conducting therapy with homebound elders, another issue arose. What can a clinician do if a community support person does not assist when called upon by the provider? In working with one client remotely, I became concerned about intent to self-harm. Although the patient had already agreed to contact with a community support person prior to the start of treatment, the patient refused permission to contact his community support person or to go to the local emergency room for evaluation. I decided to contact the community support person against the patient's wishes as I believed there to be a potential threat to life. She was torn between the therapist's recommendation and the patient's strong refusal to seek care. After she refused to assist, it was fortunate that both patient and community support person agreed that I could call the patient's local primary care provider, who agreed to see the patient immediately. The situation resolved well and the patient was eventually relieved that his thoughts of self-harm were taken seriously. However, this was an example of how the community support person is really under no obligation to follow a therapist's wishes, and if the patient is not cooperative, this arrangement can place the community support person in a difficult position. Fortunately, in the situation described here, there was a solution that was amenable to all.

CASE EXAMPLE: ASYNCHRONOUS REMOTE MONITORING

Another type of remote emergency management that will become more common is the response to asynchronous remote monitoring. I collaborated with the Iowa Medicaid program to administer the PHQ-9, using interactive voice response, to Medicaid patients in a chronic disease management program for heart failure or diabetes (Turvey, Willyard, Hickman, Klein, & Kukoyi, 2007). In interactive voice response, patients would receive a phone call where an automated recording would ask them about each of the nine items included on the PHQ-9, and they could indicate their level of experiencing each symptom by pushing the corresponding button on their phone (i.e., 1 = *most of the time*, 2 = *some of the time*, 3 = *not at all*). Patient responses would then be stored and forwarded to a database that would be accessed by the nurse care managers. The ninth item of the PHQ-9 assesses suicidality and, therefore, indicates some risk for self-harm and warrants timely evaluation. However, in a store-and-forward model, this information may not reach the nurse care manager until the next day.

Many organizations implementing the PHQ have pragmatically omitted this ninth item because they do not have the resources to provide immediate support should someone indicate suicidal ideation (Kroenke et al., 2009; Li, Ford, Strine, & Mokdad, 2008). The Iowa Medicaid program chose not to eliminate the ninth item.

The rationale was that assessing all depressive symptoms except suicide would be comparable to assessing a cardiac patient for all symptoms of cardiac distress but specifically omitting a question about chest pain. However, we did put a protocol in place in which the nurse would be alerted if suicidality were endorsed and would follow up in a timely manner (defined as within 24 hours). Patients were also provided information about timeliness of response, and the importance of reporting emergencies directly through the 911 system.

The ninth item in the PHQ-9 about suicidal ideation was, in fact, endorsed the first day of screening, and the nurse tried to contact the patient by phone. Unfortunately, the patient did not answer the phone so a wellness check was initiated—local police officers came to his home to ensure he was well. Although the patient was surprised by the wellness check, he was not angry or upset. He seemed pleased at how seriously his distress was taken, and he worked with the nurse to get appropriate treatment.

The issue of asynchronous communication of suicidal ideation is not new. Providers have experience with reviewing suicidal voicemail messages or other electronic communications hours or days after they were communicated; no provider or organization can guarantee timely response. Clear communication about expectations around time and responsiveness, as well as the patient's role in maintaining his or her own safety, has always been the standard of care when patients not in a clinical setting choose to reveal potential harmful behavior.

Before starting treatment, clinicians must evaluate the degree to which the patient, particularly those receiving care in nonclinical settings, will likely be cooperative in working with the provider should the risk for self- or other harm arise. However, similar to telemental health care with psychotic and older patients, many telemental health providers have worked successfully with high-risk patients.

Ensuring That Remote Care Falls Within the Provider's Scope of Practice

Though much attention has been devoted to the evaluation of patient appropriateness for telemental health in nonclinical settings, less discussion has focused on the appropriateness of the provider. This is a particular concern in online telemental health because the broadened access to care may result in providers treating either patients whose conditions are novel or unfamiliar to them or patients from cultures about which the clinician knows little. Clinicians may be tempted to broaden their self-identified scope of practice to include a broader age range or specific cultural subgroups. A clinician's scope of practice must be the same for telemental health as it is for same-room care. If one does not have experience working with adolescents in same-room care, one cannot provide it through telemental health simply because the patient would not receive any care otherwise. Cultural competence is also required, and continuing education may be needed if the broader access afforded by the new technology increases representation of cultural subgroups unfamiliar to the clinician.

Similarly, telemental health and concerns about appropriateness of the provider point to the controversial issue of interjurisdictional practice. Professional licensing is still primarily issued by states, and practice is limited to the geographic area designated within a specific license. Though some states allow practice across state boundaries under certain circumstances, most limit providers to practice within the geographic boundaries of their state. Taken to its logical conclusion, most recommend that telemental health providers be licensed to practice both in the state where they are located and the state where the patient is physically located while receiving treatment. Therefore, if a provider in Illinois is using online telemental health to provide care to a patient in Iowa, the provider should be licensed in both Iowa and Illinois.

Managing Data Security With Videoconferencing Software

One of the most frequently asked questions regarding online telemental health is, is it HIPAA compliant? This question cannot be answered with a simple yes or no. Many Internet-based video software packages meet advanced encryptions standards, although none can offer a full guarantee that a hacker will not intercept the video transmission. Moreover, live streaming is harder to protect from hacking than transmission of discrete data. Encryption standards can vary and are evolving over time as hackers become more sophisticated. The most recognized standard is the Federal Information Processing Standard (FIPS 140-2), which is the U.S. Government security standard used to accredit encryption standards of software and lists encryption such as AES (Advanced Encryption Standard) as providing acceptable levels of security. As may be obvious, clinicians embarking on telemental health should seek consultation from professionals who specialize in privacy and security and who are familiar with these accepted but changing standards. In addition, frank discussion with patients at the beginning of treatment about what the provider can and cannot guarantee regarding privacy of the electronic submission is recommended.

As is often the case, concerns about privacy and security have focused on the technical aspects of secure video transmission. Yet telemental health, particularly when conducted with patients in nonclinical settings, raises other concerns that are far more likely to compromise privacy than the off-chance that a hacker will intentionally intercept a video stream to learn about someone's mental health problems.

Managing Other Privacy Issues With Telemental Health Care

Providers using videoconferencing to provide care to patients in remote settings must rely on the support at the remote setting to ensure that the session is conducted in private. In clinic-to-clinic transmission, the telepresenter at the remote site often arranges for a private room, the same room used for same-room care in other instances. However, the telepresenter often takes a more active collaborative role in managing the session, which does lead to more sharing of the patient's health information than may occur in same room care. For example, the telepresenter may distribute and collect symptom measures the clinician uses to corroborate their clinical interview. Sometimes the telepresenter will need to help the patient manage prescriptions or other recommended treatment that would normally be managed by the clinician himself in same-room care.

At our VA-to-campus clinic, one psychiatrist established secure messaging with the remote telepresenter and relies on this heavily to conduct sessions. The telepresenter texts the therapist when the patient arrives, and the psychiatrist texts the telepresenter during sessions if she needs assistance in collecting information from the patient or providing other assistance related to the treatment. In addition, if for any reason the remote psychiatrist becomes concerned about the patient's safety, she will text the telepresenter to assist in emergency management. This model has the telepresenter function as a collaborator with the clinician for optimal care and coordination, yet it does involve greater sharing of clinical information than might occur in a same-room care setting where a nurse or other staff member simply leads the patient to the correct office.

The implications of relying on remote staff to manage privacy are even larger when conducting mental health care directly to patients in their homes or other nonclinical settings. Quite simply, when providing care to patients in nonclinical settings, there is no remote staff. One must rely on the patient to ensure that the session is conducted in a private and confidential setting. Depending on the circumstances, this can be a lot to ask. To start, if the patient is using a desktop computer, these are often located in the more public places in a house and are not easily moved to more private locations. In addition, the patient will need to arrange for other residents of the household to not be present or within earshot. Making this request can be very uncomfortable for some patients.

In my work with homebound older adults, I would start the treatment with a discussion of the importance of privacy of the session. I would explain that part of the benefit of the therapy comes from the patient's feeling comfortable saying whatever comes to mind. Often, particularly when working with older adults, our patients would state, "It's okay if my wife hears the session. We have no secrets." Regardless of whether this is true, it is likely the therapeutic discussion will take a different tenor if the entire session is conducted within earshot of the spouse. One could argue that this is a good thing or that engaging the spouse may be more therapeutic, but there is a difference between purposely engaging a spouse as part of the treatment plan and it occurring haphazardly because the patient does not want to take steps to ensure full privacy of the session. In our telemental health work, we ask patients to ensure that the session is private to make the discussion as similar to a session conducted in same-room care as possible. Many of our older patients complied once we addressed this issue in a matter-of-fact professional matter.

Unfortunately, lapses, whether intentional or not, do occur. I worked with a patient in his home for 10 weeks (where it was reasonably certain the sessions were conducted in private). However, toward the end of our treatment, we wanted to schedule a meeting 1 month out—longer than our usual between-session break. As the patient started to search for his schedule to make the appointment, a hand holding a calendar that clearly did not belong to the patient became visible in the left half of the screen—his spouse was within earshot and lent a helping hand in direct response to our discussion.

In spite of the best of intentions and the specific protocols followed by the therapist, providing care to patients in nonclinical settings must allow for the possibility that the session is not as private as same-room care or telemental health in a clinic setting where remote staff can ensure privacy. With all the intense focus on the HIPAA compliance of the technology supporting telemental health conducted using the Internet, these other issues receive surprisingly little attention. Granted, these breaches of privacy occur due to patient, not provider, behavior, and therefore they may not be held against the treatment provider. Moreover, to date, the research literature supports telemental health delivered to the home, indicating this issue may not impact the effectiveness of the treatment. However, clinicians must evaluate this issue in light of specific circumstances and characteristics of the patient to determine if the possibility of such privacy breaches are acceptable.

Conclusion

Online telemental health has the potential to improve access to and quality of care for a broad range of underserved patients. However, this is still in many ways a young field, particularly pertaining to therapy delivered directly to patients in private settings. Further development of best practices is needed in several areas.

For example, the limits of interjurisdictional practice pose a significant barrier to the broad expansion of telemental health conducted online. Several professional and advocacy organizations are grappling with this issue, exploring ideas like interstate compacts in which specific states agree to allow providers from other designated states to practice within their jurisdiction (Association of State and Provincial Psychology Boards, 2015). Among telemental health clinicians, opinions run strongly in favor of national licensure. Unfortunately, this discussion has not addressed in sufficient detail how the functions of state-based licensing will be taken over in one of the newer proposed systems. With national licensure, how are geographic differences in institutionalization or duty-to-warn going to be negotiated? How about geographic differences in prescription of controlled substances? These are not small issues as they are at the heart of care quality at critical points in care and regulatory boards differ greatly by region. Until a satisfactory argument and strategy to address these issues is formulated, discussion of national licensure will remain simply discussion.

Currently, another issue related to the appropriateness of the provider is being discussed in terms of developing specific credentials for providing mental health care through videoconferencing. To date, there are no specific professional organizations or licensing requirements specific to the practice of telemental health, although the VA does include internal training requirements for providers who intend to make this part of their practice. The prospect of formal credential programs is a double-edged sword. Though there are some basic guidelines that should be reviewed and understood before embarking on telemental health, it is generally very similar to same-room care, and the concept of credentials may deter providers from adopting telemental health. Ironically, provider adoption is recognized as one of the greatest barriers to widespread use of telemental health (Brooks, Turvey, & Augusterfer, 2013), so putting up barriers to its practice should not be taken lightly. Moreover, as in other aspects of medicine, credentialing can at times develop into more of a money-making business than a good faith mechanism for establishing and maintaining high-quality care.

Finally, as with any innovation, identifying optimal use cases (e.g., the use of telemedicine to deliver behavioral therapy to families of autistic children) will speed the adoption and promote the development of best practices in the context of what best suits patients' needs for truly patient-centered care.

Essential Resources

CLINICAL PRACTICE GUIDELINES

American Psychological Association. (2013). *Guidelines for the practice of telepsychology.* Retrieved from http://www.apa.org/practice/guidelines/telepsychology.aspx

Australian Psychological Association. (2011). *Guidelines for providing psychological services and products using the Internet and telecommunications technologies.* Retrieved from https://aaswsocialmedia.wikispaces.com/file/view/EG-Internet.pdf

National Association of Social Workers & Association of Social Work Boards. (2005). *Standards for technology and social work practice.* Retrieved from https://www.aswb.org/wp-content/uploads/2013/10/TechnologySWPractice.pdf

Turvey C., Coleman, M., Dennison, O., Drude, K., Goldenson, M., Hirsch, P., . . . Bernard, J. (2013). *ATA practice guidelines for video-based online mental health services.* Retrieved from https://www.integration.samhsa.gov/operations-administration/practice-guidelines-for-video-based-online-mental-health-services_ATA_5_29_13.pdf

WEBSITE RESOURCES

Center for Telehealth and e-Health Law: http://ctel.org/
Telehealth Resource Centers: Main website: http://www.telehealthresourcecenter.org/

References

American Psychological Association. (2013). *Guidelines for the practice of telepsychology.* Retrieved from http://www.apa.org/practice/guidelines/telepsychology.aspx

Andersson, G., & Cuijpers, P. (2009). Internet-based and other computerized psychological treatments for adult depression: A meta-analysis. *Cognitive Behaviour Therapy, 38*, 196–205. http://dx.doi.org/10.1080/16506070903318960

Association of State and Provincial Psychology Boards. (2015). *Psychology interjuris-dictional Compact (PSYPACT) Announced.* [Press release]. Retrieved from http://c.ymcdn.com/sites/www.asppb.net/resource/resmgr/PSYPACT_Docs/PSYPACT_Press_Release_3_16_2.pdf

Australian Psychological Society. (2011). *Guidelines for providing psychological services and products using the Internet and telecommunications technologies.* Retrieved from https://aaswsocialmedia.wikispaces.com/file/view/EG-Internet.pdf

Brooks, E., Turvey, C., & Augusterfer, E. F. (2013). Provider barriers to telemental health: Obstacles overcome, obstacles remaining. *Telemedicine and e-Health, 19,* 433–437. http://dx.doi.org/10.1089/tmj.2013.0068

Carlbring, P., Maurin, L., Törngren, C., Linna, E., Eriksson, T., Sparthan, E., . . . Andersson, G. (2011). Individually-tailored, Internet-based treatment for anxiety disorders: A randomized controlled trial. *Behaviour Research and Therapy, 49,* 18–24. http://dx.doi.org/10.1016/j.brat.2010.10.002

Chakrabarti, S. (2015). Usefulness of telepsychiatry: A critical evaluation of video-conferencing-based approaches. *World Journal of Psychiatry, 5,* 286–304.

Choi, N. G., Hegel, M. T., Marti, C. N., Marinucci, M. L., Sirrianni, L., & Bruce, M. L. (2014). Telehealth problem-solving therapy for depressed low-income homebound older adults. *The American Journal of Geriatric Psychiatry, 22,* 263–271. http://dx.doi.org/10.1016/j.jagp.2013.01.037

Choi, N. G., Marti, C. N., Bruce, M. L., Hegel, M. T., Wilson, N. L., & Kunik, M. E. (2014). Six-month postintervention depression and disability outcomes of in-home telehealth problem-solving therapy for depressed, low-income homebound older adults. *Depression and Anxiety, 31,* 653–661. http://dx.doi.org/10.1002/da.22242

Choi, N. G., Wilson, N. L., Sirrianni, L., Marinucci, M. L., & Hegel, M. T. (2014). Acceptance of home-based telehealth problem-solving therapy for depressed, low-income homebound older adults: Qualitative interviews with the participants and aging-service case managers. *The Gerontologist, 54,* 704–713. http://dx.doi.org/10.1093/geront/gnt083

Christensen, H., Griffiths, K. M., Mackinnon, A. J., & Brittliffe, K. (2006). Online randomized controlled trial of brief and full cognitive behaviour therapy for depression. *Psychological Medicine, 36,* 1737–1746. http://dx.doi.org/10.1017/S0033291706008695

Cucciare, M. A., Weingardt, K. R., & Humphreys, K. (2009). How Internet technology can improve the quality of care for substance use disorders. *Current Drug Abuse Reviews, 2,* 256–262. http://dx.doi.org/10.2174/1874473710902030256

Day, S. X., & Schneider, P. L. (2002). Psychotherapy using distance technology: A comparison of face-to-face, video, and audio treatment. *Journal of Counseling Psychology, 49,* 499–503. http://dx.doi.org/10.1037/0022-0167.49.4.499

Fortney, J. C., Pyne, J. M., Edlund, M. J., Williams, D. K., Robinson, D. E., Mittal, D., & Henderson, K. L. (2007). A randomized trial of telemedicine-based collaborative care for depression. *Journal of General Internal Medicine, 22,* 1086–1093. http://dx.doi.org/10.1007/s11606-007-0201-9

Fortney, J. C., Pyne, J. M., Kimbrell, T. A., Hudson, T. J., Robinson, D. E., Schneider, R., . . . Schnurr, P. P. (2015). Telemedicine-based collaborative care for posttraumatic stress disorder: A randomized clinical trial. *JAMA Psychiatry, 72*, 58–67. http://dx.doi.org/10.1001/jamapsychiatry.2014.1575

Frueh, B.C., Monnier, J., Yim, E., Grubaugh, A.L., Hamner, M.B., & Knapp, R.G. (2007). A randomized trial of telepsychiatry for post-traumatic stress disorder. *Journal of Telemedicine and Telecare, 13*, 142–147. http://dx.doi.org/10.1258/135763307780677604

Gainsbury, S., & Blaszczynski, A. (2011). A systematic review of Internet-based therapy for the treatment of addictions. *Clinical Psychology Review, 31*, 490–498. http://dx.doi.org/10.1016/j.cpr.2010.11.007

Grady, B., Myers, K.M., Nelson, E.-L., Belz, N., Bennett, L., Carnahan, L., . . . Voyles, D. (2011). Evidence-based practice for telemental health. *Telemedicine and e-Health, 17*, 131–148. http://dx.doi.org/10.1089/tmj.2010.0158

Hilty, D.M., Ferrer, D.C., Parish, M.B., Johnston, B., Callahan, E.J., & Yellowlees, P.M. (2013). The effectiveness of telemental health: A 2013 review. *Telemedicine and e-Health, 19*, 444–454. http://dx.doi.org/10.1089/tmj.2013.0075

Holden, D., & Dew, E. (2008). Telemedicine in a rural gero-psychiatric inpatient unit: Comparison of perception/satisfaction to onsite psychiatric care. *Telemedicine and e-Health, 14*, 381–384. http://dx.doi.org/10.1089/tmj.2007.0054

Knaevelsrud, C., Brand, J., Lange, A., Ruwaard, J., & Wagner, B. (2015). Web-based psychotherapy for posttraumatic stress disorder in war-traumatized Arab patients: Randomized controlled trial. *Journal of Medical Internet Research, 17*(3), e71. http://dx.doi.org/10.2196/jmir.3582

Kroenke, K., Strine, T.W., Spitzer, R.L., Williams, J.B.W., Berry, J.T., & Mokdad, A.H. (2009). The PHQ-8 as a measure of current depression in the general population. *Journal of Affective Disorders, 114*, 163–173. http://dx.doi.org/10.1016/j.jad.2008.06.026

Li, C., Ford, E.S., Strine, T.W., & Mokdad, A.H. (2008). Prevalence of depression among U.S. adults with diabetes: Findings from the 2006 behavioral risk factor surveillance system. *Diabetes Care, 31*, 105–107. http://dx.doi.org/10.2337/dc07-1154

Lindgren, S., Wacker, D., Suess, A., Schieltz, K., Pelzel, K., Kopelman, T., . . . Waldron, D. (2016). Telehealth and autism: Treating challenging behavior at lower cost. *Pediatrics, 137*, S167–S175. http://dx.doi.org/10.1542/peds.2015-2851O

Lopez, A.M., Cruz, M., Lazarus, S., Webster, P., Jones, E.G., & Weinstein, R.S. (2004). Case report: Use of American Sign Language in telepsychiatry consultation. *Telemedicine Journal and e-Health, 10*, 389–391.

Luxton, D.D., Sirotin, A.P., & Mishkind, M.C. (2010). Safety of telemental healthcare delivered to clinically unsupervised settings: A systematic review. *Telemedicine and e-Health, 16*, 705–711. http://dx.doi.org/10.1089/tmj.2009.0179

Mitchell, J.E., Crosby, R.D., Wonderlich, S.A., Crow, S., Lancaster, K., Simonich, H., . . . Cook Myers, T. (2008). A randomized trial comparing the efficacy of cognitive-behavioral therapy for bulimia nervosa delivered via telemedicine versus face-to-face. *Behaviour Research and Therapy, 46*, 581–592. http://dx.doi.org/10.1016/j.brat.2008.02.004

Mohr, D.C., Duffecy, J., Ho, J., Kwasny, M., Cai, X., Burns, M.N., & Begale, M. (2013). A randomized controlled trial evaluating a manualized TeleCoaching protocol for improving adherence to a web-based intervention for the treatment of depression. *PLoS One, 8*(8), e70086. http://dx.doi.org/10.1371/journal.pone.0070086

Moreno, F. A., Chong, J., Dumbauld, J., Humke, M., & Byreddy, S. (2012). Use of standard Webcam and Internet equipment for telepsychiatry treatment of depression among underserved Hispanics. *Psychiatric Services, 63*, 1213–1217. http://dx.doi.org/10.1176/appi.ps.201100274

Myers, K., Vander Stoep, A., Zhou, C., McCarty, C. A., & Katon, W. (2015). Effectiveness of a telehealth service delivery model for treating attention-deficit/hyperactivity disorder: A community-based randomized controlled trial. *Journal of the American Academy of Child & Adolescent Psychiatry, 54*, 263–274. http://dx.doi.org/10.1016/j.jaac.2015.01.009

Myers, K. M., Palmer, N. B., & Geyer, J. R. (2011). Research in child and adolescent telemental health. *Child and Adolescent Psychiatric Clinics of North America, 20*, 155–171. http://dx.doi.org/10.1016/j.chc.2010.08.007

Myers, K. M., & Turvey, C. L. (Eds.). (2012). *Telemental health: Clinical, technical, and administrative foundations for evidence-based practice.* London, England: Elsevier.

National Association of Social Workers & Association of Social Work Boards. (2005). *Standards for technology and social work practice.* Retrieved from https://www.aswb.org/wp-content/uploads/2013/10/TechnologySWPractice.pdf

Nelson, E.-L., & Bui, T. (2010). Rural telepsychology services for children and adolescents. *Journal of Clinical Psychology, 66*, 490–501. http://dx.doi.org/10.1002/jclp.20682

O'Reilly, R., Bishop, J., Maddox, K., Hutchinson, L., Fisman, M., & Takhar, J. (2007). Is telepsychiatry equivalent to face-to-face psychiatry? Results from a randomized controlled equivalence trial. *Psychiatric Services, 58*, 836–843. http://dx.doi.org/10.1176/ps.2007.58.6.836

Rabinowitz, T., Murphy, K. M., Amour, J. L., Ricci, M. A., Caputo, M. P., & Newhouse, P. A. (2010). Benefits of a telepsychiatry consultation service for rural nursing home residents. *Telemedicine and e-Health, 16*, 34–40. http://dx.doi.org/10.1089/tmj.2009.0088

Sharp, I. R., Kobak, K. A., & Osman, D. A. (2011). The use of videoconferencing with patients with psychosis: A review of the literature. *Annals of General Psychiatry, 10*, 14. http://dx.doi.org/10.1186/1744-859X-10-14

Shim, R., Ye, J., & Yun, K. (2012). Treating culturally and linguistically isolated Koreans via telepsychiatry. *Psychiatric Services, 63*, 946. http://dx.doi.org/10.1176/appi.ps.20120p946

Shore, J. H., Brooks, E., Savin, D., Orton, H., Grigsby, J., & Manson, S. M. (2008). Acceptability of telepsychiatry in American Indians. *Telemedicine and e-Health, 14*, 461–466. http://dx.doi.org/10.1089/tmj.2007.0077

Tuerk, P. W., & Shore, P. (Eds.). (2015). *Clinical videoconferencing in telehealth.* Cham, Switzerland: Springer. http://dx.doi.org/10.1007/978-3-319-08765-8

Turvey, C., Coleman, M., Dennison, O., Drude, K., Goldenson, M., Hirsch, P., . . . Bernard, J. (2013). ATA practice guidelines for video-based online mental health services. *Telemedicine and e-Health, 19*, 722–730. http://dx.doi.org/10.1089/tmj.2013.9989

Turvey, C. L., Willyard, D., Hickman, D. H., Klein, D. M., & Kukoyi, O. (2007). Telehealth screen for depression in a chronic illness care management program. *Telemedicine and e-Health*, *13*, 51–56. http://dx.doi.org/10.1089/tmj.2006.0036

Wacker, D. P., Lee, J. F., Padilla Dalmau, Y. C., Kopelman, T. G., Lindgren, S. D., Kuhle, J., . . . Waldron, D. B. (2013). Conducting functional communication training via telehealth to reduce the problem behavior of young children with autism. *Journal of Developmental and Physical Disabilities*, *25*, 35–48. http://dx.doi.org/10.1007/s10882-012-9314-0

Ye, J., Shim, R., Lukaszewski, T., Yun, K., Kim, S. H., & Rust, G. (2012). Telepsychiatry services for Korean immigrants. *Telemedicine and e-Health*, *18*, 797–802. http://dx.doi.org/10.1089/tmj.2012.0041

Yellowlees, P. M., Odor, A., Iosif, A.-M., Parish, M. B., Nafiz, N., Patrice, K., . . . Hilty, D. (2013). Transcultural psychiatry made simple—Asynchronous telepsychiatry as an approach to providing culturally relevant care. *Telemedicine and e-Health*, *19*, 259–264. http://dx.doi.org/10.1089/tmj.2012.0077

David D. Luxton

Behavioral and Mental Health Apps

3

Mobile health (mHealth) software applications, or *apps*, are software programs that operate on mobile devices such as smartphones and tablet computers (Luxton, McCann, Bush, Mishkind, & Reger, 2011). The numbers of behavioral and mental health-related mobile apps have increased exponentially over the last decade—at present, several thousand are available for download. mHealth apps are used in diverse health care settings, from small practices to large systems, and they are also used by individuals who seek to improve their health and well-being. Although you the clinician may have not yet incorporated mHealth apps into your practice, the chances are that many of your colleagues and maybe even your clients are already using them.

Mobile apps provide a diverse array of useful and powerful tools for both care seekers and care providers. For care seekers, they provide a convenient way to access self-care information and functions, such as resource locators, self-assessments, and treatments that are immediately available seven days a week (Luxton, Hansen, & Stanfill, 2014; Luxton et al., 2011). Mobile devices also provide a convenient method for communication between care seekers and providers, such as the capability of sending behavioral reminders via Short Message Service (SMS) texting, scheduling and appointment reminders,

http://dx.doi.org/10.1037/0000085-004
Using Technology in Mental Health Practice, J. J. Magnavita (Editor)

43

and the capability for synchronous video telemental health services (Luxton et al., 2011; Luxton, Mishkind, Crumpton, Ayers, & Mysliwiec, 2012). For care providers, mHealth apps can assist with clinical decision support, practice management, coding and billing, and e-learning, as well as health research, education, communication, and reference (Martínez-Pérez et al., 2014; Terry, 2010). Mobile apps can also provide an innovative way to collect rich behavioral data in real time to facilitate clinical assessment and research (Luxton, June, Sano, & Bickmore, 2015).

For clinicians, evaluating and selecting appropriate apps for use in practice can at first seem daunting. The practitioner must not only weed through the vast number of apps available on the market but must also consider the technical requirements and factors associated with their use (e.g., compatibility, network connection availability), as well as the important issues of data security, privacy, and the appropriate management of crises and other potential patient safety issues. In this chapter, I aim to ease concerns of care providers by providing useful, need-to-know information on how to select these technologies and apply them to behavioral and mental health services.

This chapter begins with a brief history of this technology and a review of the available data regarding the clinical effectiveness of mHealth apps. I then discuss the clinical use of mHealth apps across diverse populations and clinical applications. Next, I discuss the general benefits of mHealth apps in clinical practice and essential steps for integrating them into care. I also present relevant privacy, regulatory, and ethical considerations specific to the use of mHealth technologies. Finally, the chapter concludes with a list of helpful resources that provide additional information regarding the integration of mental and behavioral health apps into clinical practice.

Mobile Health Apps: Background

Smart mobile devices, such as smartphones and tablet computers (e.g., iPads), are essentially portable personal computers with wireless connectivity (typically cellular, Wi-Fi, or both). Like conventional desktop personal computers, these devices typically have a central processing unit, memory, input and output interfaces (e.g., keyboard or touchscreen, audio input and output, Universal Serial Bus ports), and a power supply (i.e., a battery). Mobile apps are the software programs or "applications" that provide a particular service or function on a mobile device. An operating system (OS) is the software that provides the backbone functionality on a mobile device, which allows the device to execute applications and controls its hardware. As of 2015, the most widely used mobile device OSs were, in order of market share: Android, iOS, Windows Phone, Blackberry OS (Gartner, 2015). It is important to note that not all apps are available for all OSs and, therefore, cannot be used with every type of mobile device. This must be considered when selecting the apps to use in your practice.

Commercially available handheld mobile electronic devices have been used in health care since the early 1990s. Early examples included Apple's first handheld device—the Apple Newton—followed by personal digital assistants (e.g., Palm Pilots), and early smartphones (e.g., Ericsson's GS88; Luxton et al., 2011). In summer 2007,

Apple released the first iPhone. This device had the touch-screen feature of tablets but with the size and functionality of a mobile cellular phone. The phone also had the ability to support third-party software apps. The Apple iPhone led the smartphone revolution, with ensuing smartphone device offerings from Samsung, Ericsson, Motorola, Nokia, Blackberry (previously Research In Motion), and others. In April 2010, Apple introduced its iPad tablet, which was followed by tablets that run on the Google Android OS.

The continual improvements in computing power, wireless technologies, software development, as well as the consistent reduction of costs, have facilitated a boom in modern mHealth technologies. According to estimates from the Global Mobile Health Market Report 2010–2015 (research2guidance, 2013), there are 500 million smartphone users worldwide (including health care professionals, patients, and other consumers) who are using health care–related apps. By 2018, 50% of the more than 3.4 billion smartphone and tablet users will have downloaded a health-related app. Also, research suggests that mental health patients' rates of smartphone ownership is near the national average in the United States, and that they have a strong interest in using their phones to monitor mental health (Torous, Chan, et al., 2014a; Torous, Friedman, & Keshavan, 2014b).

Wearable technologies are also an important part of the mHealth boom. Wearable technologies used in mHealth include smartwatches, smartglasses, and smartclothing (Luxton, June, Sano, et al., 2015). One of the principal benefits of these technologies is that they are in physical contact with users for an extended time and do not require users to interact with a keyboard or touch screen (e.g., on a mobile phone) while they are wearing them. Wearable technologies can be integrated with smartphone technology to collect physiological or other data for behavioral and mental health applications. For example, the accelerometer on a smartwatch can be used to measure and track a person's physical activity throughout the day and sleep patterns at night, which then can be integrated with behavioral self-assessments surveys delivered via a smartphone. Emergent wearable technologies include intelligent devices that are worn on the eyes (i.e., smart contact lenses) or embedded beneath the skin (Luxton, 2014; Luxton, June, Sano, et al., 2015).

Evidence Base for Behavioral and Mental Health Apps

Several published qualitative and quantitative reviews have evaluated the use and efficacy of mobile health apps in behavioral and mental health (see Free et al., 2013; Harrison et al., 2011; Luxton et al., 2011; Luxton, June, & Chalker, 2015; Mohr, Burns, Schueller, Clarke, & Klinkman, 2013; Terry, 2010). Some of these reviews have focused specifically on mental health apps, whereas others have focused more broadly on general health and included psychiatric conditions.

Most of the extant reviews provide at least some degree of encouraging support for the use of apps in clinical care. Donker et al.'s (2013) systematic review, for example, included trials that examined the effects of mental health apps (for anxiety, depression, substance use, sleep disturbances, suicidal behavior, self-harm, psychotic disorders, eating disorders, stress, and gambling) with a pre- to posttest design or compared with a control group (wait list, treatment-as-usual, or another recognized treatment). The final review consisted of eight published papers, describing five apps that targeted depression, anxiety, and substance abuse. Four apps provided support from a mental health professional. The results showed significant reductions in depression, stress, and substance use with within-group and between-group (intent-to-treat effect sizes ranging from 0.29 to 2.28 and from 0.01 to 0.48 at posttest and follow-up) patients. However, only two of the five evidence-based mental health apps were currently available in app stores. Donker et al. concluded that mobile apps have the potential to be effective and may improve treatment accessibility. Nevertheless, these researchers note that the findings should be interpreted with caution given the few studies and participants included in the review and the unknown efficacy of long-term follow-up.

Other research has focused on willingness-to-use, acceptability, and adherence. For example, Torous, Friedman, and Keshavan (2014b) examined smartphone ownership and interest in mobile apps to monitor symptoms of mental health conditions. They surveyed 320 psychiatric outpatients from four clinics around the United States (i.e., a state clinic in Massachusetts, a county clinic in California, a hybrid public and private clinic in Louisiana, and a private/university clinic in Wisconsin) with the goal of capturing a geographically and socioeconomically diverse patient population. The results indicated that the rate of ownership of smartphones among psychiatric outpatients was near the national average, and that overall patient interest in using smartphones to monitor their mental health was high. Their results also suggested that psychiatric outpatients had favorable responses to the idea of using their own smartphones to monitor their mental health (70.6% favored this assessment modality). Similar to national trends for smartphone ownership, these researchers found that the youngest generation (defined as persons under 30 years of age in their study) had the highest rates of both ownership and willingness to use mobile apps for assessment.

A challenge associated with delivering behavioral mental health treatment via smartphone apps is long-term adherence (Ainsworth et al., 2013). Ainsworth et al. (2013) conducted a review and found that less than one third of patients with schizophrenia were willing to complete a smartphone assessment for 5 weeks or longer. However, many of the studies were only short-term interventions, and some of the longer studies experienced high dropout rates. Other studies have shown very favorable adherence and acceptability of mental health-related mobile apps (e.g., Depp et al., 2010). Contributing factors to adherence and acceptability may include the target population and whether (or to what degree) app users receive clinician guidance or coaching.

Most existing reviews note the limitation of existing studies and the need for more quality research, including randomized controlled trials that evaluate mobile technologies that augment traditional interventions to improve health outcomes (Mohr et al., 2013; Powell, Landman, & Bates, 2014). As pointed out by de Beurs, Kirtley, Kerkhof, Portzky, and O'Connor (2015), most experimental studies rely on convenience samples—typically students or patients from a local hospital—thereby limiting the ability to generalize the findings. There is also a universal lack of data from larger program evaluations of mHealth apps.

In recognizing the evidence gap, the U.S. National Institutes of Health (NIH) held an mHealth evidence workshop in 2013 to address the issue and encourage research "needed to assess when, where, and for whom mHealth devices, apps, and systems are efficacious" (Kumar et al., 2013, p. 228). Some of the primary challenges identified during the workshop included the need for collection of enormous quantities of real-world patient-generated data and the problems associated with the rapid development and obsolescence of the new technologies to be studied. Indeed, by the time a trial or large program evaluation has been completed, the technology may have advanced or been superseded, making it difficult to comprehensively evaluate the efficacy of any particular app. Thus, the field could benefit from faster evaluation and dissemination methods (Schueller, Muñoz, & Mohr, 2013).

Although the available literature is beginning to show promising results for evidence-based mental health apps, clinicians should consider the gaps in the available research specific to their particular need (i.e., to address a particular health condition or population). Fortunately, more and more research is being conducted on the efficacy of apps used in behavioral and mental health care. Clinicians can, therefore, expect to benefit from a more extensive evidence base in the years ahead.

Scope of Applications

Apps are available to assist with the treatment and management of just about every mental health condition, including anxiety disorders, depression, eating disorders, psychosis, and for suicide prevention, as well as for the management of health-related behaviors such as diet, exercise, smoking cessation, sleep, relaxation, and medication adherence (Donker et al., 2013; Luxton et al., 2011). Apps are also designed for specific demographic populations, such as children, adolescents, young adults, and older persons. Some are gender specific and others are for varied cultural groups. While the majority of apps available for download from the major storefronts are in English, some developers have specially versioned apps for people who speak non-English languages.

Relevance of the Apps in Behavioral and Mental Health Care

CLINICAL ASSESSMENT AND SYMPTOM MONITORING

Mobile apps provide a convenient tool for conducting assessment with standardized measures, clinical measures, and surveys (Luxton et al., 2011). Self-assessment data can, in some instances, can be integrated with other functions of the app, such as display of data on graphs to track change over time (e.g., change in mood, stress, or pain levels). Moreover, data collected via electronic survey can be used by the app to alert or direct users to engage in a particular behavior. For example, several available suicide prevention apps can direct users to review a safety plan or contact help resources when the user self-reports increased levels of depression or suicidal thinking (see Luxton, June, & Chalker, 2015).

SELF-CARE: NONCLINICAL BEHAVIOR CHANGE AND IMPROVEMENT

One of the most popular uses of mobile apps is end-user self-care. Apps facilitate this with tools that are available at any time that they may be needed. Mobile apps also provide opportunities for users to measure, track, and share data about health, wellness, and health-related behaviors with other people. The Quantified Self movement, for example, allows people to obtain a broad range of data about themselves (e.g., behavioral patterns, physiological and mood states, environmental information) from mobile self-tracking apps and wearable technologies, and share and compare them with the data of millions of other people via the Internet (Wolf, 2011). The goal of collecting these data is for self-monitoring and self-reflection to facilitate change or improvement.

INFORMATIONAL RESOURCES

Mobile apps provide a convenient platform to provide psychoeducation, clinical information, and training to care seekers and health care providers. For example, many apps provide information of the signs and symptoms of health conditions. Some apps provide interactive or adaptive virtual training tools that coach skill rehearsal in order to facilitate skill acquisition. Other apps assist clinicians with the provision of evidence-based treatments (e.g., *PTSD Coach* and *CBT-i* apps, which are available at https://mobile.va.gov/appstore).

RESOURCE LOCATION AND CRISIS SUPPORT

Some apps are designed to assist with help services resource location and crisis support. Some of the primary features of these apps include "emergency-buttons," crisis support resource locators, and information and peer support functions. The emergency-button (sometimes referred to as "hot-button" or "red-button") feature makes use of the mobile device's cellular, e-mail, or Internet connection for immediate connection to a crisis line (or other resources) whenever and wherever a person may feel the need. The resource location and emergency-button features of these apps are particularly useful, considering that a patient may need help in off-hours. Moreover, users, including family members or other persons supporting a client in crisis, may also appreciate the simplicity and ease-of-use of the emergency-button feature and the peace-of-mind of knowing that it is there, if it is ever needed (Luxton, June, & Chalker, 2015).

The *ReliefLink* app (Emory University, Woodruff Health Sciences Center, 2013), for example, is an app with resource location and crisis support features. It is intended to facilitate continuity of care and follow-up care for patients after discharge from an inpatient unit or emergency department (ED). The app uses a map feature and global positioning system (GPS) to locate help resources that are in proximity to the user. The app also features mood/behavior monitoring and tracking features, a safety-planning feature, built-in coping tools (i.e., relaxation and mindfulness exercises, relaxing radio music), medication and appointment reminders, an emergency-button that can connect patients to helplines, a 911 feature, and contact information for health care providers, friends, and/or family members.

SYNCHRONOUS VIDEO AND TEXTING APPLICATIONS

Most modern smartphones and tablets have built-in video and audio capabilities; videoconference apps make use of these capabilities to enable mobile synchronous video telehealth capacities. Examples of popular video apps include Facetime, Skype, and Vidyo. This mobile video capability has opened new doors for a range of tele-mental health services, including treatments, consultation, and remote assessment (Luxton et al., 2011). Smartphones and tablets provide new opportunities for behavioral health care that is low cost, flexible, and mobile. However, wireless devices must generally use either cellular or wi-fi network connections and, thus, videoconferencing connection quality will depend on available network bandwidth (Luxton, Mishkind, et al., 2012).

Smartphones can also be used to provide patients with psychoeducation via SMS text messaging (Cole-Lewis & Kershaw, 2010). Text and e-mail in health care can be used to send appointment reminders, behavioral reminders, and to provide individual-level support (Free et al., 2013). Texting has a number of advantages, including high popularity and low cost. Texting is also asynchronous; thus, users can access text messages at their convenience. The use of this technology may be especially useful for addressing suicide risk among patients following treatment, including after release from psychiatric inpatient units or EDs (Luxton, June, & Chalker, 2015). For example, Caring Contacts (Luxton, June, & Comtois, 2013; Motto, 1976) is a suicide prevention intervention that sends brief caring messages to high-risk patients following discharge from treatment.

Practitioners must remain aware of Health Insurance Portability and Accountability Act (HIPAA) and data security requirements when using video and/or texting apps. Not all mobile video apps, including Skype, are presently HIPAA compliant (Luxton, Nelson, & Maheu, 2016). Thus, if you are considering integrating these types of apps into care, a review of HIPAA compliance regulations is a must.

MOMENTARY ASSESSMENT AND PREDICTIVE ANALYTICS

Mobile technologies also provide opportunities for sophisticated data collection to detect risk in real time and to recommend intervention (Luxton, June, Sano, et al., 2015). Ecological momentary assessment involves the sampling of current behaviors and experiences in real time in the natural environment (Moskowitz & Young, 2006), and predictive analytics entails extracting information from existing data sets to determine patterns and to predict emerging (i.e., future) outcomes (Luxton, 2015). Data inputs may include Internet and social media usage (i.e., a measure of social activity), surveys provided on a mobile device (i.e., to collect symptom data or attitudes), behavioral data (e.g., exercise- and sleep-pattern data collected by smartwatches), and environmental data (e.g., location). These data inputs can be used to develop context-aware systems that automatically detect when clients/patients need assistance, automatically deliver tailored assistance during problematic situations, and/or alert health care providers and/or the user to apply a safety plan and coping skills (Burns et al., 2011; Luxton, June, Sano, et al., 2015).

For example, Burns et al. (2011) developed and evaluated the *Mobilyze!* app that is intended to help people to manage depressive symptoms. The mobile phone app and supporting architecture make use of mobile device–sensed data (e.g., GPS, ambient light, recent calls) and data entered by the user (e.g., patients' mood, emotions, and cognitive/motivational states) that are encrypted and transmitted to several server-based software components. Machine learning algorithms are used to generate a user-specific model to predict the client's future state from sensed data, while also discarding irrelevant information not of predictive value in the model. The output can then be used to automatically assist the client or clinician in identifying whether further intervention is needed. According to the authors, the *Mobilyze!* app is the first ecological momentary intervention for unipolar depression, as well as one of the first attempts to use context sensing to identify mental health–related states.

Benefits of Incorporating Behavioral and Mental Health Apps

One of the greatest benefits of mHealth devices (i.e., smartphones and tablets) and the apps that operate on them is increased access to point-of-use tools (Luxton, June, & Chalker, 2015). Mobile apps also provide the benefit of clinical and behavioral data collection, such as mood states or sleep patterns, in real time. Other benefits include patient-centered customization, the ability to upload and use data from the cloud, and cost savings.

POINT-OF-USE AVAILABILITY

Clients/patients can carry their devices with them throughout the day (and night) and can use mobile apps whenever and wherever they want. Thus, mobile apps can provide immediate access to self-care resources, whether it be coping tools or red-button access to crisis services. Mobile apps can also improve access to information for healthcare providers, including electronic health records and informational databases. This immediately available access to information has been shown to improve clinical decision making and patient outcomes (Martínez-Pérez et al., 2014; Ventola, 2014).

REAL-TIME DATA COLLECTION AND MONITORING

Data can be collected passively via a mobile (or wearable) device's sensors and by surveys administered via apps, with the potential for sharing those data with health care providers for review between or during treatment sessions. This certainly has advantages over the traditional methods of asking clients/patients to document and monitor their symptoms and behaviors in a paper-and-pencil survey, checklist, or journal.

PATIENT-CENTERED CUSTOMIZATION

Mobile apps can be designed or "versioned" by developers to appeal to and best fit the needs of specific client or patient populations. App content can be provided in different languages or designed to improve accessibility for persons with disabilities. For example, some apps provide both visual- and audio-based instructions and feature navigational functions that can assist persons with hearing or visual impairments. Many mobile apps also have the capability for end users to customize features and functions based on their own preferences and needs. For example, visual appearance or choice of male or female voice narration can be adjusted on some apps.

TECHNOLOGICAL INTEGRATION AND INTEROPERABILITY

One of the greatest benefits of mobile devices is the ability to link the functionality and data of mobile apps to other devices via the cloud. The Internet, and more specifically cloud computing, are the principal technologies that enable this connectivity and integration. In cloud computing, data processing and data storage are not based on one local computer or device, but accessed via the internet. The use of wireless technologies (e.g., wi-fi, Bluetooth, cellular) allows multiple types of hardware devices (e.g., smartphones and intelligent wearables) to connect to and integrate with other devices and data via the cloud (Luxton, June, Sano, et al., 2015). Ultimately, mobile apps can be integrated as part of comprehensive systems that support patient-centered care. For example, some health care systems enable patients to upload the data from their mobile device to their electronic health records and for health care providers to access that data on their mobile devices.

LOWER COSTS

Mobile apps can contribute to significant cost savings. For example, the automated access to information, billing, or other office management needs provided on mobile devices can improve the efficiency of health care delivery and, thus, lower costs. Mobile apps can also help to reduce costs of health care via the "stepped-care" model. In stepped care, patients receive treatment at increasing "steps" or levels of intensity (i.e., the amount and type) depending on their needs (Bower & Gilbody, 2005). For example, patients may initially be provided with low-cost guided self-help/self-management via a mobile app and be progressed to more intensive behavioral health options, such as therapy or inpatient treatment, if needed. Moreover, mobile apps can facilitate the stepped care model by providing options for close and more immediate monitoring of symptoms and outcomes, thereby informing when the next step of care may be necessary (Luxton et al., 2014).

A CASE EXAMPLE

A patient who is being treated for a physical health condition is also experiencing ongoing stress and occasional problems with sleep. The patient is referred to a psychologist on the team for assessment. The psychologist determines that, at the present time, the patient does not meet the criteria for behavioral health treatment services. The patient is shown how to download and use a stress management app that they may utilize on their own. The app provides specific training and guided demonstration on how to apply and practice evidence-based relaxation breathing techniques. The patient can customize the app to speed up or slow down the guided breathing exercises to their preferred comfort level. The patient self-monitors their symptoms at home via self-assessments provided within the app. Symptom self-assessment data is automatically uploaded to the medical record and shared with their health care provider (if HIPAA compliant) or shown to the provider on a follow-up visit. If the patient's symptoms persist or worsen, he or she is again evaluated by a health-care provider and progressed to the next level of care (e.g., a sleep study and traditional in-office treatment for insomnia). The patient is encouraged to continue to use the app in between outpatient sessions.

Advice for Incorporating Apps Into Mental Health Practice

Luxton, June, and Chalker (2015) provided recommendations for selecting apps and integrating them into care (see Table 3.1 for the checklist). These recommendations are discussed and elaborated upon in this section.

1. IDENTIFY CLINICAL NEED AND APPROPRIATENESS

An initial step is to assess what the individual client needs and to match the appropriate intervention and tools to these needs. Mobile apps are typically intended to augment clinical care and, thus, how they may best accomplish this may differ from one clinical situation to another based on the client's needs. For example, some clients/patients may benefit solely from the informational component of a mobile app (e.g., evidence-based coping strategies presented therein), whereas others may benefit from symptom-tracking features or interactive coaching that requires active participation and practice from the client.

TABLE 3.1

Checklist for Selecting and Integrating Mobile Health Apps for Use in Clinical Care

Step	Specific considerations
1. Identify clinical needs.	■ Determine what tool or application may benefit patient needs: 　■ Treatment need 　■ Symptom monitoring 　■ Information only ■ Determine patient preference for use of technology tool: 　■ Assess experience with technologies. 　■ Determine access to technologies (e.g., smartphones).
2. Determine what apps are available and assess quality of the tool/application.	■ Visit resources. ■ Search app stores. ■ Read available literature regarding mobile health apps. ■ Review information about the application. ■ Review published scientific literature. ■ Review user feedback. ■ Receive training (if available). ■ Discuss with colleagues.
3. Review regulatory and data security requirements.	■ Does application fall under medical device requirements? ■ Does application meet HIPAA requirements? ■ Review local policies. ■ Review safety risks.
4. Evaluate/test it.	■ Test it yourself before use. ■ Get feedback from your individual patients.
5. Plan use/develop protocols.	■ Discuss safety/expectations with patient. ■ Plan protocols for use: 　■ Review existing, or 　■ Develop protocols (how who and when to use the application).

Note. From "Mobile Health Technologies for Suicide Prevention: Feature Review and Recommendations for Use in Clinical Care," by D. D. Luxton, J. D. June, and S. A. Chalker, 2015, *Current Treatment Options in Psychiatry*, *2*, p. 356. Copyright 2015 by Springer. Adapted with permission.

Clients' preferences for using the technology must also be assessed. This should include an assessment of their experience with technology, access to technology (e.g., phone ownership and/or access to wireless connection), or any other concerns that they may have (e.g., how any collected data may be used and secured). As Luxton, June, and Chalker (2015) suggested, this information is important for ascertaining the fit between patient and technology, as well as determining what additional training or coaching may be required to help the client to feel comfortable and confident with the technology. Clinicians should also be mindful of any cognitive deficits or physical challenges (e.g., inadequate vision, hearing, or hand or finger movement) that may impede use of the technology. It is important for care providers to discuss usability issues with their clients, consider options for customizing the tools when possible, or suggest appropriate alternatives.

2. DETERMINE WHAT APPS ARE AVAILABLE AND ASSESS THEIR QUALITY

Perhaps the most difficult step is determining what app or apps are most appropriate for use in clinical care, given the sheer number available. An internet search, as well as a search of the app storefront, is a logical starting point. Keep in mind that even if an app is advertised as "evidence based" because it consists of content from a tested therapeutic approach, it does not mean that use of the app is evidence based (Luxton, June, & Chalker, 2015). Presently, there is not an established mobile health app certification or accreditation process that involves formal review of apps for appropriateness for any given use. Thus, it is necessary to review the available information about any app of interest to assess its quality and appropriateness for your intended application.

A literature review of the app or a program that has used apps for a target condition or population of interest is highly recommended. A review of any information from the manufacturer or organization that produced the app, along with user manuals or clinical guides, is also a good idea. The app description available at the mobile applications store (i.e., iTunes, Google Play, Amazon Appstore), user reviews, and sometimes the number of downloads of the app can provide indicators of its quality and user friendliness. However, a disadvantage of this strategy alone is that it does not consider the evidence base, validity, or accuracy of the app (Boudreaux et al., 2014). Review of mobile app clearinghouses websites is also recommended (Boudreaux et al., 2014). Clearinghouses, such as MobiHealthNews (http://mobihealthnews.com), often provide structured evaluations and recommendations from health care providers that are consolidated in one place. Talking with colleagues who may have experience with the app in their practice, as well as the attendance at training workshops or conference proceedings regarding the use of the mobile app(s), can also be helpful.

Because the majority of apps are freely available to the public, patients may download and use them without collaboration with a clinician. It is, therefore, a good idea to ask clients or patients about their awareness of and use of apps and other resources, such as self-care websites and social media groups. A review of a patient's use of and experience with mHealth apps and social media can be helpful for determining additional resources and potential exposures to risks (Luxton, June, & Chalker, 2015).

3. REGULATORY, DATA SECURITY, AND POLICY REVIEW

One of the most important steps to integrating mobile apps into a practice is the careful review of regulatory, data security, and applicable policy requirements. In the United States, the Food and Drug Administration (FDA) provides regulatory control and guidance concerning mobile devices that function as medical devices, and defines them as a device "intended to be used as an accessory to a regulated medical device, or transform a mobile platform into a regulated medical device" (Food and Drug Administration, 2015b). The FDA presently considers a medical device to be a product intended to prevent or treat any aspect of human functioning. For an mHealth app to fall under current FDA regulation, it must meet this definition and be intended to be used as an accessory to an already-regulated medical device or to transform a mobile platform into a regulated medical device (Food and Drug Administration, 2015a). The FDA stipulates that not all mobile health apps will meet these criteria, and it gives several examples of types of mobile apps that it does not intend to regulate. These typically include apps that are classified as being solely education/training tools or those that automate office operations (e.g., an electronic billing function). A review of the FDA requirements and any documentation provided by the manufacturer of an mHealth app is a prudent step for clinicians and health care organizations to take.

Clinicians should also review applicable institutional-level policy regarding the use of mobile technologies. Some institutions may have developed specific protocols or identified and approved particular apps as part of the standard of care. For example, the U.S. Department of Veterans Affairs supports the use of several apps as part of their standards of care in behavioral health services (for more information, visit https://mobile.va.gov/appstore).

The responsible use of mobile apps during clinical practice also requires that individual practitioners and health care organizations remain cognizant of risks to patient privacy and data security. Some mHealth apps have the capability to collect, store, and transmit Protected Health Information (PHI). Patients may do whatever they choose with their own data that are collected, stored, or transmitted on mobile devices. However, when a patient transmits or shares any electronic PHI with a HIPAA-covered entity, then the health care professional becomes responsible for HIPAA compliance (Luxton, Kayl, & Mishkind, 2012). Since 2013, upon the enactment of the Health Information Technology for Economic and Clinical Health (HITECH) Act, the penalties for HIPAA noncompliance have become more severe (U.S. Government Printing Office, 2013). A summary of the new rules, as well as additional helpful information regarding HIPAA requirements, is available from the American Medical Association (see https://www.ama-assn.org/practice-management/hipaa-compliance).

Keep in mind that when using synchronous video apps for telemental health clinical services, most laws and regulations define the originating site (i.e., site-of-care delivery) as where the client or patient is located. It is necessary for health professionals who are providing telemental health services to be familiar with the individual state requirements of this originating site. This is because some states have specific telemedicine laws, and these laws vary from state to state as to the types and circumstances of care that can be provided across state lines. Moreover, telemental health services across state lines are potentially under the regulation of both the state where the provider is located and the state where the patient is located, making knowledge of more than just one state law a requirement (Luxton et al., 2016).

4. EVALUATE AND TEST

It is also a good idea to pilot test any app of interest before using it in clinical practice (Boudreaux et al., 2014; Luxton, June, & Chalker, 2015). This should include a review and test of all of the features, limitations, and information within the app to determine its accuracy. Additionally, solicit feedback from your clients regarding their experiences with the app, as this will be helpful for determining what may work best for them and whether nontechnological alternatives (e.g., paper-and-pencil assessments) may be more appropriate. Specific questions that are important to ask patients when soliciting their feedback include whether they used the app and, if so, how often; whether they experienced any problems with the app (e.g., finding features or experiencing technical problems); and whether they felt that use of it was beneficial to them.

5. PLAN USE AND DEVELOP PROTOCOLS

Health care providers must consider safety issues and expectations regarding the use of mobile apps when incorporating them into practice. One of the topics that should be discussed during the informed-consent process and throughout care, as needed, is the expectation regarding contact via electronic means. Electronic forms of communication, such as e-mail and texting, are instant and, thus, there may be an expectation by patients of immediate response by health care providers (Luxton, June, & Comtois, 2013). It is, thus, important to discuss expectations, including typical response times and limits to availability (e.g., whether or not a response can be expected during off-hours or on weekends). A discussion of the risks and a plan for what happens if the battery runs out of power, wireless signal is lost, or a patient loses their smartphone should also be discussed during the informed-consent process.

LIMITATIONS OF MOBILE HEALTH TECHNOLOGY

Several limitations need to be considered when incorporating mHealth technologies into care. As noted earlier, technology can quickly become obsolete. A more significant limitation, however, is that not all clients or patients will have access to these technologies. Access to wireless networks in some areas or countries is also a potential limitation. Fortunately, access is improving worldwide—it estimated that by 2017, 85% of the world's population will be covered by a commercial wireless signal (Savitz, 2012). The adoption of mHealth technologies in health care organizations can also be hindered due to a lack of awareness or knowledge of their capabilities, concerns about patient privacy (i.e., electronic data security), lack of supporting technology infrastructure, or economic barriers (Luxton, June, & Chalker, 2015). Identification of a local mobile health "champion" who can help to educate an organization and train other clinicians may be helpful.

The Future of Mobile Health Technology

Technological innovation will continue to improve mHealth capabilities. Future mobile apps will take advantage of larger databases and more powerful integration with cloud computing. Improvements in sensing and affect-detection technologies will allow for more adaptive mobile operating systems and applications that adjust to the needs of users (Luxton, June, Sano, et al., 2015). Artificial Intelligence techniques also provide an opportunity to improve the accuracy and efficiency of mHealth apps, while also making them more interactive and user-friendly (Luxton, June, Sano, et al., 2015). For example, speech recognition and natural language processing technologies (e.g., those used by Apple's Siri, Microsoft's Cortana, or IBM's Watson) make interaction with technology much more natural, efficient, and engaging.

Virtual reality is another exciting emergent technology with implications for mHealth. For example, augmented reality (also called mixed reality) combines virtual reality with the real world by superimposing computer-generated graphics on live video imagery (Luxton, 2015). The technology can also be used with GPS capabilities that can provide real-time location data to the user. Several mobile apps have this capability, as do wearable devices such as Google's Glass (wearable intelligent glasses). Also, virtual intelligent agents, such as virtual humans, can be used on mobile devices to provide real-time feedback about behavioral patterns and coaching (Luxton, June, Sano, et al., 2015). A primary benefit of this technology is that virtual humans are available to provide advice and supportive motivation to users anytime and anywhere it is needed. The extended contact time with clients, along with the perception that the virtual human is sharing more of their personal experience, has the potential to establish what clients perceive to be a trusting, working alliance with them (Luxton, June, Sano, et al., 2015).

Conclusion

Mobile apps designed for behavioral and mental health have the potential to improve clinical care and overall health. Not only do they provide an opportunity to increase access to evidence-based mental health care, they also empower care seekers by providing them with 24/7 access to evidence-based tools that give them more control over the management of their care and health. Mobile apps also help improve the everyday function of care providers and entire health care systems by increasing the efficiency of office management and access to information. Mobile apps can be used as part of stepped care approaches to providing healthcare that help in the process of addressing provider shortages. These tools also provide opportunities to gather rich data on individual behavior, emotional states, and social context that can be used to inform interventions aimed at behavior change unlike any technological tool or approach used in the past.

Mobile apps are here to stay, and their use will only continue to expand in behavioral and mental healthcare. Indeed, a new trend can be seen with some health-care providers in both behavioral health and primary care who are prescribing apps to patients as a part of a larger treatment plan (Lippman, 2013). Just as with any other technology used in health care, providers must be familiar with best practices to ensure competent and ethical practice. With appropriate training and hands-on practice, providers can assure that their patients are getting the best possible care through the use of technology to improve health and well-being.

Essential Resources

Boudreaux, E. D., Waring, M. E., Hayes, R. B., Sadasivam, R. S., Mullen, S., & Pagoto, S. (2014). Evaluating and selecting mobile health apps: Strategies for healthcare providers and healthcare organizations. *Translational Behavioral Medicine, 4,* 363–371. http://dx.doi.org/10.1007/s13142-014-0293-9

Luxton, D. D., June, J. D., & Chalker, S. (2015). Mobile health technologies for suicide prevention: Feature review and recommendations for use in clinical care. *Current Treatment Options in Psychiatry, 2,* 349–362. http://dx.doi.org/10.1007/s40501-015-0057-2

Luxton, D. D., June, J. D., Sano, A., & Bickmore, T. (2015). Mobile, wearable, and ambient intelligence in behavioral health care. In D. D. Luxton (Ed.), *Artificial intelligence in behavioral and mental health care.* Cambridge, MA: Academic Press.

Luxton, D. D., McCann, R. A., Bush, N. E., Mishkind, M. C., & Reger, G. M. (2011). mHealth for mental health: Integrating smartphone technology in behavioral healthcare. *Professional Psychology: Research & Practice, 42,* 505–512. http://dx.doi.org/10.1037/a0024485

Mohr, D. C., Burns, M. N., Schueller, S. M., Clarke, G., & Klinkman, M. (2013). Behavioral intervention technologies: Evidence review and recommendations for future research in mental health. *General Hospital Psychiatry, 35,* 332–338. http://dx.doi.org/10.1016/j.genhosppsych.2013.03.008

References

Ainsworth, J., Palmier-Claus, J. E., Machin, M., Barrowclough, C., Dunn, G., Rogers, A., . . . Lewis, S. (2013). A comparison of two delivery modalities of a mobile phone-based assessment for serious mental illness: Native smartphone application vs text-messaging only implementations. *Journal of Medical Internet Research, 15*(4), e60. http://dx.doi.org/10.2196/jmir.2328

Boudreaux, E. D., Waring, M. E., Hayes, R. B., Sadasivam, R. S., Mullen, S., & Pagoto, S. (2014). Evaluating and selecting mobile health apps: Strategies for healthcare providers and healthcare organizations. *Translational Behavioral Medicine, 4,* 363–371. http://dx.doi.org/10.1007/s13142-014-0293-9

Bower, P., & Gilbody, S. (2005). Stepped care in psychological therapies: Access, effectiveness and efficiency. Narrative literature review. *The British Journal of Psychiatry, 186,* 11–17. http://dx.doi.org/10.1192/bjp.186.1.11

Burns, M. N., Begale, M., Duffecy, J., Gergle, D., Karr, C. J., Giangrande, E., & Mohr, D. C. (2011). Harnessing context sensing to develop a mobile intervention for depression. *Journal of Medical Internet Research, 13*(3), e55. http://dx.doi.org/10.2196/jmir.1838

Cole-Lewis, H., & Kershaw, T. (2010). Text messaging as a tool for behavior change in disease prevention and management. *Epidemiologic Reviews, 32,* 56–69. http://dx.doi.org/10.1093/epirev/mxq004

de Beurs, D., Kirtley, O., Kerkhof, A., Portzky, G., & O'Connor, R. C. (2015). The role of mobile phone technology in understanding and preventing suicidal behavior. *Crisis, 36,* 79–82. http://dx.doi.org/10.1027/0227-5910/a000316

Depp, C. A., Mausbach, B., Granholm, E., Cardenas, V., Ben-Zeev, D., Patterson, T. L., . . . Jeste, D. V. (2010). Mobile interventions for severe mental illness: Design and preliminary data from three approaches. *Journal of Nervous and Mental Disease, 198,* 715–721. http://dx.doi.org/10.1097/NMD.0b013e3181f49ea3

Donker, T., Petrie, K., Proudfoot, J., Clarke, J., Birch, M. R., & Christensen, H. (2013). Smartphones for smarter delivery of mental health programs: A systematic review. *Journal of Medical Internet Research, 15*(11), e247. http://dx.doi.org/10.2196/jmir.2791

Emory University, Woodruff Health Sciences Center. (2013). *Suicide prevention app awarded $50,000 prize at White House conference.* Retrieved from http://news.emory.edu/stories/2013/09/kaslow_relieflink_app/campus.html

Food and Drug Administration. (2015a, September 22). *Mobile medical applications.* Retrieved from https://www.fda.gov/MedicalDevices/DigitalHealth/MobileMedicalApplications/ucm255978.htm#a

Food and Drug Administration. (2015b, July 20). *What is a medical device?* Retrieved from http://www.fda.gov/AboutFDA/Transparency/Basics/ucm211822.htm

Free, C., Phillips, G., Galli, L., Watson, L., Felix, L., Edwards, P., . . . Haines, A. (2013). The effectiveness of mobile-health technology-based health behaviour change or disease management interventions for health care consumers: A systematic review. *PLoS Medicine, 10*(1), e1001362. Advance online publication. http://dx.doi.org/10.1371/journal.pmed.1001362

Gartner. (2015, November 18). *Gartner says emerging markets drove worldwide smartphone sales to 15.5 percent growth in third quarter of 2015.* Retrieved from https://www.gartner.com/newsroom/id/3169417

Harrison, V., Proudfoot, J., Wee, P. P., Parker, G., Pavlovic, D. H., & Manicavasagar, V. (2011). Mobile mental health: Review of the emerging field and proof of concept study. *Journal of Mental Health, 20,* 509–524. http://dx.doi.org/10.3109/09638237.2011.608746

Kumar, S., Nilsen, W. J., Abernethy, A., Atienza, A., Patrick, K., Pavel, M., . . . Swendeman, D. (2013). Mobile health technology evaluation: The mHealth evidence workshop. *American Journal of Preventive Medicine, 45,* 228–236. http://dx.doi.org/10.1016/j.amepre.2013.03.017

Lippman, H. (2013). How apps are changing family medicine: Clinicians' reviews. *Journal of Family Practice, 62,* 362–367. Retrieved from https://www.mdedge.com/sites/default/files/Document/September-2017/6207_JFP_Article4.pdf

Luxton, D. D. (2014). Artificial intelligence in psychological practice: Current and future applications and implications. *Professional Psychology: Research & Practice, 45,* 332–339. http://dx.doi.org/10.1037/a0034559

Luxton, D. D. (Ed.). (2015). *Artificial intelligence in behavioral and mental health care.* Cambridge, MA: Academic Press.

Luxton, D. D., Hansen, R. N., & Stanfill, K. (2014). Mobile app self-care versus in-office care for stress reduction: A cost minimization analysis. *Journal of Telemedicine and Telecare, 20*, 431–435. http://dx.doi.org/10.1177/1357633X14555616

Luxton, D. D., June, J. D., & Chalker, S. (2015). Mobile health technologies for suicide prevention: Feature review and recommendations for use in clinical care. *Current Treatment Options in Psychiatry, 2*, 349–362. http://dx.doi.org/10.1007/s40501-015-0057-2

Luxton, D. D., June, J. D., & Comtois, K. A. (2013). Can postdischarge follow-up contacts prevent suicide and suicidal behavior? A review of the evidence. *Crisis, 34*, 32–41. http://dx.doi.org/10.1027/0227-5910/a000158

Luxton, D. D., June, J. D., Sano, A., & Bickmore, T. (2015). Intelligent mobile, wearable, and ambient technologies in behavioral health care. In D. D. Luxton (Ed.), *Artificial intelligence in behavioral and mental health care.* San Diego, CA: Elsevier Academic Press.

Luxton, D. D., Kayl, R. A., & Mishkind, M. C. (2012). mHealth data security: The need for HIPAA-compliant standardization. *Telemedicine and e-Health, 18*, 284–288. http://dx.doi.org/10.1089/tmj.2011.0180

Luxton, D. D., McCann, R. A., Bush, N. E., Mishkind, M. C., & Reger, G. M. (2011). mHealth for Mental Health: Integrating Smartphone Technology in Behavioral Healthcare. *Professional Psychology Research and Practice, 42*, 505–512. http://dx.doi.org/10.1037/a0024485

Luxton, D. D., Mishkind, M. C., Crumpton, R. M., Ayers, T. D., & Mysliwiec, V. (2012). Usability and feasibility of smartphone video capabilities for telehealth care in the U.S. military. *Telemedicine and e-Health, 18*, 409–412. http://dx.doi.org/10.1089/tmj.2011.0219

Luxton, D. D., Nelson, E.-L., & Maheu, M. (2016). *A practitioner's guide to telemental health.* Washington, DC: American Psychological Association.

Martínez-Pérez, B., de la Torre-Díez, I., López-Coronado, M., Sainz-de-Abajo, B., Robles, M., & García-Gómez, J. M. (2014). Mobile clinical decision support systems and applications: A literature and commercial review. *Journal of Medical Systems, 38*, 4. http://dx.doi.org/10.1007/s10916-013-0004-y

Mohr, D. C., Burns, M. N., Schueller, S. M., Clarke, G., & Klinkman, M. (2013). Behavioral intervention technologies: Evidence review and recommendations for future research in mental health. *General Hospital Psychiatry, 35*, 332–338. http://dx.doi.org/10.1016/j.genhosppsych.2013.03.008

Moskowitz, D. S., & Young, S. N. (2006). Ecological momentary assessment: What it is and why it is a method of the future in clinical psychopharmacology. *Journal of Psychiatry & Neuroscience, 31*, 13–20.

Motto, J. A. (1976). Suicide prevention for high-risk persons who refuse treatment. *Suicide & Life Threatening Behavior, 6*, 223–230.

Powell, A. C., Landman, A. B., & Bates, D. W. (2014). In search of a few good apps. *JAMA, 311*, 1851–1852. http://dx.doi.org/10.1001/jama.2014.2564

Research2Guidance. (2013). *Mobile health market report 2013–2017: The commercialization of mHealth applications* (Vol. 3). Retrieved from http://research2guidance.com/product/mobile-health-market-report-2013-2017/

Savitz, E. (2012, June). Ericsson: 85% global 3G coverage by 2017; 50% for 4G. *Forbes.* Retrieved from http://www.forbes.com/sites/ericsavitz/2012/06/05/ericsson-sees-85-global-3g-wireless-coverage-by-2017-50-4g-coverage

Schueller, S. M., Muñoz, R. F., & Mohr, D. C. (2013). Realizing the potential of behavioral intervention technologies. *Current Directions in Psychological Science, 22,* 478–483. http://dx.doi.org/10.1177/0963721413495872

Terry, M. (2010). Medical apps for smartphones. *Telemedicine and e-Health, 16,* 17–22. http://dx.doi.org/10.1089/tmj.2010.9999

Torous, J., Chan, S. R., Yee-Marie Tan, S., Behrens, J., Mathew, I., Conrad, E. J., . . . Keshavan, M. (2014a). Patient smartphone ownership and interest in mobile apps to monitor symptoms of mental health conditions: A survey in four geographically distinct psychiatric clinics. *Journal of Medical Internet Research, 1,* 1–7.

Torous, J., Friedman, R., & Keshavan, M. (2014b). Smartphone ownership and interest in mobile applications to monitor symptoms of mental health conditions. *Journal of Medical Internet Research, 2*(1), e2. http://dx.doi.org/10.2196/mhealth.2994

U.S. Government Printing Office. (2013). Modification to the HIPAA privacy, security, enforcement, and breach notification rules under the Health Information Technology for Economic and Clinical Health Act and the Genetic Information Nondiscrimination Act; other medication to the HIPAA rules, *78 Fed Reg. 5565* (January 25, 2013). Retrieved from http://www.gpo.gov/fdsys/granule/FR-2013-01-25/2013-01073/content-detail.html

Ventola, C. L. (2014). Mobile devices and apps for health care professionals: Uses and benefits. *Pharmacy & Therapeutics, 39,* 356–364.

Wolf, G. (2011, March 3). *What is the quantified self?* Retrieved from http://quantifiedself.com/2011/03/what-is-the-quantified-self/

TECHNOLOGY-BASED TREATMENTS | II

Liza C. Zwiebach, Laura Loucks, Devika Fiorillo, and Marat V. Zanov

Virtual Reality Psychotherapy 4

irtual reality (VR) is a form of human-computer interaction that provides the user a heightened level of immersion in the computer-generated environment (Rizzo, Buckwalter, & Neumann, 1997). In contrast to the experience of, for example, viewing a film on a screen or a video on a computer monitor, the VR user encounters sensory information typically delivered through a head-mounted display, specialized interface devices, and sophisticated graphics, through which the user derives a sense of presence in the computer-generated scene (Rizzo et al., 2015). For example, a user of a VR scenario simulating an airline flight will likely feel as though he or she is on an airline flight. Depending on the particular configuration of VR equipment, the user can expect not merely the visual and auditory cues associated with a particular scene but also evocative vibrotactile and/or olfactory stimuli. For example, the VR flight simulator might impart the sights, sounds, and smells of being in flight, as well as the vibrations a passenger might feel as a result of the jet engine.

The use of VR as a tool in mental health treatment is the focus of this chapter. In this chapter, we (a) review the emergence of VR in this capacity and its continued development as a facilitator of psychotherapy, (b) describe the empirical evidence demonstrating its effectiveness across a range of

Marat Zanov is director of training, sales, and support for Virtually Better, Inc., which develops virtual reality applications for behavioral health care.

http://dx.doi.org/10.1037/0000085-005
Using Technology in Mental Health Practice, J. J. Magnavita (Editor)

clinical presentations, (c) offer clinical case examples in which VR has been utilized, and (d) provide information on incorporating VR into mental health practice. To date, VR has found application in many contexts and settings. In this chapter, we focus on those applications of VR targeted specifically at psychiatric disorders; however, VR may have benefits in psychological treatment for conditions commonly considered more of a physiological nature (e.g., fibromyalgia; García-Palacios et al., 2015). To demonstrate the scope in which VR may be employed, we include a case example in which pain in a pediatric patient is the target for intervention.

Emergence of Virtual Reality Therapy

In the 1950s and 1960s, inventions such as the simulation device, interactive multi-media theater, and head-mounted display marked the advent of the basic structures and processes underlying VR technology. Amongst other developments in the 1970s, the creation of advanced interactive audience experiences was put forth by Krueger, setting the path for immersion in computer-generated worlds occupied by other human and virtual characters. The term *virtual reality*, referring to a computer-simulated environment within which people can interact, came into use in 1989 beginning with Jaron Lanier. By the early 1990s, behavioral health professionals began taking interest in the application of VR simulations to enhance clinical assessment and interventions. Recognizing the greater opportunities afforded by VR-simulation technology to create controllable, multisensory, and interactive three-dimensional stimulus environments, unattainable through previously existing clinical approaches. In addition, media interest in the concept of VR also soared, as movies like *The Lawnmower Man* (1992) and *Virtuosity* (1995) popularized the application of the technology amongst the general public. Much of the popular interest in VR faded quickly though, as the technological state of VR at the time (characterized by hardware limitations and expensive equipment) underwhelmed public expectations. However, research and development in clinical behavioral health persisted, and within two and a half decades, VR in this realm has progressed from being relatively unknown to holding an important role.

The application and study of VR to address psychological disorders began in the mid-1990s. At the time, cognitive behavioral therapies emphasizing exposure to feared stimuli had been in use for the treatment of anxiety for decades, and exposures were conducted primarily in two ways: in vivo and imaginal. VR therapy was thought of as being capable of providing patients with environments that could be more realistic than imagination and more easily accessible than in vivo exposure; thus, it had the potential to be a powerful tool for activating and modifying pertinent fears in the treatment of specific phobias. In 1995, the first study to examine the effectiveness of VR therapy for acrophobia or the fear of heights was published by an Emory University team, led by clinical psychologist Barbara Rothbaum and Georgia Institute of Technology computer scientist Larry Hodges (Rothbaum et al., 1995a). Studies documenting the effectiveness of VR exposure therapy for other forms of specific phobias, including fear of flying and spider phobia, followed (Carlin, Hoffman, & Weghorst,

1997; Rothbaum, Hodges, Watson, Kessler, & Opdyke, 1996). Within just a couple of decades since the earliest studies on VR therapy, its development and application within behavioral health has extended to a wide range of anxiety disorders and diversified to include other areas within clinical mental and behavioral health.

The proliferation of clinical research efforts involving VR can be tied to the technological advances that took place over time. When the first studies on VR were implemented, environments were limited in quality, and setup could cost well over $250,000. In the years following, the underlying technology underwent significant improvements and decreased in cost, influenced partly by the digital gaming and entertainment industries. Advancements were made in audiovisual displays, computational speed, 3D graphics rendering, intelligence agents, tracking devices, user interface, voice recognition capabilities, and software, leading to innovations in assessment and treatment tools. Individuals from a variety of disciplines and areas of expertise, such as artificial intelligence, cognitive modeling, facial and figure animation, nonverbal communication, personality and emotion, to name a few, have played an important role in advancing the underlying technology for VR in behavioral health.

In addition, collaborative efforts were put forth to develop shareable tools, modular architecture, and interface standards to improve simulations. Virtual applications that were constructed by scientists include skyscrapers, spiders, battlefields, beaches, fantasy worlds, museums, virtual airplanes, and flight simulators. Innovations in construction of mundane functional environments that are highly relevant for clinical care such as the office, home, supermarket, school rooms, and educational materials also took place. Technological progress also generated interest in the creation of realistic human avatars. One team at the University of Southern California focused on improving facial expression in avatars (Rizzo, Neumann, Enciso, Fidaleo, & Noh, 2001). By using a performance-driven facial animation system, avatars that expressed universal primary emotions (including happiness, sadness, anger, fear, disgust, and surprise) were created, setting an example in terms of improving realism and communication. Overall, greater access to a variety of refined, yet cost-effective, VR systems with interactive and immersive environments became easily achievable with the use of typical personal computers, paving the way for psychological research and behavioral health applications in modern world.

Several other developments have contributed to the accessibility and improvement of VR for behavioral health. Although researchers first studied the use of VR for the treatment of posttraumatic stress disorder (PTSD) in the late 1990s using a virtual Vietnam scenario for male Vietnam veterans (Rothbaum, Hodges, Ready, Graap, & Alarcon, 2001), the technology progressed markedly in the context of the Afghanistan and Iraq wars, with growing concern about the large number of US military personnel returning with PTSD and other traumatic injuries. The U.S. Department of Defense (DOD) and U.S. Department of Veterans Affairs (VA), in response, played significant roles in the advancement of VR therapy by funding research and development across a broad range of applications, with implications for both military and civilian settings. These efforts have continued to greatly diversify VR scenario content and improve customizability of stimulus delivery to fit a wide range of experiences and content, while also reducing equipment costs.

Additionally, as a significant body of literature emphasized the efficacy of VR therapy, commercial ventures for manufacturing and distributing applications for clinical use developed. Although there are a number of such companies, one of the first, Virtually Better, Inc., has produced products for a number of specific phobias. The popularity of VR in recent times was made evident by the results of a poll in which VR ranked fourth out of 45 in terms of intervention predicted to increase in the next decade (Norcross, Pfund, & Prochaska, 2013).

Evidence Base for Virtual Reality in Therapy

To date, the most widely demonstrated use of VR in mental health practice has been in the field of anxiety disorder treatment. Indeed, VR in mental health first emerged as a tool to advance exposure therapy for specific phobias (Rothbaum et al., 1995a, 1995b, 1996). VR presented a novel alternative to traditional in vivo exposure, which, depending on the phobic stimulus, can involve significant barriers in terms of logistics (e.g., storms), monetary expense (e.g., flying), and/or controllability (e.g., animals such as spiders). VR offered a method of introducing the phobic stimulus in a more immersive manner than can be provided with mere imaginal exposure, thereby giving the patient more opportunity to habituate to the resulting anxiety, while still remaining relatively convenient and controllable. VR has now been used to good effect with specific phobias of flying (Kahan, Tanzer, Darvin, & Borer, 2000; Rothbaum et al., 2006; Rothbaum, Hodges, Anderson, Price, & Smith, 2002; Triscari, Faraci, Catalisano, D'Angelo, & Urso, 2015), heights (Emmelkamp et al., 2002; Rothbaum et al., 1995a, 1995b), driving (Wald & Taylor, 2003), and spiders (García-Palacios, Hoffman, Carlin, Furness, & Botella, 2002; Shiban, Pauli, & Mühlberger, 2013). Further, VR has been demonstrated to be effective in treating claustrophobia (Botella, Baños, Villa, Perpiñá, & García-Palacios, 2000); agoraphobia (Malbos, Rapee, & Kavakli, 2013; Peñate, Pitti, Bethencourt, de la Fuente, & Gracia, 2008); panic disorder with agoraphobia (Martin, Botella, García-Palacios, & Osma, 2007); and social anxiety disorder, both generalized (Anderson et al., 2013; Roy et al., 2003) and specific to public speaking (Harris, Kemmerling, & North, 2002; Safir, Wallach, & Bar-Zvi, 2012; Wallach, Safir, & Bar-Zvi, 2009). In fact, a meta-analysis suggests that VR treatment gains may surpass those of in vivo exposure for specific phobias (Powers & Emmelkamp, 2008). Additional studies suggest that VR could be useful in treating subclinical presentations, such as test anxiety (Alsina-Jurnet, Carvallo-Beciu, & Gutiérrez-Maldonado, 2007) or performance anxiety (Orman, 2004). Preliminary findings suggest that VR may also be useful in potentiating the effects of exposure and response prevention treatment for obsessive–compulsive disorder (Belloch et al., 2014).

The growing body of evidence supporting the use of VR in exposure therapy led to its adaptation for use with PTSD. Imaginal exposure has been an established and effective method to address symptoms of PTSD by allowing processing of traumatic memories to occur (Foa, Steketee, & Rothbaum, 1989); however, a subset of patients do not ultimately respond to this intervention, possibly due to insufficient level of immersion and presence in the memory as recounted in imaginal exposure. Exposure therapy for PTSD using VR is able to provide stimuli that have particular significance in a patient's traumatic memory, thus boosting the level of exposure and emotional processing that can occur (Rothbaum et al., 1999). For example, many veterans of the Vietnam War who suffer from PTSD report that the sound of helicopters is distressing, and while this sound may be incorporated into an exposure session using VR, the feasibility of having a real-life helicopter present for an exposure session would present great difficulty. As in the treatment of specific phobias, using VR to treat PTSD is extremely extensible and can include a wide range of stimulus elements pertinent to a given patient's traumatic memory. VR exposure therapy has now been used to treat PTSD in veterans of the Vietnam War (Ready, Pollack, Rothbaum, & Alarcon, 2006; Rothbaum, Hodges, Ready, et al., 2001); Operation Enduring Freedom/Operation Iraqi Freedom (Gerardi, Rothbaum, Ressler, Heekin, & Rizzo, 2008; McLay et al., 2011; Reger et al., 2011; Rothbaum et al., 2014); and conflicts fought by Portuguese soldiers in African colonies (Gamito et al., 2009); as well as in survivors of the September 11, 2001, attack on the World Trade Center (Difede & Hoffman, 2002); a motor vehicle crash (Beck, Palyo, Winer, Schwagler, & Ang, 2007); and a terrorist attack in Israel (Freedman et al., 2010).

Although the greatest evidence for VR in mental health care to date is in the area of exposure therapy specifically, it has been shown to be effective in treating a number of other types of clinical presentation as well. In particular, it has been found that eating disorders can be addressed using VR. Such treatment may entail using VR to challenge a patient's cognitive distortions around his or her body size (e.g., by presenting a scene of a room with four doors of different size and instructing the patient to choose the door corresponding to his or her body width). Other cues may include scenes that prompt an emotional response in the patient, and subsequently the patient may practice a virtual behavioral choice, such as going to the kitchen or a room with a scale. Through use of such VR-based interventions, researchers have found positive effects on the specific symptom of body image disturbance in patients with anorexia nervosa (Riva, Bacchetta, Baruffi, Rinaldi, & Molinari, 1999), bulimia nervosa (Marco, Perpiñá, & Botella, 2013), binge eating disorder (Riva et al., 2000), and eating disorder not otherwise specified (Riva, Bacchetta, Baruffi, & Molinari, 2001). The use of VR to treat eating disorders is a relatively new application and, to date, all of the work using VR to treat eating disorders has been conducted by only two research groups, located in Spain and Italy. Particularly considering the complex cultural variables related to disorders of weight and eating (Wildes, Emery, & Simons, 2001), this represents an important area for future directions in the field of therapy using VR.

A more recent area of research is the use of VR with psychotic disorders. Specifically, VR has been adapted as a tool in social skills training for patients with schizophrenia or schizoaffective disorder (Ku et al., 2007; K.-M. Park et al., 2011; Rus-Calafell, Gutiérrez-Maldonado, & Ribas-Sabaté, 2014). While social skills training has long been an intervention thought to improve social discomfort, negative symptoms, and independent living skills in people with severe mental illness (Rus-Calafell, Gutiérrez-Maldonado, Ortega-Bravo, Ribas-Sabaté, & Caqueo-Urízar, 2013), barriers persist to this population's participation in such interventions. In the clinical setting, individuals may be reluctant to engage in skills practice in a group with other patients due to anxiety or embarrassment, and practicing in a more naturalistic, nonclinical setting could be even more intimidating. VR thus can mimic a naturalistic setting in which skills practice, with virtual avatars, can occur with less perceived risk to the patient; also, the pragmatic barriers, unpredictability, and inconvenience associated with a naturalistic setting are diminished. This work is somewhat of a natural extension of the successful use of VR with nonpsychotic individuals for whom social anxiety is their primary presenting concern. Similar work also has been conducted with patients on the autism spectrum (Mitchell, Parsons, & Leonard, 2007).

The findings related to VR as used in an exposure model to treat anxiety disorders has also been extended to the field of substance use disorders and other addictive disorders. Cue exposure therapy (Heather & Bradley, 1990) posits that cravings are the result of conditioned responses that arise from the association of an environmental cue with a drug of abuse. Thus, following the same extinction learning model used in exposure therapy for anxiety, an individual may reduce cravings through repeated contact with the environmental cue in the absence of the substance. Using VR to deliver these cues may provide more sense of immersion and presence, thus bolstering the effect of the exposure. VR-based cue exposure therapy has been demonstrated with nicotine (Choi et al., 2011), as well as with gambling (C.-B. Park et al., 2015).

Scope of Application

The vast majority of research to date on VR therapy has been with an adult population. As mentioned in the previous section, a number of studies have demonstrated its use as a treatment for PTSD among veterans of the Iraq and/or Afghanistan wars; it is thought that, owing to generational characteristics, VR may actually be a draw for this population of younger adults, who have come of age in a technologically advanced world (Kramer, Savary, Pyne, Kimbrell, & Jegley, 2013). The same generational effects, however, do not disqualify older adults from participating in VR therapy, as has been demonstrated with Vietnam veterans (Ready et al., 2006; Rothbaum et al., 2001) and other samples of older adults (Gamito et al., 2010) successfully treated with this tool. Nonetheless, recruitment may be a challenge with an older population given a relative lack of familiarity and comfort with the VR technology (Ready, Gerardi, Backscheider, Mascaro, & Rothbaum, 2010). There is a limited breadth of research using VR with clinical populations of children and adolescents, although available studies (e.g., Ferrand, Ruffault, Tytelman, Flahault, & Négovanska, 2015) illustrate the feasibility of doing so.

To date, most VR therapy takes place in an outpatient setting. However, this may be attributed mostly to the types of primary presentation for which VR has been deployed; anxiety disorders and particularly specific phobias rarely warrant an inpatient or residential treatment setting. Indeed, there have been investigations of VR therapy in an inpatient context (e.g., K.-M. Park et al., 2011), to good effect.

Benefits of VR Therapy

Incorporating VR into mental health practice has numerous benefits, many of which hinge upon the virtual immersion of patients into diverse settings and scenarios beyond the limits of the clinical environment (Morina, Ijntema, Meyerbröker, & Emmelkamp, 2015; Rothbaum, Hodges, & Kooper, 1997). As mentioned, a primary benefit of VR is the creation of a multisensory experience, including imagery, sound (e.g., crowd chatter, wind, gunfire), touch (e.g., floor vibrations), and smell (e.g., diesel fuel, liquor), which elicits a sense of "presence" as the patient interacts with the virtual world (Dinh, Walker, Hodges, Song, & Kobayashi, 1999). With treatment applications for numerous mental health diagnoses (e.g., PTSD, phobias, substance use, social skills), the sense of presence that patients experience through VR augments traditional treatment elements, including (a) exposure to stimuli that, in day-to-day life, often trigger and maintain a patient's distress and symptoms (e.g., Culbertson, Shulenberger, D. L. Garza, Newton, & Brody, 2012; Gerardi, Cukor, Difede, Rizzo, & Rothbaum, 2010; Rothbaum et al., 1997); (b) distraction from physical pain (e.g., Hoffman, Patterson, Carrougher, & Sharar, 2001; Sharar et al., 2008); (c) mindfulness practice for chronic pain (Gromala, Tong, Choo, Karamnejad, & Shaw, 2015); and (d) social skills training for individuals with autism spectrum disorder (Kandalaft, Didehbani, Krawczyk, Allen, & Chapman, 2012; Lahiri, Bekele, Dohrmann, Warren, & Sarkar, 2015). Furthermore, self-report, observational, and physiological measures confirm that VR evokes the desired psychological responses in patients that are consistent with real-life exposure (e.g., Costanzo et al., 2014; García-Rodríguez, Pericot-Valverde, Gutiérrez-Maldonado, Ferrer-García, & Secades-Villa, 2012; Saladin, Brady, Graap, & Rothbaum, 2006) and promotes increased habituation and emotional processing (Powers & Emmelkamp, 2008; Rothbaum, Rizzo, & Difede, 2010). For instance, among individuals with anxiety disorders, VR effectively elicited the fear response, including increased physiological and self-reported measures of heart rate and skin conductance (Costanzo et al., 2014); among individuals with substance use disorders, VR elicited greater levels of cue reactivity than the commonly used modalities (e.g., pictures, video, paraphernalia; Kuntze et al., 2001; Lee et al., 2003). Thus, the multisensory VR experience can enhance traditional evidence-based treatments by helping patients develop a sense of presence without requiring real-world exposure.

A second benefit of VR is the clinician's ability to control the duration, sensory cues, and sequencing of the virtual environment in order to match the exposure to the patient's treatment goals and progress (Gershon, Anderson, Graap, Zimand, Hodges, & Rothbaum, 2002; Rizzo et al., 2015). In contrast, real life exposures are subject to unpredictable environmental changes (e.g., crowd levels, noises) or are limited by the natural order of an event. For example, in the fear of flying paradigm, a patient may fear the plane take-off more than the plane landing. VR enables the patient to experience and habituate to the landing before progressing to the take-off scenario (Rothbaum et al., 1997). In addition, the clinician can manage the flight conditions (e.g., weather, turbulence). Whether exposing a patient to feared situations or craving cues, the provider has the opportunity to create scenarios that enhance the clinical experience at levels that match the patient's needs.

A third benefit of VR is the opportunity to expose patients to contexts (e.g., military combat zone, drug house) that would be costly, time consuming, dangerous, or impractical through in vivo exposure (Saladin et al., 2006). Since traditional in vivo exposure methods are impractical for such scenarios, clinicians traditionally rely on the patient's willingness and ability to visually engage in a memory through imaginal exposure. Therefore, the use of VR can safely and efficiently expose patients to the target context. For instance, in the treatment of combat-related PTSD, VR can immerse veterans into the trauma context, such as a market ambush, roadside IED, or mortar attack on a forward operating base (Rizzo, Hartholt, Grimani, Leeds, & Liewer, 2014; Rothbaum et al., 2010).

Fourth, through use of VR, clinicians may coach the patient during or immediately following the exposure, which can increase engagement, habituation, and appropriate coping (e.g., Culbertson et al., 2012). Alternatively, in-the-moment coaching is not always feasible in real-life exposures, where confidentiality, stigma, and other concerns might arise for patients.

Last, in the growing age of technology, VR has potential to be a more accessible and less stigmatizing therapy format for the gaming generations (Gerardi et al., 2010). Individuals who have difficulty engaging in exposure-based treatments (e.g., traditional in vivo or imaginal exposure) or are reluctant to engage in therapy tend to be more willing to engage in VR therapy (Rizzo et al., 2015; Wilson, Onorati, Mishkind, Reger, & Gahm, 2008). Among 150 participants with specific phobias, 76% selected VR over in vivo, real-world exposure (García-Palacios, Botella, Hoffman, & Fabregat, 2007). Additionally, in the treatment of PTSD with prolonged exposure therapy, patients revisit the traumatic events through imaginal exposure in order to facilitate emotional processing. While some effectively engage with the memories, others have greater difficulty and avoidance. For these individuals, immersion into the virtual world can help patients overcome these obstacles (Rizzo et al., 2014).

Case Example: PTSD

VR can enhance traditional imaginal exposure therapy for PTSD, which includes the patient's retelling of the traumatic event repeatedly in session. With the use of VR, the clinician enhances the patient's retelling of the events with relevant images, sounds, smells, and sensations gradually across sessions. Gerardi et al. (2008) illustrated a veteran's response to prolonged exposure with VR therapy using a Virtual Iraq paradigm.

The patient was a 29-year-old, White, male veteran who served as a combat engineer in the Georgia National Guard after 10 years of active duty service. The veteran engaged in four sessions of VR exposure therapy to address combat-related PTSD. The identified index trauma included an attack on his convoy, during which two of his fellow soldiers were significantly injured. Following the trauma, the veteran reported PTSD symptoms, including intrusive memories, difficulties driving, irritability, concentration difficulties, and hypervigilance, which reportedly interfered with functioning at home and work. The VR was administered through a head-mounted display that included separate display screens for each eye, integrated head tracing, and stereo earphones. The veteran was presented with a computer-generated view of the Virtual Iraq environment (Rizzo et al., 2010) that moved in a natural way with head and body motion. To control the intensity of the VR exposure, the clinician introduced effects gradually across sessions, with the initial session including only the context of the trauma. Sounds and smells were presented in subsequent sessions, with explosions and gunfire in the final two sessions.

The following virtual effects were used in treatment:

- Treatment context: Participant was positioned as the driver of a Humvee (additional positions available: A-driver, gunner, etc.) on a desert highway in Iraq. Relevant scenes could include driving through a city, farmland, under a bridge, or through a checkpoint. Time of day and weather were set to match the context of the actual trauma.
- Sounds/sensations: Sounds included AK-47 gunfire, helicopter, explosions; a soundboard provided vibrations to simulate Humvee, explosions, medevac.
- Smells: diesel fuel, cordite.

Following VR treatment, the veteran's PTSD symptoms decreased by 56% as measured by the Clinician Administered PTSD Scale (Blake et al., 1990), with scores declining from the extreme range (106) to the moderate/threshold range (47), and the PTSD Symptom Scale, Self-Report (Foa, Riggs, Dancu, & Rothbaum, 1993), with scores declining from 35 to 10. Following treatment, the veteran reported improved daily functioning both at home and at work. He reported the VR equipment as comfortable and the use of VR as logical.

Case Example: Pain

VR paradigms have been developed as a distraction tool to divert an individual's attention from pain and anxiety due to injury and/or medical procedures (Hoffman et al., 2001). In the following case study, Gershon, Zimand, Lemos, Rothbaum, and Hodges (2003) examined the effectiveness of VR in reducing anxiety and pain among pediatric cancer patients undergoing painful procedures.

The patient was an 8-year-old Caucasian boy who was diagnosed with acute lymphocytic leukemia 2 years prior to the study. Treatment included numerous port access medical procedures, which often cause distress in children. Before the study, the patient had completed 10 port access procedures, and he completed four port access procedures during the study. The VR paradigm was a Virtual Gorilla program that enables the user to "become" an adolescent gorilla immersed in a gorilla habitat. This program allows the user to explore the habitat, which is meant to simulate a natural gorilla habitat that one might find at a zoo, and participate in social interaction with other gorilla avatars (Allison, Wills, Bowman, Wineman, & Hodges, 1997). Assessment of anxiety and pain included (a) pulse rate before, during, and after the procedure; (b) child, parent, and nurse reports of the child's pain and anxiety before and after the procedure, using a horizontal ruler depicting pain and anxiety on a scale from 1 to 10 (Visual Analogue Scale; e.g., Varni, Walco, & Katz, 1989); and (c) researcher's behavioral observation of pain using the Children's Hospital of Eastern Ontario Pain Scale (CHEOPS; McGrath, Johnson, Goodman, Schillinger, Dunn, & Chapman, 1985), which includes ratings of behavior (e.g., crying, facial expression, verbalization, posture, touch, and leg movement) on a scale of 1 to 3 (0 = *opposite of pain behavior*, 3 = *severe level of the behavior*). Study procedures followed an A-B-C-A design (A = no distraction, B = watching the VR program on a computer but not with the head-mounted display, C = engaging in the Virtual Gorilla Program through the head-mounted display), respectively across the four port access procedures.

Results from each condition indicated that the lowest level of pain occurred during the VR condition (C) as assessed by the CHEOPS and VAS, and pulse rate also was lowest during the VR condition. When compared with other conditions, the nurse and parents reported the lowest anxiety during the VR condition (C). The child reported the least amount of anxiety while watching the VR on a computer without a head mount (B). Results demonstrated that VR serves as an effective anxiety and pain management tool for use during invasive procedures.

Case Example: Fear of Flying

Treating the fear of flying is particularly challenging with traditional exposure therapy, due to the cost, time, rigidity, and impracticality of conducting repeated exposures with an actual airplane flight. Thus, using VR to immerse individuals into the flying experience may serve as an accessible alternative that facilitates emotional processing and habituation.

Rothbaum et al. (1996) examined the effectiveness of a VR program designed to treat the fear of flying. The participant was a 42-year-old woman who met *DSM–IV* (*Diagnostic and Statistical Manual of Mental Disorders*, fourth ed.; American Psychiatric Association, 1994) criteria for specific phobia related to fear of flying, which reportedly had increased over the 5 years prior to the study. She had not flown for 2 years and previously used antihistamines and anxiolytics to manage her anxiety. As a result of her anxiety, she had missed family vacations and was seeking treatment because she was expected to fly for a new job. The participant did not endorse general anxiety at preassessment, as measured by the State-Trait Anxiety Inventory (STAI; Spielberger, Gorsuch, & Lushene, 1970). Before being referred for the VR treatment study, she engaged in seven paid outpatient sessions with one of the study therapists, during which she used bibliotherapy and learned anxiety management techniques, including brief breathing relaxation, thought-stopping, cognitive restructuring, and preparing for a stressor.

VR sessions were conducted over 35 to 45 minutes. Effects included sounds, sights, and vibrations consistent with various stages of a flight. The patient progressed through the fear hierarchy at her own pace and completed the following VR situations: sitting in an airplane, taking off, landing, flying in calm weather, and flying in stormy weathers. Specific sounds that matched the situation included take-off, landing, rain, and thunder. She completed six sessions of VR therapy and terminated after reporting no further distress related to the exposures. She completed a live flight with her family 2 days after terminating therapy.

The participant's posttreatment scores indicated clinically significant declines in fear of flying when compared to pre-anxiety management training (seven sessions) and postanxiety management and pre-VR therapy, as assessed by Subjective Units of Distress (SUDs) ratings, the Questionnaire on Attitudes toward Flying (QAF; Howard, Murphy, & Clarke, 1983), Fear of Flying Inventory (FFI; Scott, 1987), and the Self-Survey of Stress Responses (SSR; Forgione & Bauer, 1980). Declines were maintained at the 1-month follow-up assessment. During the live flight, the participant reported SUDs no greater than 30/100 for each flight. Reflecting on the flight, she reported that the plane experienced "10 minutes of strong turbulence but I stayed pretty calm" (Rothbaum et al., 1996, p. 480).

Tips for Incorporating Virtual Reality Into Mental Health Practice

A typical VR system may consist of a computer with a powerful video processor, two monitors (one for the clinician's interface and another for the clinician's orientation to the patient's position in the virtual environment), a head-mounted display for the patient, an amplifier and a vibrotactile platform, a scent machine, and necessary peripheral devices. While there is no uniform certification process on conducting VR exposure therapy, some vendors offer structured training to their customers, which covers the salient theory of prolonged exposure therapy and involves hands-on experience in using the VR exposure system. Readers are encouraged to verify information coming directly from the technology vendor about how to conduct the therapy and the clinical indications for which VR would be recommended. Prices for comprehensive VR systems may vary between $20,000 and $50,000, depending on the configuration. This will normally include the cost of a formal training for the onsite clinical personnel. Some VR companies offer significant discounts to military and research institutions as well. It should be noted that more affordable solutions for private practitioners are also available, including smartphone-based VR therapy systems priced at around $600 and above. Some vendors may have a subscription model, while others would only have a one-time fee.

Whatever path the reader may choose to pursue, integrating VR into one's mental health practice can serve to the mutual benefit of clinician and consumer. VR offers an entirely new level of therapeutic intervention that is often based on a traditional (e.g., prolonged exposure therapy) approach, which may provide a cost-effective way of addressing phobias, addictions, and PTSD. It is important to be familiar with the strengths as well as the challenges of each particular approach. Appropriate training and consultation with experienced colleagues will position one well to be successful.

Essential Resources

The following is a list of resources to guide the reader in the incorporation of this technology:

- Laboratory of Psychology and Technology, http://www.labpsitec.uji.es/eng/index.php
- University of Southern California Institute for Creative Technologies, http://ict.usc.edu/
- The Virtual Reality Medical Center, http://www.vrphobia.com/index.htm
- Virtually Better, Inc., http://www.virtuallybetter.com/sales

References

Allison, D., Wills, B., Bowman, D., Wineman, J., & Hodges, L. F. (1997). The virtual reality gorilla exhibit. *IEEE Computer Graphics and Applications, 17*, 30–38. http://dx.doi.org/10.1109/38.626967

Alsina-Jurnet, I., Carvallo-Beciu, C., & Gutiérrez-Maldonado, J. (2007). Validity of virtual reality as a method of exposure in the treatment of test anxiety. *Behavior Research Methods, 39*, 844–851. http://dx.doi.org/10.3758/BF03192977

American Psychiatric Association. (1994). *Diagnostic and statistical manual of mental disorders* (4th ed.). Washington, DC: Author.

Anderson, P. L., Price, M., Edwards, S. M., Obasaju, M. A., Schmertz, S. K., Zimand, E., & Calamaras, M. R. (2013). Virtual reality exposure therapy for social anxiety disorder: A randomized controlled trial. *Journal of Consulting and Clinical Psychology, 81*, 751–760. http://dx.doi.org/10.1037/a0033559

Beck, J. G., Palyo, S. A., Winer, E. H., Schwagler, B. E., & Ang, E. J. (2007). Virtual reality exposure therapy for PTSD symptoms after a road accident: An uncontrolled case series. *Behavior Therapy, 38*, 39–48. http://dx.doi.org/10.1016/j.beth.2006.04.001

Belloch, A., Cabedo, E., Carrió, C., Lozano-Quilis, J. A., Gil-Gómez, J. A., & Gil-Gómez, H. (2014). Virtual reality exposure for OCD: Is it feasible? *Revista de Psicopatología y Psicología Clínica, 19*(1), 37. http://dx.doi.org/10.5944/rppc.vol.19.num.1.2014.12981

Blake, D. D., Weathers, F., Nagy, L. M., Kaloupek, D. G., Klauminzer, G., Charney, D. S., & Keane, T. M. (1990). A clinician rating scale for assessing current and lifetime PTSD: The CAPS-1. *Behavior Therapist, 13*, 187–188.

Botella, C., Baños, R. M., Villa, H., Perpiñá, C., & García-Palacios, A. (2000). Virtual reality in the treatment of claustrophobic fear: A controlled, multiple-baseline design. *Behavior Therapy, 31*, 583–595. http://dx.doi.org/10.1016/S0005-7894(00)80032-5

Carlin, A. S., Hoffman, H. G., & Weghorst, S. (1997). Virtual reality and tactile augmentation in the treatment of spider phobia: A case report. *Behaviour Research and Therapy, 35*, 153–158. http://dx.doi.org/10.1016/s0005-7967(96)00085-x

Choi, J. S., Park, S., Lee, J.-Y., Jung, H.-Y., Lee, H.-W., Jin, C.-H., & Kang, D.-H. (2011). The effect of repeated virtual nicotine cue exposure therapy on the psychophysiological responses: A preliminary study. *Psychiatry Investigation, 8*, 155–160. http://dx.doi.org/10.4306/pi.2011.8.2.155

Costanzo, M. E., Leaman, S., Jovanovic, T., Norrholm, S. D., Rizzo, A. A., Taylor, P., & Roy, M. J. (2014). Psychophysiological response to virtual reality and subthreshold posttraumatic stress disorder symptoms in recently deployed military. *Psychosomatic Medicine, 76*, 670–677. http://dx.doi.org/10.1097/PSY.0000000000000109

Culbertson, C. S., Shulenberger, S., D. L. Garza, R., Newton, T. F., & Brody, A. L. (2012). Virtual reality cue exposure therapy for the treatment of tobacco dependence. *Journal of Cyber Therapy and Rehabilitation, 5*(1), 57–64.

Difede, J., & Hoffman, H. G. (2002). Virtual reality exposure therapy for World Trade Center post-traumatic stress disorder: A case report. *Cyberpsychology & Behavior, 5*, 529–535. http://dx.doi.org/10.1089/109493102321018169

Dinh, H. Q., Walker, N., Hodges, L. F., Song, C., & Kobayashi, A. (1999). Evaluating the importance of multi-sensory input on memory and the sense of presence in virtual environments. *Proceedings of IEEE Virtual Reality,* 222–228. Retrieved from http://ieeexplore.ieee.org/document/756955/

Emmelkamp, P. M. G., Krijn, M., Hulsbosch, A. M., de Vries, S., Schuemie, M. J., & van der Mast, C. A. P. G. (2002). Virtual reality treatment versus exposure in vivo: A comparative evaluation in acrophobia. *Behaviour Research and Therapy, 40*, 509–516. http://dx.doi.org/10.1016/S0005-7967(01)00023-7

Ferrand, M., Ruffault, A., Tytelman, X., Flahault, C., & Négovanska, V. (2015). A cognitive and virtual reality treatment program for the fear of flying. *Aerospace Medicine and Human Performance, 86*, 723–727. http://dx.doi.org/10.3357/AMHP.4211.2015

Foa, E. B., Riggs, D. S., Dancu, C. V., & Rothbaum, B. O. (1993). Reliability and validity of a brief instrument for assessing post-traumatic stress disorder. *Journal of Traumatic Stress, 6*, 459–473. http://dx.doi.org/10.1002/jts.2490060405

Foa, E. B., Steketee, G., & Rothbaum, B. O. (1989). Behavioral/cognitive conceptualizations of post-traumatic stress disorder. *Behavior Therapy, 20*, 155–176. http://dx.doi.org/10.1016/S0005-7894(89)80067-X

Forgione, A. G., & Bauer, F. M. (1980). *Fearless flying: The complete program for relaxed air travel.* Boston, MA: Houghton Mifflin.

Freedman, S. A., Hoffman, H. G., García-Palacios, A., Tamar Weiss, P. L., Avitzour, S., & Josman, N. (2010). Prolonged exposure and virtual reality-enhanced imaginal exposure for PTSD following a terrorist bulldozer attack: A case study. *Cyberpsychology, Behavior, and Social Networking, 13*, 95–101. http://dx.doi.org/10.1089/cyber.2009.0271

Gamito, P., Oliveira, J., Morais, D., Oliveira, S., Duarte, N., Saraiva, T., . . . Rosa, P. (2009). Virtual reality therapy controlled study for war veterans with PTSD: Preliminary results. *Studies in Health Technology and Informatics, 144,* 269–272.

Gamito, P., Oliveira, J., Rosa, P., Morais, D., Duarte, N., Oliveira, S., & Saraiva, T. (2010). PTSD elderly war veterans: A clinical controlled pilot study. *Cyberpsychology, Behavior, and Social Networking, 13,* 43–48. http://dx.doi.org/10.1089/cyber.2009.0237

García-Palacios, A., Botella, C., Hoffman, H., & Fabregat, S. (2007). Comparing acceptance and refusal rates of virtual reality exposure vs. in vivo exposure by patients with specific phobias. *CyberPsychology & Behavior, 10,* 722–724. http://dx.doi.org/10.1089/cpb.2007.9962

García-Palacios, A., Herrero, R., Vizcaino, Y., Belmonte, M. A., Castilla, D., Molinari, G., . . . Botella, C. (2015). Integrating virtual reality with activity management for the treatment of fibromyalgia: Acceptability and preliminary efficacy. *The Clinical Journal of Pain, 31,* 564–572. http://dx.doi.org/10.1097/ajp.0000000000000196

García-Palacios, A., Hoffman, H., Carlin, A., Furness, T. A., III, & Botella, C. (2002). Virtual reality in the treatment of spider phobia: A controlled study. *Behaviour Research and Therapy, 40,* 983–993. http://dx.doi.org/10.1016/S0005-7967(01)00068-7

García-Rodríguez, O., Pericot-Valverde, I., Gutiérrez-Maldonado, J., Ferrer-García, M., & Secades-Villa, R. (2012). Validation of smoking-related virtual environments for cue exposure therapy. *Addictive Behaviors, 37,* 703–708. http://dx.doi.org/10.1016/j.addbeh.2012.02.013

Gerardi, M., Cukor, J., Difede, J., Rizzo, A., & Rothbaum, B. O. (2010). Virtual reality exposure therapy for post-traumatic stress disorder and other anxiety disorders. *Current Psychiatry Reports, 12,* 298–305. http://dx.doi.org/10.1007/s11920-010-0128-4

Gerardi, M., Rothbaum, B. O., Ressler, K., Heekin, M., & Rizzo, A. (2008). Virtual reality exposure therapy using a virtual Iraq: Case report. *Journal of Traumatic Stress, 21,* 209–213. http://dx.doi.org/10.1002/jts.20331

Gershon, J., Anderson, P., Graap, K., Zimand, E., Hodges, L., & Rothbaum, B. O. (2002). Virtual reality exposure therapy in the treatment of anxiety disorders. *The Scientific Review of Mental Health Practice, 1,* 78–83.

Gershon, J., Zimand, E., Lemos, R., Rothbaum, B. O., & Hodges, L. (2003). Use of virtual reality as a distractor for painful procedures in a patient with pediatric cancer: A case study. *CyberPsychology & Behavior, 6,* 657–661. http://dx.doi.org/10.1089/109493103322725450

Gromala, D., Tong, X., Choo, A., Karamnejad, M., & Shaw, C. D. (2015). The virtual meditative walk: Virtual reality therapy for chronic pain management. *Proceedings of the 33rd Annual ACM Conference on Human Factors in Computing Systems,* 521–524. Retrieved from https://dl.acm.org/citation.cfm?doid=2702123.2702344

Harris, S. R., Kemmerling, R. L., & North, M. M. (2002). Brief virtual reality therapy for public speaking anxiety. *CyberPsychology & Behavior, 5,* 543–550. http://dx.doi.org/10.1089/109493102321018187

Heather, N., & Bradley, B. P. (1990). Cue exposure as a practical treatment for addictive disorders: Why are we waiting? *Addictive Behaviors, 15,* 335–337. http://dx.doi.org/10.1016/0306-4603(90)90043-W

Hoffman, H. G., Patterson, D. R., Carrougher, G. J., & Sharar, S. R. (2001). Effectiveness of virtual reality-based pain control with multiple treatments. *The Clinical Journal of Pain, 17,* 229–235. http://dx.doi.org/10.1097/00002508-200109000-00007

Howard, W. A., Murphy, S. M., & Clarke, J. C. (1983). The nature and treatment of fear of flying: A controlled investigation. *Behavior Therapy, 14,* 557–567. http://dx.doi.org/10.1016/S0005-7894(83)80078-1

Kahan, M., Tanzer, J., Darvin, D., & Borer, F. (2000). Virtual reality-assisted cognitive-behavioral treatment for fear of flying: Acute treatment and follow-up. *CyberPsychology & Behavior, 3,* 387–392. http://dx.doi.org/10.1089/10949310050078832

Kandalaft, M. R., Didehbani, N., Krawczyk, D. C., Allen, T. T., & Chapman, S. B. (2012). Virtual reality social cognition training for young adults with high-functioning autism. *Journal of Autism and Developmental Disorders, 43,* 34–44. http://dx.doi.org/10.1007/s10803-012-1544-6

Kramer, T. L., Savary, P. E., Pyne, J. M., Kimbrell, T. A., & Jegley, S. M. (2013). Veteran perceptions of virtual reality to assess and treat posttraumatic stress disorder. *Cyberpsychology, Behavior, and Social Networking, 16,* 293–301. http://dx.doi.org/10.1089/cyber.2013.1504

Ku, J., Han, K., Lee, H. R., Jang, H. J., Kim, K. U., Park, S. H., . . . Kim, S. I. (2007). VR-based conversation training program for patients with schizophrenia: A preliminary clinical trial. *CyberPsychology & Behavior, 10,* 567–574. http://dx.doi.org/10.1089/cpb.2007.9989

Kuntze, M. F., Stoermer, R., Mager, R., Roessler, A., Mueller-Spahn, F., & Bullinger, A. H. (2001). Immersive virtual environments in cue exposure. *CyberPsychology & Behavior, 4,* 497–501. http://dx.doi.org/10.1089/109493101750527051

Lahiri, U., Bekele, E., Dohrmann, E., Warren, Z., & Sarkar, N. (2015). A physiologically informed virtual reality based social communication system for individuals with autism. *Journal of Autism and Developmental Disorders, 45,* 919–931. http://dx.doi.org/10.1007/s10803-014-2240-5

Lee, J. H., Ku, J., Kim, K., Kim, B., Kim, I. Y., Yang, B.-H., . . . Kim, S. I. (2003). Experimental application of virtual reality for nicotine craving through cue exposure. *CyberPsychology & Behavior, 6,* 275–280. http://dx.doi.org/10.1089/109493103322011560

Malbos, E., Rapee, R. M., & Kavakli, M. (2013). A controlled study of agoraphobia and the independent effect of virtual reality exposure therapy. *Australian and New Zealand Journal of Psychiatry, 47,* 160–168. http://dx.doi.org/10.1177/0004867412453626

Marco, J. H., Perpiñá, C., & Botella, C. (2013). Effectiveness of cognitive behavioral therapy supported by virtual reality in the treatment of body image in eating disorders: One year follow-up. *Psychiatry Research, 209,* 619–625. http://dx.doi.org/10.1016/j.psychres.2013.02.023

Martin, H. V., Botella, C., García-Palacios, A., & Osma, J. (2007). Virtual reality exposure in the treatment of panic disorder with agoraphobia: A case study. *Cognitive and Behavioral Practice, 14,* 58–69. http://dx.doi.org/10.1016/j.cbpra.2006.01.008

McGrath, P. J., Johnson, G., Goodman, J. T., Schillinger, J., Dunn, J., & Chapman, J. (1985). CHEOPS: A behavioral scale for rating postoperative pain in children. In H. L. Fields, R. Dubner, & F. Cervero (Eds.), *Advances in pain research and therapy* (Vol. 9, pp. 395–402). New York, NY: Raven Press.

McLay, R. N., Wood, D. P., Webb-Murphy, J. A., Spira, J. L., Wiederhold, M. D., Pyne, J. M., & Wiederhold, B. K. (2011). A randomized, controlled trial of virtual reality-graded exposure therapy for post-traumatic stress disorder in active duty service members with combat-related post-traumatic stress disorder. *Cyberpsychology, Behavior, and Social Networking, 14*, 223–229. http://dx.doi.org/10.1089/cyber.2011.0003

Mitchell, P., Parsons, S., & Leonard, A. (2007). Using virtual environments for teaching social understanding to 6 adolescents with autistic spectrum disorders. *Journal of Autism and Developmental Disorders, 37*, 589–600. http://dx.doi.org/10.1007/s10803-006-0189-8

Morina, N., Ijntema, H., Meyerbröker, K., & Emmelkamp, P. M. G. (2015). Can virtual reality exposure therapy gains be generalized to real-life? A meta-analysis of studies applying behavioral assessments. *Behaviour Research and Therapy, 74*, 18–24. http://dx.doi.org/10.1016/j.brat.2015.08.010

Norcross, J. C., Pfund, R. A., & Prochaska, J. O. (2013). Psychotherapy in 2022: A Delphi poll on its future. *Professional Psychology: Research and Practice, 44*, 363–370. http://dx.doi.org/10.1037/a0034633

Orman, E. K. (2004). Effect of virtual reality graded exposure on anxiety levels of performing musicians: A case study. *Journal of Music Therapy, 41*, 70–78. http://dx.doi.org/10.1093/jmt/41.1.70

Park, C.-B., Park, S. M., Gwak, A. R., Sohn, B. K., Lee, J.-Y., Jung, H. Y., . . . Choi, J.-S. (2015). The effect of repeated exposure to virtual gambling cues on the urge to gamble. *Addictive Behaviors, 41*, 61–64. http://dx.doi.org/10.1016/j.addbeh.2014.09.027

Park, K.-M., Ku, J., Choi, S.-H., Jang, H.-J., Park, J.-Y., Kim, S. I., & Kim, J.-J. (2011). A virtual reality application in role-plays of social skills training for schizophrenia: A randomized, controlled trial. *Psychiatry Research, 189*, 166–172. http://dx.doi.org/10.1016/j.psychres.2011.04.003

Peñate, W., Pitti, C. T., Bethencourt, J. M., de la Fuente, J., & Gracia, R. (2008). The effects of a treatment based on the use of virtual reality exposure and cognitive-behavioral therapy applied to patients with agoraphobia. *International Journal of Clinical and Health Psychology, 8*, 5–22.

Powers, M. B., & Emmelkamp, P. M. G. (2008). Virtual reality exposure therapy for anxiety disorders: A meta-analysis. *Journal of Anxiety Disorders, 22*, 561–569. http://dx.doi.org/10.1016/j.janxdis.2007.04.006

Ready, D. J., Gerardi, R. J., Backscheider, A. G., Mascaro, N., & Rothbaum, B. O. (2010). Comparing virtual reality exposure therapy to present-centered therapy with 11 U.S. Vietnam veterans with PTSD. *Cyberpsychology, Behavior, and Social Networking, 13*, 49–54. http://dx.doi.org/10.1089/cyber.2009.0239

Ready, D. J., Pollack, S., Rothbaum, B. O., & Alarcon, R. D. (2006). Virtual reality exposure for veterans with posttraumatic stress disorder. *Journal of Aggression, Maltreatment & Trauma, 12*, 199–220. http://dx.doi.org/10.1300/J146v12n01_11

Reger, G. M., Holloway, K. M., Candy, C., Rothbaum, B. O., Difede, J., Rizzo, A. A., & Gahm, G. A. (2011). Effectiveness of virtual reality exposure therapy for active duty soldiers in a military mental health clinic. *Journal of Traumatic Stress, 24*, 93–96. http://dx.doi.org/10.1002/jts.20574

Riva, G., Bacchetta, M., Baruffi, M., & Molinari, E. (2001). Virtual reality-based multidimensional therapy for the treatment of body image disturbances in obesity: A controlled study. *CyberPsychology & Behavior, 4,* 511–526. http://dx.doi.org/ 10.1089/109493101750527079

Riva, G., Bacchetta, M., Baruffi, M., Rinaldi, S., & Molinari, E. (1999). Virtual reality based experiential cognitive treatment of anorexia nervosa. *Journal of Behavior Therapy and Experimental Psychiatry, 30,* 221–230. http://dx.doi.org/10.1016/ S0005-7916(99)00018-X

Riva, G., Bacchetta, M., Baruffi, M., Rinaldi, S., Vincelli, F., & Molinari, E. (2000). Virtual reality-based experiential cognitive treatment of obesity and binge-eating disorders. *Clinical Psychology & Psychotherapy, 7,* 209–219. http://dx.doi.org/ 10.1002/1099-0879(200007)7:3<209::AID-CPP232>3.0.CO;2-V

Rizzo, A., Cukor, J., Gerardi, M., Alley, S., Reist, C., Roy, M., . . . Difede, J. (2015). Virtual reality exposure for PTSD due to military combat and terrorist attacks. *Journal of Contemporary Psychotherapy, 45,* 255–264. http://dx.doi.org/10.1007/ s10879-015-9306-3

Rizzo, A., Hartholt, A., Grimani, M., Leeds, A., & Liewer, M. (2014). Virtual reality exposure therapy for combat-related posttraumatic stress disorder. *Computer, 47,* 31–37. Retrieved from http://doi.ieeecomputersociety.org/10.1109/MC.2014.199

Rizzo, A. A., Buckwalter, J. G., & Neumann, U. (1997). Virtual reality and cognitive rehabilitation: A brief review of the future. *The Journal of Head Trauma Rehabilitation, 12,* 1–15. http://dx.doi.org/10.1097/00001199-199712000-00002

Rizzo, A. A., Neumann, U., Enciso, R., Fidaleo, D., & Noh, J. Y. (2001). Performance-driven facial animation: Basic research on human judgments of emotional state in facial avatars. *CyberPsychology and Behavior, 4,* 471–487. http://dx.doi.org/10.1089/ 109493101750527033

Rizzo, A. S., Difede, J., Rothbaum, B. O., Reger, G., Spitalnick, J., Cukor, J., & McLay, R. (2010). Development and early evaluation of the virtual Iraq/Afghanistan exposure therapy system for combat-related PTSD. *Annals of the New York Academy of Sciences, 1208,* 114–125. http://dx.doi.org/10.1111/j.1749-6632.2010.05755.x

Rothbaum, B. O., Anderson, P., Zimand, E., Hodges, L., Lang, D., & Wilson, J. (2006). Virtual reality exposure therapy and standard (in vivo) exposure therapy in the treatment of fear of flying. *Behavior Therapy, 37,* 80–90. http://dx.doi.org/10.1016/ j.beth.2005.04.004

Rothbaum, B. O., Hodges, L., Alarcon, R., Ready, D., Shahar, F., Graap, K., . . . Baltzell, D. (1999). Virtual reality exposure therapy for PTSD Vietnam veterans: A case study. *Journal of Traumatic Stress, 12,* 263–271. http://dx.doi.org/10.1023/ A:1024772308758

Rothbaum, B. O., Hodges, L., Anderson, P. L., Price, L., & Smith, S. (2002). Twelve-month follow-up of virtual reality and standard exposure therapies for the fear of flying. *Journal of Consulting and Clinical Psychology, 70,* 428–432. http://dx.doi.org/ 10.1037/0022-006X.70.2.428

Rothbaum, B. O., Hodges, L., & Kooper, R. (1997). Virtual reality exposure therapy. *The Journal of Psychotherapy Practice and Research, 6,* 219–226.

Rothbaum, B. O., Hodges, L. F., Kooper, R., Opdyke, D., Williford, J. S., & North, M. (1995a). Effectiveness of computer-generated (virtual reality) graded exposure in the treatment of acrophobia. *American Journal of Psychiatry, 152,* 626–628. http://dx.doi.org/10.1176/ajp.152.4.626

Rothbaum, B. O., Hodges, L. F., Kooper, R., Opdyke, D., Williford, J. S., & North, M. (1995b). Virtual reality graded exposure in the treatment of acrophobia: A case report. *Behavior Therapy, 26,* 547–554. http://dx.doi.org/10.1016/S0005-7894(05)80100-5

Rothbaum, B. O., Hodges, L. F., Ready, D., Graap, K., & Alarcon, R. D. (2001). Virtual reality exposure therapy for Vietnam veterans with posttraumatic stress disorder. *The Journal of Clinical Psychiatry, 62,* 617–622. http://dx.doi.org/10.4088/JCP.v62n0808

Rothbaum, B. O., Hodges, L., Watson, B. A., Kessler, G. D., & Opdyke, D. (1996). Virtual reality exposure therapy in the treatment of fear of flying: A case report. *Behaviour Research and Therapy, 34,* 477–481. http://dx.doi.org/10.1016/0005-7967(96)00007-1

Rothbaum, B. O., Price, M., Jovanovic, T., Norrholm, S. D., Gerardi, M., Dunlop, B., . . . Ressler, K. J. (2014). A randomized, double-blind evaluation of D-cycloserine or alprazolam combined with virtual reality exposure therapy for posttraumatic stress disorder in Iraq and Afghanistan War veterans. *The American Journal of Psychiatry, 171*(6), 640–648. http://dx.doi.org/10.1176/appi.ajp.2014.13121625

Rothbaum, B. O., Rizzo, A. S., & Difede, J. (2010). Virtual reality exposure therapy for combat-related posttraumatic stress disorder. *Annals of the New York Academy of Sciences, 1208,* 126–132. http://dx.doi.org/10.1111/j.1749-6632.2010.05691.x

Roy, S., Klinger, E., Légeron, P., Lauer, F., Chemin, I., & Nugues, P. (2003). Definition of a VR-based protocol to treat social phobia. *CyberPsychology & Behavior, 6,* 411–420. http://dx.doi.org/10.1089/109493103322278808

Rus-Calafell, M., Gutiérrez-Maldonado, J., Ortega-Bravo, M., Ribas-Sabaté, J., & Caqueo-Urízar, A. (2013). A brief cognitive-behavioural social skills training for stabilised outpatients with schizophrenia: A preliminary study. *Schizophrenia Research, 143,* 327–336. http://dx.doi.org/10.1016/j.schres.2012.11.014

Rus-Calafell, M., Gutiérrez-Maldonado, J., & Ribas-Sabaté, J. (2014). A virtual reality-integrated program for improving social skills in patients with schizophrenia: A pilot study. *Journal of Behavior Therapy and Experimental Psychiatry, 45,* 81–89. http://dx.doi.org/10.1016/j.jbtep.2013.09.002

Safir, M. P., Wallach, H. S., & Bar-Zvi, M. (2012). Virtual reality cognitive-behavior therapy for public speaking anxiety: One-year follow-up. *Behavior Modification, 36,* 235–246. http://dx.doi.org/10.1177/0145445511429999

Saladin, M. E., Brady, K. T., Graap, K., & Rothbaum, B. O. (2006). A preliminary report on the use of virtual reality technology to elicit craving and cue reactivity in cocaine dependent individuals. *Addictive Behaviors, 31,* 1881–1894. http://dx.doi.org/10.1016/j.addbeh.2006.01.004

Scott, W. (1987). A fear of flying inventory. In P. R. A. Kellar & S. R. Hayman (Eds.), *Innovations of clinical practice* (Vol. 7). Sarasota, FL: Professional Resource Exchange.

Sharar, S. R., Miller, W., Teeley, A., Soltani, M., Hoffman, H. G., Jensen, M. P., & Patterson, D. R. (2008). Applications of virtual reality for pain management in burn-injured patients. *Expert Review of Neurotherapeutics, 8,* 1667–1674. http://dx.doi.org/10.1586/14737175.8.11.1667

Shiban, Y., Pauli, P., & Mühlberger, A. (2013). Effect of multiple context exposure on renewal in spider phobia. *Behaviour Research and Therapy, 51*, 68–74. http://dx.doi.org/10.1016/j.brat.2012.10.007

Spielberger, C. D., Gorsuch, R. L., & Lushene, R. E. (1970). *Manual for the State-Trait Anxiety Inventory.* Buffalo, NY: University of Buffalo.

Triscari, M. T., Faraci, P., Catalisano, D., D'Angelo, V., & Urso, V. (2015). Effectiveness of cognitive behavioral therapy integrated with systematic desensitization, cognitive behavioral therapy combined with eye movement desensitization and reprocessing therapy, and cognitive behavioral therapy combined with virtual reality exposure therapy methods in the treatment of flight anxiety: A randomized trial. *Neuropsychiatric Disease and Treatment, 11*, 2591–2598. https://dx.doi.org/10.2147/NDT.S93401

Varni, J. W., Walco, G. A., & Katz, E. R. (1989). A cognitive-behavioral approach to pain associated with pediatric chronic diseases. *Journal of Pain and Symptom Management, 4*, 238–241. http://dx.doi.org/10.1016/0885-3924(89)90048-1

Wald, J., & Taylor, S. (2003). Preliminary research on the efficacy of virtual reality exposure therapy to treat driving phobia. *CyberPsychology & Behavior, 6*, 459–465. http://dx.doi.org/10.1089/109493103769710488

Wallach, H. S., Safir, M. P., & Bar-Zvi, M. (2009). Virtual reality cognitive behavior therapy for public speaking anxiety: A randomized clinical trial. *Behavior Modification, 33*, 314–338. http://dx.doi.org/10.1177/0145445509331926

Wildes, J. E., Emery, R. E., & Simons, A. D. (2001). The roles of ethnicity and culture in the development of eating disturbance and body dissatisfaction: A meta-analytic review. *Clinical Psychology Review, 21*, 521–551. http://dx.doi.org/10.1016/S0272-7358(99)00071-9

Wilson, J. A. B., Onorati, K., Mishkind, M., Reger, M. A., & Gahm, G. A. (2008). Soldier attitudes about technology-based approaches to mental health care. *CyberPsychology & Behavior, 11*, 767–769. http://dx.doi.org/10.1089/cpb.2008.0071

Jeffrey A. Marksberry and Daniel L. Kirsch

Cranial Electrotherapy Stimulation 5

Harnessing electricity for medicinal purposes predates Benjamin Franklin and his famous kite experiment. The ancient Greeks used the shock of a torpedo ray fish (also known as an electric eel), which can deliver up to 220 volts for pain relief during surgery and childbirth, as well as for the treatment of headaches. Scribonius Largus, the court physician to the Roman emperor Claudius, was the first to record such use of electricity to treat headaches and gout pain in 46 AD (Bullock, Hopkins, Popper, & Ray, 2005). Fast forward 2 millennia and practitioners are now using an elegant version of microcurrent to treat the body and mind. Cranial electrotherapy stimulation (CES) is a Food and Drug Administration (FDA)–approved modality for the treatment of anxiety, insomnia, and depression (Cranial electrotherapy stimulator, 21 *Code of Federal Regulations* [CFR], § 882.5800, 2013). CES research has made remarkable advances over the last 100 years, paralleling the direction of modern health care science, with the most recent studies being double-blind, sham-controlled randomized clinical trials (RCT), the gold standard in evidence-based medicine.

As Henry Nasrallah pointed out in his description of the future of behavioral health, neurostimulation for brain repair is one of the top six trends in clinical practice, along with pharmacogenomics, targeting neuroplasticity

Dr. Kirsch is the CEO and Dr. Marksberry is the vice president of Electromedical Products International, which is a company that manufactures the CES device called Alpha-Stim.

http://dx.doi.org/10.1037/0000085-006
Using Technology in Mental Health Practice, J. J. Magnavita (Editor)

and unravelling the connection between physical and mental disorders (Nasrallah, 2009). CES offers a noninvasive, safe, and effective form of neurostimulation that can be performed by the clinician, or the patient at home, and is cost-effective. This is in stark contrast to vagal nerve stimulation (VNS) and to deep brain stimulation (DBS), which requires neurosurgery, or transcranial magnetic stimulation (TMS), which is cost-prohibitive for most patients as it is not covered by insurance and must be performed in the practitioner's office. All of these modalities also have a much bigger adverse-effects profile than CES.

This chapter covers the history of CES and the clinical evidence supporting its use in practice, including safety, effectiveness, and the scope of applications. We also explain the logistics of including this technology in a practitioner's armamentarium and what it takes to develop a CES treatment room to multiply the efforts of your practice.

Cranial Electrotherapy Stimulation Past to Present

Electromedicine may have begun with the ancient Greeks and Romans, but it wasn't considered a viable option by practitioners in the United States until the 1970s. However, CES started in Russia in the 1950s and gained popularity in parts of Europe, where it was originally called "electrosleep" before making its way to the United States in the 1960s. Psychopharmaceutical treatment was not prevalent then, so intense interest was generated by the possibilities that this new method offered for treating difficult psychiatric cases. Clinical studies commenced with the intent of discovering the best waveform configuration, mechanisms of action, safety profile, and potential clinical usefulness.

In 1978, the FDA's Neurological Panel suggested the modality be called cranial electrotherapy stimulation, rather than "electrosleep." The FDA also determined that CES would only be available by prescription, making the United States one of only two countries in which an order from a licensed health care practitioner must be obtained for its use. This restriction continues today (Cranial electrotherapy stimulator, 21 CFR, § 882.5800, 2013). However, a license to order pharmaceuticals is not required—practitioners can use and order a CES device for a patient if their license allows them to diagnose and treat the particular condition. Currently, psychologists are the largest group of practitioners and researchers who utilize CES.

As technology has progressed over the decades, so have CES devices. This progression started with early 1970s CES units, which were the size of a carry-on suitcase designed to be used by practitioners in a clinical setting. It required tying a band around the head to hold wet sponges initially directly on the eyes, then against the forehead or temples, to deliver the treatment (Kirsch, 2002). Today, CES devices (Alpha-Stim, Nexalin, and CES Ultra) have made significant technological strides— the size of the equipment has been reduced to the size of a smartphone with digital LCD screens designed to be quick and easy to use by a practitioner or by the patient at home. The current is now delivered via electrodes that clip onto the earlobes, as opposed to the antiquated 1970s sponges. Besides being easier to use and having an appearance similar to earbud headphones, the earlobes provide a better electrode placement because they drive the current more directly to the target areas in the brain stem that control emotions (e.g., hypothalamus, limbic system). Figure 5.1 illustrates the technological advances to the Alpha-Stim CES device since it was first introduced in 1981.

How Cranial Electrotherapy Stimulation Works

The mechanisms of action of CES have not been clearly elucidated; however, several mechanisms have been postulated. CES is thought to be derived from a direct mode of action, and, thus, it has been described largely from a neurobiological standpoint with respect to its effect on electrical brain activity, neurotransmitters, and hormones. Table 5.1 summarizes some of the mechanistic studies carried out to better understand the physiological responses to CES since 1967.

In the past decade, research has shifted to imaging studies to increase knowledge about the physiological processes that occur during CES. A functional magnetic resonance imaging (fMRI) study by Feusner et al. (2012) found that CES causes cortical deactivation in the midline frontal and parietal regions of the brain of anxiety patients after just one 20-minute treatment. A second fMRI study reported decreased activity in the pain processing regions of the brain in patients with fibromyalgia (Taylor, Anderson, Riedel, Lewis, & Bourguignon, 2013; Taylor, Anderson, Riedel, Lewis, Kinser, et al., 2013).

The most recent fMRI study to date (Qiao et al., 2015) showed balancing of nerve clusters in Tourette's patients under 12 years old, confirming the putative mechanism of brain balancing, or normalization, proposed by Giordano (Kirsch, 2006). In this Tourette's study, after a series of Alpha-Stim CES treatments, subjects exhibited altered spontaneous functional connectivity in brain areas within cortico-striato-thalamo-cortical (CSTC) circuits involved in motor generation or control. The functional activity and connectivity in motor pathways was suppressed, while activations in the control portions of the CSTC loop were increased. There was also a decrease in the Yale Global Tic Severity Scale indicating a decrease in motor and vocal tics from baseline to the end of 24 weeks of CES treatment that was highly significant ($p = < .01$) for both the subset of subjects ($n = 8$) who had fMRIs and the total group ($N = 42$). The authors, in China and the United States, concluded that the normalization of the balance between motor and control portions of the CSTC circuit may result in the recovery of adolescents with Tourette's syndrome.

Electroencephalogram analysis of subjects who received one 20-minute treatment of CES showed significant increases in alpha activity (increased relaxation) and decreases in delta activity (increased alertness) and theta activity (increased ability to focus; Kennerly, 2004). The changes in brainwave patterns are thought to represent a calm, relaxed, alert state. These imaging changes, coupled with the older neurochemical research, help to explain the positive clinical responses reported with CES in mood and sleep disorders.

FIGURE 5.1

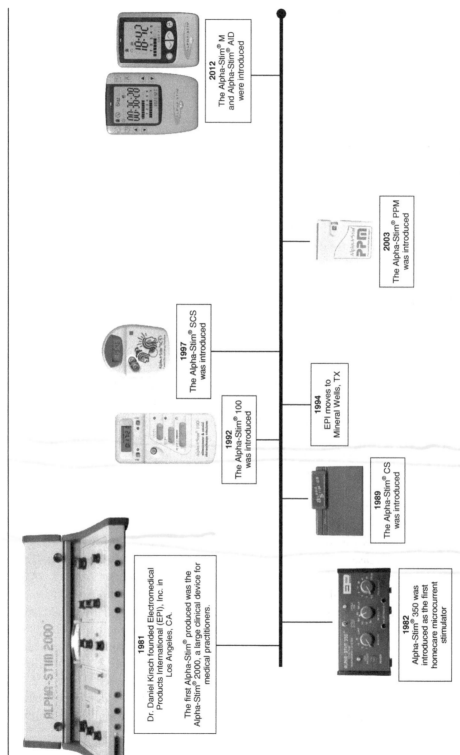

1981
Dr. Daniel Kirsch founded Electromedical Products International (EPI), Inc. in Los Angeles, CA.

The first Alpha-Stim® produced was the Alpha-Stim® 2000, a large clinical device for medical practitioners.

1982
Alpha-Stim® 350 was introduced as the first homecare microcurrent stimulator

1989
The Alpha-Stim® CS was introduced

1992
The Alpha-Stim® 100 was introduced

1994
EPI moves to Mineral Wells, TX

1997
The Alpha-Stim® SCS was introduced

2003
The Alpha-Stim® PPM was introduced

2012
The Alpha-Stim® M and Alpha-Stim® AID were introduced

Technological advances to the Alpha-Stim cranial electrotherapy stimulation device since it was first introduced in 1981. From *History of the waveform: The clinical history of the Alpha-Stim® waveform technology.* Retrieved from http://www.alpha-stim.com/healthcare-professionals/history-of-the-waveform/. Copyright 2017 by Electromedical Products International, Inc. Adapted with permission.

TABLE 5.1

Summary of Mechanistic Cranial Electrotherapy Stimulation Research

Findings	Study type	Reference
Increase neurotransmitter release and resynthesis	Open label	Siegesmund et al., 1967
Increased inhibitory process resulting in analgesia and sleep	Open label	Pozos et al., 1968 Pozos et al., 1969
Increase blood serotonin levels	Pilot study	Shealy et al., 1989
Increased MAO-B and GABA	Double blind	Krupitsky et al., 1991
Increased serotonin and beta-endorphins in spinal fluid	Open label	Liss & Liss, 1996
Increased GABA and beta-endorphins	Open label	Shealy et al., 1998
Increased alpha and decreased delta activity on qEEG	Open label pilot study	Kennerly, 2004
Cortical deactivation in frontal and parietal regions on fMRI	Open label	Fuesner et al., 2012
Decreased pain processing in fibromyalgia patients on fMRI	Double blind	Taylor, Anderson, Riedel, Lewis, & Bourguignon, 2013
Balancing of cortical brain clusters in adolescent Tourette's patients on fMRI	Double blind	Qiao et al., 2015

Safety of Cranial Electrotherapy Stimulation

The FDA cleared CES for the treatment of anxiety, depression, and insomnia in 1979. CES is noninvasive and has an excellent safety profile. The FDA publicly commented on CES safety in an announcement in the *Federal Register* reclassifying CES to a Class II device and stating that "in terms of safety, there is little evidence of device risk," and "in general, CES devices appear to have a favorable long-term safety profile" (Kux, 2016). The only precautions to CES include pregnancy and having a pacemaker, spinal cord stimulator, or other implanted electrical device (Phillips, 1997). Adverse effects of CES occur infrequently and are mild and self-limiting. These include vertigo, skin irritation at the electrode sites, and headaches. Headaches and vertigo are usually experienced when the current is set too high for a particular individual. These effects resolve when the current is reduced or within minutes to hours following treatment. Skin irritation at the electrode site can be avoided by moving electrodes around slightly during treatments. No serious adverse effects have ever been reported from using CES (Kirsch, 2002). In an Alpha-Stim survey of service members and veterans, 99% of subjects ($n = 152$) considered CES technology to be safe (Kirsch, Price, Nichols, Marksberry, & Platoni, 2014). An important safety benefit of CES is that it leaves the user alert and relaxed after treatment, in contrast to drugs that can have adverse effects on service members' ability to function on missions that require intense focus and attention (Kennerly, 2006).

Evidence Base for Cranial Electrotherapy Stimulation

In the last 5 years, CES studies have been carried out at major American medical institutions (e.g., Walter Reed National Military Medical Center, MD Anderson Cancer Center, The University of Texas Health Science Center, UCLA's David Geffen School of Medicine, the University of Virginia). At the time of this writing, over 60% of Alpha-Stim CES sales in the United States go to the U.S. Department of Defense and Veterans Affairs Medical Centers, both of which are conducting well-planned research projects. The uptick in research is not confined to the approved indications of anxiety, insomnia, and depression, but also includes treatment areas such as restless leg syndrome, attention-deficit/hyperactivity disorder, fibromyalgia, the aforementioned Tourette's syndrome, and addictions. The exploration of these off-label treatment areas is an indicator that CES is still in the infancy stage and that researchers are just starting to understand the normalization effects of CES to the brain.

ANXIETY

In a double-blind, sham-controlled RCT that studied anxiety and depression, 115 subjects suffering from a treatment-resistant anxiety disorder, many with comorbid depression, received 5 weeks of active or sham CES (Barclay & Barclay, 2014). The Hamilton Anxiety Rating Scale (HAM-A; Hamilton, 1959) and Hamilton Depression Rating Scale (HAM-D; Hamilton, 1960) were obtained at baseline and at the end of weeks 1, 3, and 5. At the end of the study, when compared with scores at baseline, anxiety and depression scores decreased significantly in the treatment group but not in the sham group. The CES treatment group decreased their initial anxiety scores by 50% in 83% of the subjects ($p = .001$) and in 82% of the initial depression scores ($p = .001$). In the CES treatment group, the decrease in anxiety scores was more than 3 times that of the sham group, and the decrease in depression scores was more than 12 times the decrease seen in the sham control.

The results reported by Barclay and Barclay (2014) are consistent with seven similar double-blind, sham-controlled RCTs using CES to treat acute and chronic anxiety disorders (Cork et al., 2003; Hill, 2015; Lee et al., 2013; Mellen & Mackey, 2008; Strentzsch, 2008; Voris, 1995; Winick, 1999). These anxiety studies represent a unique cross-section of patients, including college students, preoperative and dental anxiety patients, sheriff and security officers, people with chronic mental illness, outpatient psychology and psychiatry patients, and chronic pain patients. The diversity of patient populations studied sheds light on the potential uses for CES.

In an RCT ($n = 120$) comparing the effects of paroxetine (Paxil) with paroxetine and CES in anxiety patients over a 6-week period, there was significantly more improvement ($p < .01$) in the CES group on the HAM-A (L. Lu & Hu, 2014) than in the group that took paroxetine alone (although both groups improved significantly). The CGI-SI, as a secondary measure, confirmed the between-group differences in favor of the CES group ($p < .05$).

Four additional single-blind RCTs on anxiety yielded significant findings in favor of the treatment group (Chen et al., 2007; Gibson & O'Hair, 1987; Kim et al., 2008; Kolesos, Osionwo, & Akkhigbe, 2013). Four open-label and retrospective analyses also reported that CES significantly decreased anxiety (Gong et al., 2016; Libretto, Hilton, Gordon, Zhang, & Wesch, 2015; X. Y. Lu, Wang, Li, Zhang, & Liu, 2005; Overcash, 1999).

A prominent research and academic psychiatrist has said that "CES melts away anxiety" (M. Woodbury, personal communication to the FDA at the American Psychiatric Association annual meeting, New Orleans, May 2010). Indeed, the effects in state or situational anxiety are almost immediate in most people, or at least achievable within a single 20- to 40-minute treatment session. CES is used as an anxiolytic by dentists just prior to and throughout procedures (Kolesos, Osionwo, & Akkhigbe, 2013; Winick, 1999), as well as by physicians and psychologists (Lee et al., 2013). A single treatment can increase alpha brain waves, while decreasing delta and theta waves (Kennerly, 2004).

Achieving significant effects in trait anxiety or generalized anxiety disorder (GAD) could take up to 6 weeks of treatment. Two or three treatments per week are usually sufficient. After the anxiety is under control, CES may be used on an as-needed basis.

Clinical Vignette: Generalized Anxiety Disorder

Donald is a 55-year-old man with long-standing GAD. He had suffered with worsening anxiety for more than 20 years, and, during most of that time, he had seen a psychiatrist who prescribed several anxiolytics, sleep medications, and an antidepressant. Donald felt as though these medications had little effect; however, he continued to take them as directed. He also saw a psychologist who instructed him on relaxation techniques and deep breathing. Over the period of a year, after a minor cardiac event, the patient's anxiety worsened. He became increasingly anxious, which led to panic attacks and other disruptions in daily life, and he began to demonstrate agoraphobic behavior (his leg was shaking and both his family life and career began to erode).

He learned about CES through a new psychologist he was referred to by a friend, and together they decided to try a series of treatments in the office. The first few CES treatments took place during the patient's normal cognitive behavioral therapy (CBT) visit each week, and each visit tended to calm him down. Donald called it his "brain spa" time. After the encouraging preliminary results seen in the office trial, the psychologist instructed Donald on how to properly use the device and ordered one for 20-minute daily home use. At first, Donald was concerned the CES device was making him worse, because more suppressed negative feelings were coming to the surface. The psychologist explained that CES helps to normalize the brain, which can include processing previously repressed feelings, and advised him to continue CES therapy on a reduced schedule of two to three 20-minute treatments per week. After 1 month, Donald reported a decrease in his anxiety, an improved sex life, and the ability to do more tasks that require concentration. He also noted a higher overall quality of life, and his family noticed the positive changes in him as well. He was then instructed to continue using CES one or two times a week and whenever he started to feel stressed. After 6 weeks, his leg stopped shaking and by 90 days, Donald considered himself cured of his anxiety.

DEPRESSION

Two double-blind, sham-controlled RCTs using Alpha-Stim CES technology yielded significant findings for depression in favor of the treatment group in (a) 115 GAD patients ($p < .001$) with comorbid depression (Barclay & Barclay, 2014), and (b) in 21 sheriff officers ($p < .01$) in Alabama (Mellen & Mackey, 2009). In addition, Chen et al. (2007), in a single-blind, sham-controlled RCT of 60 children ages 8 to 16 with mixed anxiety-depression disorder, reported that CES significantly decreased depression ($p < .001$) in the treatment group, when compared with the sham group. Six open-label studies and retrospective analyses reported that CES significantly decreased depression from baseline to the endpoint of the study (Amr, El-Wasify, Elmaadawi, Roberts, & El-Mallakh, 2013; Bystritsky, Kerwin, & Feusner, 2008; Gong et al., 2016; Libretto et al., 2015; Lichtbroun, Raicer, & Smith, 2001; X. Y. Lu et al., 2005).

Similar to the course of treatment in trait anxiety, CES could take 3 to 6 weeks of treatment to notice significant effects in depressed patients. When depression is comorbid with anxiety, the anxiety also may not show improvement for the first week or two. Two or three treatments per week are usually sufficient at first, although some cases require daily treatment. After the first 6 weeks, the schedule may be reduced to one to two treatments per week.

Insomnia

One double-blind, sham-controlled RCT using Alpha-Stim CES technology ($n = 46$) for 8 weeks found that CES significantly ($p < .001$) decreased insomnia in favor of the treatment (Taylor, Anderson, Riedel, Lewis, & Bourguignon, 2013; Taylor, Anderson, Riedel, Lewis, Kinser, et al., 2013). Another double-blind, sham-controlled, randomized, 5-day study of military service members in a partial psychiatric hospitalization program ($n = 57$) using Alpha-Stim CES technology reported significant improvements ($p < .04$) on Days 1 and 4, and almost significant findings ($p = .079$) on Day 5 (Lande & Gragnani, 2013). In that study, the actively treated service members slept 43 minutes more, and the sham-treated subjects slept 19 minutes less, per night, over the 5-day period. An open-label study of pain patients also found that CES significantly improved sleep (Lichtbroun et al., 2001).

Insomnia has a wide range of etiologies, and, depending on the cause and comorbid conditions, it can take anywhere from one treatment to 2 months of treatments before an improvement is seen. The 20- to 60-minute treatment session should be done at least 3 hours before going to bed, as CES has the paradoxical effect of increasing alertness immediately following a treatment. However, some people can use it when waking in the night and fall back asleep while the treatment is still active (the device will turn itself off at the conclusion of the preset treatment period).

FIBROMYALGIA

There have been three studies of the use of Alpha-Stim CES on fibromyalgia patients conducted at major U.S. universities. In a double-blind, sham-controlled RCT of CES for fibromyalgia ($n = 46$), subjects in the active CES and sham groups were instructed to use the device for 60 continuous minutes each day for 8 weeks (Taylor, Anderson, Riedel, Lewis, & Bourguignon, 2013). Pain was decreased significantly in the active group ($p = .023$) but not in the sham group.

In a 6-week study, a 3-week double-blind, sham-controlled RCT of CES for fibromyalgia ($n = 60$) was followed by a 3-week open-label crossover arm in which subjects in the sham and control groups could elect to participate in a more typical treatment course of CES (Lichtbroun et al., 2001). Results were significant in the CES group over the sham-treated group for sleep quality ($p = .02$), anxiety ($p = .04$), anger ($p = .04$), tender point scores ($p = .02$), self-rated pain ($p = .004$), fatigue ($p = .03$), feelings of well-being ($p = .007$), and quality of life ($p = 0.001$). Changes in depression, vigor, and confusion were not significant in this study. The findings for anxiety and sleep quality in this study were consistent with the findings of other Alpha-Stim studies indicating CES significantly decreases anxiety and improves sleep quality.

The third double-blind, sham-controlled RCT of CES evaluated the effect of a specified treatment course of CES for patients with fibromyalgia (Cork et al., 2003). This 6-week study included a 3-week, double-blind, randomized, sham-controlled arm, followed by a 3-week, open-label arm in which subjects in the sham group participated in a usual course of treatment of CES. Results were significant in the CES group over the sham-treated group for anxiety ($p = .001$), tender point scores ($p = .001$), self-rated pain ($p = .001$), but changes in functional impairment as measured by the Oswestry test (Fairbank & Pynsent, 2000) were not significant.

With these three RCT trials and one fMRI study showing decreased activity in the pain-processing regions of the brain (e.g., cingulate gyrus, insula, prefrontal cortex) in patients with fibromyalgia (Taylor, Anderson, Riedel, Lewis, Kinser, et al., 2013), there is more evidence that CES is a more effective treatment for fibromyalgia than any other intervention. Fibromyalgia patients must have patience in both treatment duration and course. Because they are particularly sensitive to the current, they must use a low level of current (e.g., 100 microamperes) for at least an hour per day. Then, it will be approximately 3 to 4 weeks before they begin to notice significant improvements in pain levels, sleep patterns, and mood.

POSTTRAUMATIC STRESS DISORDER

Posttraumatic stress disorder (PTSD) can take many forms, with some patients suffering from debilitating anxiety, depression, anger, headaches, and depression. As these symptoms manifest and worsen over time, we see stress levels increase, relationships deteriorate, and quality of life erode. Patients are often prescribed several medications to address each one of their symptoms. This polypharmacy approach dramatically increases the risks of harmful side effects.

The Warrior Combat Stress Reset Program (WCSRP) at Fort Hood, Texas, has been using Alpha-Stim CES since 2008. This integrative program was evaluated by a third party for effectiveness for treating PTSD (Libretto et al., 2015). The evaluation results were very positive, with significant reduction ($p < .001$) reported in PTSD, depression, anxiety, and pain. The WCSRP is an integrative program that uses individual and group therapy sessions, acupuncture, massage, yoga, CES, and other treatment modalities to treat PTSD patients who have recently returned from deployment. The goal is to prepare them to return to combat. Patient satisfaction for each modality was also measured, with Alpha-Stim CES scoring 100% in the final year of the evaluation.

A case series conducted at Creighton University tested the utility of CES in treating PTSD symptoms in two war veterans (Bracciano et al., 2012). The patients reported significant reduction in PTSD symptoms after 28 days of treatment, going from 34 to 13 and 29 to 10 on the PTSD Symptom Scale-Interview (PSS-I; Foa, Riggs, Dancu, & Rothbaum, 1993). There were also noticeable reductions in hyperarousal, avoiding certain situations and flashbacks.

A service member and veteran survey examined the perceptions of the effectiveness and safety of CES in 152 respondents (Kirsch et al., 2014). The findings were not only highly significant overall, but unexpectedly, the CES-plus-medication group did not do as well as the CES-only group treatment in anxiety, PTSD, insomnia and depression.

Victims of domestic violence also often experience PTSD in a manner similar to service members. A brief 5-day study was conducted with 10 women who were victims of domestic violence and living in a shelter (Mellen, Case, & Ruiz, 2016). The average age was 45 years, and most reported either being married to or living with the abuser. Two of three scales in the Behavior Rating Inventory of Executive Function—Adult Version (BRIEF-A; Roth, Isquith, & Gioia, 1996) found significant reductions in stress levels for the 10 sheltered residents. These were the Global Executive Composite Score ($p = .028$) and the Behavior Regulation Scale ($p = .009$); Metacognition fell just out of range ($p = .06$). The nine clinical measures of the Brief Symptom Inventory (Derogatis, 1993) did not quite achieve statistical significance either within the 5-day course of therapy, however, the trend lines indicated positive changes in all nine of the clinical variables, suggesting movement toward more normalized functioning in each category. Specifically, there were reductions seen in somatization and obsessive–compulsive thinking; reduced levels of depression, anxiety, hostility; and improved ability to relate interpersonally. There were also reductions in phobic anxiety, paranoid ideation, and psychoticism. The authors concluded that CES may contribute to reductions in psychological stress experienced by victims of domestic abuse. The results from the BRIEF-A suggest improvements in global functioning within the cortical and subcortical areas of the brain that may improve victims' abilities to think more clearly and make better decisions. PTSD patients should expect to use CES daily until the symptoms subside and then continue on a reduced schedule indefinitely.

Incorporating Cranial Electrotherapy Stimulation Into Clinical Practice

Mental health practitioners should begin by learning about CES. There are free live webinars and recorded training sessions are given frequently. There is a test after the webinar that earns a certificate of proficiency in continuing medical education and offers continuing education credits in some fields. Practitioners can then implement CES as a treatment option for patients with anxiety, insomnia, and/or depression, as well as for so-called off-label uses, either as a first-line treatment or a synergistic modality used with CBT, eye movement desensitization and reprocessing, biofeedback or neurofeedback, hypnosis, prolonged exposure, meditation, or talk therapy. Some clinicians have their patients use the CES device in the waiting room, prior to treatment, although more commonly CES is applied during a talk session (as it tends to open up the patient to talk more freely). Once positive results are seen, the practitioner can write an order for either the purchase or rental of a CES device for the patient's home use. There are practitioners who order CES devices in quantity to have on hand to immediately dispense them when it is indicated. Many of these practitioners usually pass along most, if not all, of the bulk discount to their patients as a courtesy.

A newer concept being adopted by some practitioners is to have a specialized CES treatment room with five to 10 comfortable chairs where patients can come in and use CES whenever they feel the need. This concept was first implemented in an army hospital in Texas, because it was the most cost-effective way to administer treatment to the most service members, using the minimal number of staff. One room monitor can supervise 10 chairs per seating, with up to three seatings per hour, or 240 treatments per 8-hour shift. From there, it was taken up by a Veterans Affairs Medical Center where Alpha-Stim CES was studied along with four other devices for safety, effectiveness, veteran compliance, and practicality (Tan, Dao, Smith, Robinson, & Jensen, 2010). Although the veterans were trained in the use of all five devices, and were encouraged to use any one at each visit, they chose CES 73% of the time. Of course, the government does not charge service members or veterans for health care, but this same concept can be quite lucrative when applied to a private practice, clinic, or hospital for a very nominal fee to the patient. And there is no impending shortage of patients with mood and sleep disorders. Using a figure of just $20 as the lowest reasonable fee for this service, and assuming a maximum capacity of 240 treatments per day, such a room would generate gross revenues of $4,800 per day, or $1,267,200 per year. The costs would be one employee, 10 comfortable lounge or massage chairs, and 10 CES devices, which cost under $1,000 each. Of course there would also be replenishable supplies (e.g., electrodes, conducting solution, batteries), but those costs are negligible. Realistically, the room would not likely be at full capacity for 22 days per month as calculated into the above numbers. So, a practitioner is more likely to make $250,000 to $500,000 annual net income from a CES treatment room. Once an order is provided for the patients to use or purchase a CES device, they like the low cost and convenience of such a therapy room and tend to refer their friends. The $20 cost is cheaper than a few drinks at a bar, and the mood-enhancing effects are better and certainly healthier.

Using CES is easy. The ear clip electrodes have replaceable pads that are moistened with a specialized conducting solution and then clipped onto the earlobes. The device is then turned on, and the current is slowly raised until the patient experiences an altered state, typically described as a light or floating feeling. If the current is uncomfortable, it can be reduced. As a rule of thumb, people who can comfortably tolerate 250 microamperes or more can complete a treatment in 20 minutes. Under 250 microamperes usually requires longer treatment, generally 30 to 40 minutes or until at least 2 minutes after the patient feels light. If the patient feels heavy, continue treatment until that gives way to a light feeling. The same procedure is used for all indications, as CES tends to have a balancing or normalizing effect on the brain.

Conclusion

CES is a well-researched, safe, effective, and cost-effective means to manage mood and sleep disorders. With mental health care moving away from pharmaceuticals and toward a new set of devices, it is time for CES to be the first-line of treatment for many disorders, as it is safer and at least as effective as other forms of therapy.

Essential Resources

The American Institute of Stress Learning Center, http://www.stress.org.

Electromedical Products International, Inc., manufacturer of Alpha-Stim technology, http://www.alpha-stim.com

Kirsch D. L. (2002). *The science behind cranial electrotherapy stimulation* (2nd ed.). Edmonton, Alberta, Canada: Medical Scope.

Kirsch, D. L., & Marksberry, J. A. (2015). The evolution of cranial electrotherapy stimulation for anxiety, insomnia, depression and pain and its potential for other indications. In Rosch, P. J. (Ed.), *Bioelectromagnetic and subtle energy medicine* (2nd ed.). Boca Raton, FL: CRC Press.

References

Amr, M., El-Wasify, M., Elmaadawi, A. Z., Roberts, R. J., & El-Mallakh, R. S. (2013). Cranial electrotherapy stimulation for the treatment of chronically symptomatic bipolar patients. *The Journal of ECT, 29*, e31–e32. http://dx.doi.org/10.1097/YCT.0b013e31828a344d

Barclay, T. H., & Barclay, R. D. (2014). A clinical trial of cranial electrotherapy stimulation for anxiety and comorbid depression. *Journal of Affective Disorders, 164*, 171–177. http://dx.doi.org/10.1016/j.jad.2014.04.029

Bracciano, A. G., Chang, W.-P., Kokesh, S., Martinez, A., Meier, M., & Moore, K. (2012). Cranial electrotherapy stimulation in the treatment of posttraumatic stress disorder: A pilot study of two military veterans. *Journal of Neurotherapy, 16*, 60–69. http://dx.doi.org/10.1080/10874208.2012.650100

Bullock, T. H., Hopkins, C. D., Popper, A. N., & Fay, R. R. (2005). *Electroreception.* New York, NY: Springer.

Bystritsky, A., Kerwin, L., & Feusner, J. (2008). A pilot study of cranial electrotherapy stimulation for generalized anxiety disorder. *The Journal of Clinical Psychiatry, 69*, 412–417. http://dx.doi.org/10.4088/JCP.v69n0311

Chen, Y., Yu, L., Zhang, J., Li, L., Chen, T., & Chen, Y. (2007). Results of cranial electrotherapy stimulation to children with mixed anxiety and depressive disorder. *Shanghai Archives of Psychiatry, 19*, 203–205.

Cork, R. C., Wood, P., Ming, N., Shepherd, C., Eddy, J., & Price, L. (2003). The effect of cranial electrotherapy stimulation (CES) on pain associated with fibromyalgia. *The Internet Journal of Anesthesiology, 8*(2), 1–8.

Cranial electrotherapy stimulator, 21 C.F.R. § 882.5800 (2013).

Derogatis, L. R. (1993). *BSI Brief Symptom Inventory: Administration, scoring, and procedure manual* (4th ed.). Minneapolis, MN: National Computer Systems.

Electromedical Products International, Inc. (2017). *History of the waveform: The clinical history of the Alpha-Stim® waveform technology.* Retrieved from http://www.alpha-stim.com/healthcare-professionals/history-of-the-waveform/

Fairbank, J. C. T., & Pynsent, P. B. (2000). The Oswestry Disability Index. *Spine, 25*, 2940–2953.

Feusner, J. D., Madsen, S., Moody, T. D., Bohon, C., Hembacher, E., Bookheimer, S. Y., & Bystritsky, A. (2012). Effects of cranial electrotherapy stimulation on resting state brain activity. *Brain and Behavior, 2*, 211–220. http://dx.doi.org/10.1002/brb3.45

Foa, E., Riggs, D., Dancu, C., & Rothbaum, B. (1993). Reliability and validity of a brief instrument for assessing post-traumatic stress disorder. *Journal of Traumatic Stress, 6*, 459–474. http://dx.doi.org/10.1007/BF00974317

Gibson, T. H., & O'Hair, D. E. (1987). Cranial application of low level transcranial electrotherapy vs. relaxation instructions in anxious patients. *American Journal of Electromedicine, 4*, 18–21.

Gong, B. Y., Ma, H. M., Zang, X. Y., Wang, S. Y., Zhang, Y., Jiang, N., . . . Zhao, Y. (2016). Efficacy of cranial electrotherapy stimulation combined with biofeedback therapy in patients with functional constipation. *Journal of Neurogastroenterology and Motility, 22*, 497–508. http://dx.doi.org/10.5056/jnm15089

Hamilton, M. (1959). The assessment of anxiety states by rating. *British Journal of Medical Psychology, 32*, 50–55. http://dx.doi.org/10.1111/j.2044-8341.1959.tb00467.x

Hamilton, M. (1960). A rating scale for depression. *Journal of Neurology, Neurosurgery, and Psychiatry, 23*, 56–62. http://dx.doi.org/10.1136/jnnp.23.1.56

Hill, N. T. (2015). *The effects of alpha stimulation on induced anxiety* (Master's thesis). Available from Digital Commons @ ACU, Electronic Theses and Dissertations. (Paper 6).

Kennerly, R. (2004). qEEG analysis of cranial electrotherapy: A pilot study. *Journal of Neurotherapy, 8*(2), 112–113.

Kennerly, R. (2006). *Changes in quantitative EEG and low resolution tomography following cranial electrotherapy stimulation* (Unpublished doctoral dissertation). *University of North Texas*, Denton.

Kim, H. J., Kim, W. Y., Lee, Y. S., Chang, M. S., Kim, J. H., & Park, Y. C. (2008). The effect of cranial electrotherapy stimulation on preoperative anxiety and hemodynamic responses. *Korean Journal of Anesthesiology, 55*, 657–661. http://dx.doi.org/10.4097/kjae.2008.55.6.657

Kirsch, D. L. (2002). *The science behind cranial electrotherapy stimulation* (2nd ed.), Edmonton, Alberta, Canada: Medical Scope.

Kirsch, D. L. (2006). Cranial electrotherapy stimulation for the treatment of anxiety, depression, insomnia and other conditions. *Nature Medicine, 23*, 118–120.

Kirsch, D. L., Price, L. R., Nichols, F., Marksberry, J. A., & Platoni, K. T. (2014). Military service member and veteran self reports of efficacy of cranial electrotherapy stimulation for anxiety, posttraumatic stress disorder, insomnia, and depression. *US Army Medical Department Journal, Oct–Dec, 46*–54.

Kolesos, O. N., Osionwo, H. O., & Akkhigbe, K. O. (2013). The role of relaxation therapy and Cranial Electrotherapy Stimulation in the management of dental anxiety in Nigeria. *ISOR Journal of Dental Practices, 10*, 51–57.

Krupitsky, E. M., Burakov, A. M., Karan-ova, G. F., Katsnelson, J. S., Lebedev, V. P., Grinenko, A. J., & Borodkin, J. S. (1991). The administration of transcranial electric treatment for affective disturbances therapy in alcoholic patients. *Drug and Alcohol Dependence, 27*, 1–6. http://dx.doi.org/10.1016/0376-8716(91)90080-I

Kux, L. (2016). Neurological devices; Reclassification of cranial electrotherapy stimulator intended to treat insomnia and/or anxiety; Effective date of requirement for premarket approval for cranial electrotherapy stimulator intended to treat depression. *Federal Register Number*: 2016-01173.

Lande, R. G., & Gragnani, C. (2013). Efficacy of cranial electric stimulation for the treatment of insomnia: A randomized pilot study. *Complementary Therapies in Medicine, 21*, 8–13. http://dx.doi.org/10.1016/j.ctim.2012.11.007

Lee, S.-H., Kim, W.-Y., Lee, C.-H., Min, T.-J., Lee, Y.-S., Kim, J.-H., & Park, Y.-C. (2013). Effects of cranial electrotherapy stimulation on preoperative anxiety, pain and endocrine response. *The Journal of International Medical Research, 41*, 1788–1795. http://dx.doi.org/10.1177/0300060513500749

Libretto, S., Hilton, L., Gordon, S., Zhang, W., & Wesch, J. (2015). Effects of integrative PTSD treatment in a military health setting. *Energy Psychology, 7*, 33–44. http://dx.doi.org/10.9769/EPJ.2015.11.01.SL

Lichtbroun, A. S., Raicer, M.-M. C., & Smith, R. B. (2001). The treatment of fibromyalgia with cranial electrotherapy stimulation. *Journal of Clinical Rheumatology, 7*, 72–78. http://dx.doi.org/10.1097/00124743-200104000-00003

Liss, S., & Liss, B. (1996). Physiological and therapeutic effects of high frequency electrical pulses. *Integrative Physiological and Behavioral Science, 31*, 88–96.

Lu, L., & Hu, J. A. (2014). Comparative study of anxiety disorders treatment with paroxetine in combination with cranial electrotherapy stimulation therapy. *Medical Innovation of China, 11*, 080–082.

Lu, X. Y., Wang, A. H., Li, Y., Zhang, J. S., & Liu, B. X. (2005). Safety and effectiveness of Cranial Electrotherapy Stimulation in treating children with emotional disorders. *Chinese Journal of Clinical Rehabilitation, 9*, 96–97.

Mellen, R. R., Case, J., & Ruiz, D. J. (2016). Cranial Electrotherapy Stimulation (CES) as a treatment for reducing stress and improving prefrontal cortex functioning in victims of domestic violence. *International Association for Correctional and Forensic Psychology Newsletter, 48*, 12–15.

Mellen, R. R., & Mackey, W. (2008). Cranial electrotherapy stimulation (CES) and the reduction of stress symptoms in a sheriff's jail security and patrol officer population: A pilot study. *American Jails, 22*, 32–38.

Mellen, R. R., & Mackey, W. (2009). Reducing sheriff's officers' symptoms of depression using Cranial Electrotherapy Stimulation (CES): A control experimental study. *The Correctional Psychologist, 41*, 9–15.

Nasrallah, H. A. (2009). Psychiatry's future is here: Here are 6 trends that will affect your practice. *Current Psychiatry, 8*, 16–18.

Overcash, S. J. (1999). Cranial Electrotherapy Stimulation in patients suffering from acute anxiety disorders. *American Journal of Electromedicine, 16*, 49–51.

Phillips, P. (1997, July 25). *510(k)* (Number: K903014). Retrieved from https://www.accessdata.fda.gov/scripts/cdrh/cfdocs/cfpmn/pmn_template.cfm?id=k903014

Pozos, R. S., Richardson, A. W., & Kaplan, H. M. (1968). Low wattage electroanesthesia in dogs: Modification by synaptic drugs. *Anesthesia and Analgesia, 47*, 342–344. http://dx.doi.org/10.1213/00000539-196807000-00007

Pozos, R. S., Richardson, A. W., & Kaplan, H. M. (1969). Mode of production and locus of action of electroanesthesia in dogs. *Anesthesia and Analgesia, 48*, 342–345. http://dx.doi.org/10.1213/00000539-196905000-00007

Qiao, J., Weng, S., Wang, P., Long, J., & Wang, Z. (2015). Normalization of intrinsic neural circuits governing Tourette's Syndrome using Cranial Electrotherapy Stimulation. *IEEE Transactions on Biomedical Engineering, 62*, 1272–1280. http://dx.doi.org/10.1109/TBME.2014.2385151

Roth, R. M., Isquith, P. K., & Gioia, G. A. (1996). *BRIEF-A: Behavior rating inventory of executive function—Adult version*. Psychological Assessment Resources: Lutz, FL.

Shealy, C. N., Cady, R. K., Culver-Veehoff, D., Cox, R., & Liss, S. (1998). Cerebrospinal fluid and plasma neurochemicals: Response to Cranial Electrical Stimulation. *Journal of Neurological and Orthopedic Surgery and Medicine, 18*, 94–97.

Shealy, C. N., Cady, R. K., Wilkie, R. G., Cox, R., Liss, S., & Clossen, W. (1989). Depression: A diagnostic, neurochemical profile and therapy with cranial electrotherapy stimulation (CES). *The Journal of Neurological & Orthopaedic Medicine & Surgery, 10*, 319–321.

Siegesmund, K. A., Sances, A., Jr., & Larson, S. J. (1967). The effects of electrical currents on synaptic vesicles in monkey cortex. In A. M. Wageneder and S. T. Schuy (Eds.), *Electrotherapeutic sleep and electroanesthesia proceedings* (Vol. 1, pp. 31–33). Amsterdam, The Netherlands: Excerpta Medica Foundation.

Strentzsch, J. A. (2008). *An examination of cranial electrotherapy stimulation (CES) on alpha-amylase levels, cortisol levels and state-trait anxiety scores in the chronically mentally ill*

(Doctoral dissertation, Saint Mary's University). Retrieved from https://www. stress.org/an-examination-of-cranial-electrotherapy-stimulation-ces-on-alpha-amylase-levels-cortisol-levels-and-state-trait-anxiety-scores-in-the-chronically-mentally-ill/

Tan, G., Dao, T. K., Smith, D. L., Robinson, A., & Jensen, M. P. (2010). Incorporating complementary and alternative medicine (CAM) therapies to expand psychological services to veterans suffering from chronic pain. *Psychological Services, 7,* 148–161. http://dx.doi.org/10.1037/a0020304

Taylor, A. G., Anderson, J. G., Riedel, S. L., Lewis, J. E., & Bourguignon, C. (2013). A randomized, controlled, double-blind pilot study of the effects of Cranial Electrical Stimulation on activity in brain pain processing regions in individuals with fibromyalgia. *EXPLORE: The Journal of Science and Healing, 9,* 32–40. http://dx.doi.org/10.1016/j.explore.2012.10.006

Taylor, A. G., Anderson, J. G., Riedel, S. L., Lewis, J. E., Kinser, P. A., & Bourguignon, C. (2013). Cranial electrical stimulation improves symptoms and functional status in individuals with fibromyalgia. *Pain Management Nursing, 14,* 327–335. http://dx.doi.org/10.1016/j.pmn.2011.07.002

Voris, M. D. (1995). *An investigation of the effectiveness of cranial electrotherapy stimulation in the treatment of anxiety disorders among outpatient psychiatric patients, impulse control parolees, and pedophiles.* Corpus Christi, TX: Delos Mind/Body Institute Newsletter.

Winick, R. L. (1999). Cranial Electrotherapy Stimulation (CES): A safe and effective low cost means of anxiety control in a dental practice. *General Dentistry, 47,* 50–55.

Ed Hamlin

Growing the Evidence Base for Neurofeedback in Clinical Practice

6

Neurofeedback refers to a type of biofeedback using brain/computer inter-face technology that permits an individual to learn to change the pattern of activity of his or her electroencephalogram (EEG). In this technique, relevant aspects of brain wave activity are accessed and converted in real time into visual and/or auditory displays, allowing the trainee to learn to volitionally alter them. The EEG is dynamic and its activity patterns are con-stantly fluctuating. Ordinarily, a person would not have any direct awareness of his or her brain wave activity and its fluctuations and, thus, would have no idea of how to change it. However, as with other forms of biofeedback, the feedback display provides the information necessary for reinforcement to be received when fluctuations are in the desired direction. Learning to change brain wave activity modifies how the brain is functioning. Initially, these learned modifications may be very short-lived, but as a person contin-ues to practice making desired alterations in their brain waves, the changes begin to last longer.

Investigations and applications of neurofeedback training began in the 1960s. Since then, the technique has been widely used in the treatment of a variety of disorders, including seizures, attention-deficit/hyperactivity dis-order (ADHD), substance abuse, posttraumatic stress disorder (PTSD), anxi-ety, depression, insomnia, learning disabilities, and more (Hammond, 2011; Hirshberg, Chiu, & Frazier, 2005). Additionally, it has been applied as an aid in

http://dx.doi.org/10.1037/0000085-007
Using Technology in Mental Health Practice, J. J. Magnavita (Editor)

personal enhancement or peak performance training. However, for much of the time since its inception, mental health disciplines and academic training programs have largely ignored it. Some have suggested that "there persists a level of distrust and/or bias in the medical and research communities in the USA toward neurofeedback and other functional interventions" (Orndorff-Plunkett, Singh, Aragón, & Pineda, 2017, p. 95) As a result, neurofeedback has been largely ignored or disregarded in social neuroscience (e.g., Orndorff-Plunkett et al., 2017). Currently, though, this lack of attention is changing, as there is developing interest in the application of technology in mental health practice.

History of Neurotechnology

The flood of neuroscience publications at the end of the last century was largely the result of advances in neuroimaging technology permitting the viewing of the human brain in operation. For the first time, scientists and clinicians were able to see an intact brain performing some of its various functions without invasive procedures that violated its physical integrity. Previously, brain examination largely happened postmortem and typically involved a brain compromised by injury or disease, greatly limiting the applicability of the findings. Initially in the last 2 decades of the 20th century, positron emission tomography and, later, functional magnetic resonance imaging (fMRI) technology became widely available in university medical centers, as well as in other research and clinical facilities. In 1989, then President George H. W. Bush declared the 1990s the "Decade of the Brain," providing government funding for launching a great many studies in the developing field of neuroscience. In 1978, a total of 6,500 papers regarding brain science were published in refereed journals; by 1998, that number had grown to 17,000 (Rose & Abi-Rached, 2013), in large part due to the development of new imaging technologies and increased government funding for basic neuroscience research. The number of published papers and people involved in the study of the brain has continued to grow throughout the new century. Many universities have renamed their psychology graduate study programs to include "neuroscience" in the titles, and it is a rare psychology training program that does not now include a brain science focus. The brain sciences are now informing many areas of study beyond psychology, neurology, and psychiatry, including infant development, education, economics, sociology, politics, and sports performance.

In addition to the advances associated with functional neuroimaging, other novel and exciting brain science findings were occurring during this same period. Eric Kandel, Michael Merzenich, and Marion Diamond were demonstrating the largely unrecognized capacity of brain structures and activities being altered by specific experiences, introducing the concept of *neuroplasticity* to both the academic and public arenas (Diamond & Hopson, 1999; Kandel, 2006; Merzenich, 2013). Although Hebb (1949) had largely described many of the mechanisms involved in the process of brain changes from experience decades earlier, neuroplasticity was not empirically demonstrated until the work of these pioneering scientists—work that resulted in Kandel being awarded the Nobel Prize in 2000. Prior to this time, the brain was considered to be relatively fixed in both its structure and functioning, with the exception of the recognition of gradual cell loss and functional decline over time. The discovery that the brain's structure and functioning are molded by our experiences opened entirely new avenues of thought and exploration, as well as suggesting novel possibilities for intervention.

TECHNOLOGICAL ADVANCES IN BRAIN SCIENCES

During this explosion of technological advances and scientific discoveries involving the brain and its functioning, some important previous work on the learned alteration of brain functioning has gone largely unnoticed, arguably due to being somewhat ahead of its time. Technology had been developed early in the 20th century for recording the EEG, the first physiological measure of the human brain's activity. Its developer, Hans Berger, was convinced that his tool for watching the brain's electrical activity would be embraced by psychiatry, but the field ultimately denied its utility beyond seizure identification (Schirmann, 2014; Ulrich, 2002). In the 1920s, Berger was the first to record and amplify the electrical activity of the brain by placing sensors on the scalp to measure the electrical impulses generated by brain cells. The EEG is measured in frequency and amplitude—*frequency* reflects the speed of the nerve firings and is measured in hertz (Hz) or cycles per second. More activated brain cells typically fire at a faster rate than a brain at rest. This relationship between firing rate and activation of the brain was the first observation Berger noted in the EEG.

Amplitude refers to power and reflects the magnitude of the voltage being generated at the surface of the brain area being monitored. EEG amplitude is typically measured in microvolts, or a millionth of a volt, as the signal acquired at the scalp is actually very small. The number of brain cells firing synchronously at a particular frequency determines the amplitude an individual brain cell discharges with the same voltage each time it fires.

Conventional terminology divides the EEG frequencies into bandwidths. *Delta* refers to activity below 4 Hz and is typically associated with deep, dreamless sleep. *Theta* activity, considered to exist between 4 and 8 Hz, is common when an individual is drowsy, daydreaming, or visualizing internally generated images. *Alpha* activity is defined as 8 to 12 Hz, is rhythmic (regularly oscillating), and has been shown to be associated with meditation or a relaxed focus. It is considered to represent idling in the brain, as it typically increases in amplitude in the visual centers of the brain when the eyes are closed and attenuates with eye opening. *Beta* activity is in the range of 12 to 20 Hz and is commonly associated with active processing of sensory information, as seen when someone is attentive to external stimuli. Faster beta frequencies above 20 Hz are typically seen in higher states of arousal, such as excitement, anxiety, and fear states. All of the different EEG frequencies are present all of the time. It is the proportions of the various frequencies that fluctuate throughout the day. When sleeping, there is a greater proportion (higher amplitude) of delta waves; when alert and engaged in a cognitive task, delta proportions are diminished and beta frequencies are more prevalent. Mental states are reflected in the patterns of activity seen in the EEG frequencies and amplitudes. There are no good or bad brain wave frequencies— they all are important. Adaptive functioning requires flexibility in states of arousal.

APPLICATIONS OF BRAIN SCIENCE DISCOVERIES

Slowly, brain science discoveries are now finding their way into applied psychology.

Alpha Waves and Calming the Mind and Body

In 1968, more than 20 years prior to the launching of the Decade of the Brain, two researchers were beginning to explore the possibilities for training the EEG through the use of biofeedback. Joe Kamiya, at the University of Chicago and later at the University of California at San Francisco, was exploring enhancement of alpha frequencies in the brain (Kamiya, 1968). Elmer Green, at the Menninger Foundation, had been conducting research on self-regulation of the autonomic nervous system and had discovered that adept meditators produced higher alpha amplitudes compared with nonmeditators. Kamiya began to train individuals to recognize when they were in a state where alpha activity was predominating in the EEG. Kamiya discovered that as the trainees' awareness of their state improved, the percent of time the subjects spent in alpha increased. The conscious awareness of the state associated with the brain wave activity resulted in greater access to it. Additionally, the subjects who showed enhanced spontaneous alpha control reported "mental states reflecting relaxation, 'letting go', and pleasant affect associated with maintaining alpha" (Nowlis & Kamiya, 1970, p. 476). A 1968 article published in *Psychology Today* regarding Kamiya's work generated a great deal of public and professional interest in the instrumental training of alpha activity (Kamiya, 1968). The article described the benefits of being able to reduce stress in the brain by essentially training the brain wave activity closely associated with meditation and physiological stress release. Although other forms of biofeedback were already known and were being used in practice, brain wave biofeedback appeared to offer a more fundamental approach to producing a calmer body and mind through learning to alter the functioning of the central nervous system.

In Jim Robbins's book, *A Symphony in the Brain* (2008), he recounts the history and applications of neurofeedback and tells the story of Abraham Maslow calling Kamiya at 6:00 in the morning after learning of his work just a day earlier, stating he had been unable to sleep that night because of his excitement over the implications such unprecedented learned control of the brain could offer. From such exposure, neurofeedback was popularly seen as a possible panacea for overcoming many of the ills associated with modern life. Many articles appeared in popular publications (e.g., "Behavior: Brain Wave of the Future," 1971; "Mind Over Body, Mind Over Mind," 1971), touting the potential increases in self-awareness and self-regulation offered by this newly emerging technique.

Role of Sensorimotor Rhythm

At approximately this same time, M. Barry Sterman (2000), a researcher at UCLA, was taking a less applied approach to studying the training of the EEG utilizing operant conditioning techniques. Sterman, while researching the mechanisms of sleep, discovered a particular EEG activity that occurred during the transition from wake to sleep. He was interested in the process of internal inhibition facilitating the reduction in activation of the brain necessary to trigger sleep onset. In his studies, he identified a particular brain rhythm generated in the sensory-motor circuits of the brain associated with relaxation. He named this activity the sensorimotor rhythm (SMR) and subsequently found that it was not only associated as a precursor to sleep but with motoric quiescence in general. He saw an increase in SMR activity when his research animals became very still physically, whether they were relaxing prior to falling sleep or becoming very still while fully awake and alert (e.g., prior to pouncing when at play or withholding a motor response in learning experiments). The SMR activity he found was in the beta frequency range, but resembled alpha activity in appearance due to its rhythmicity and, unlike most beta activities which signal activation, it was associated with motoric quiescence. During the period when Sterman was studying the functions of SMR, papers were being published demonstrating learned control over many physiological processes that were previously considered outside of volitional control (see, e.g., Miller & DiCara, 1967). So, Sterman wondered if the EEG was amenable to self-control. He designed a study to determine if the EEG activity of cats could be operantly conditioned. The cats were rewarded with food when they increased the amplitude of their SMR activity after being cued by a light. The cats were readily able to learn to increase the occurrence of SMR activity, and a paper was published adding brain functioning to the list of physiological responses amenable to improved volitional control (Wyrwicka & Sterman, 1968).

At the time Sterman's paper describing the conditioning of the EEG was published, biofeedback was becoming very popular as demonstrations showed that individuals could learn to alter their muscle tension, skin temperature, heart rate, blood pressure, and skin conductance, all primarily associated with relaxation and arousal reduction. However, Sterman's work showed that cats could be taught to increase the amplitude of a specific EEG frequency when presented with a reward for making the increase. Sterman's research was the first to demonstrate the alteration of electrical activity in the brain in response to operant learning techniques. Unfortunately, since his discovery preceded the development of interest in brain activity and a greater appreciation in the brain's role in function and dysfunction, the implications of the discovery that training could alter basic brain activities did not receive the immediate recognition it deserved. The prevailing focus of neurofeedback training remained largely centered on alpha training, relaxation, and stress reduction.

Neurofeedback and Seizure Control

Fortunately, as often happens in science, a set of serendipitous circumstances led to Sterman's discovering a clinical application for operant conditioning of the EEG. After he completed his experiment demonstrating the operant conditioning of the EEG in cats, he received a contract from the National Aeronautics and Space Administration to study the emergence of seizure disorders in personnel working around rocket fuel. During exposure of the cats to the seizure-inducing compounds in the rocket fuel, he noticed a group of the experimental subjects having a much longer latency for the onset of seizure activity during exposure when compared with other cats. He then found that the more seizure-resistant cats were the ones he had previously trained to enhance their SMR activity. Sterman decided that since seizures are considered to result from a failure of inhibitory activity in the brain (see, e.g., Ben-Ari, Krnjevic, & Reinhardt, 1979), the enhancement of an EEG activity associated with inhibition and motoric quiescence might prove useful in the treatment of epilepsy. He confirmed this hypothesis when several individuals with intractable epilepsy were trained to increase their production of the SMR rhythm and showed a reduction in both the frequency and the intensity of their seizures (Sterman, Macdonald, & Stone, 1974). Several subsequent studies have shown the utility of neurofeedback training for seizure control (Sterman, 2000). It was this work that helped launch the field of EEG biofeedback, or neurofeedback as it has come to more typically be called, beyond simply enhancing relaxation. However, neurofeedback had to await the explosion of professional and popular interest in the brain to begin to gain more widespread recognition.

INCREASED RANGE OF APPLICATION

The increased awareness of neurofeedback was in large part due to Joel Lubar, a biopsychologist who studied with Sterman, through his extension of the application of neurofeedback to ADHD, a much more common disorder than epilepsy. Since many individuals with ADHD show deficits in inhibitory functioning, the extension from seizure control to attentional and behavioral control seemed plausible to Lubar. With only two neurofeedback approaches having been used to this point—eyes-closed alpha training and eyes-opened SMR training—he applied the same training protocols used for seizure control and, following neurofeedback training, found improvement in both behavioral regulation and cognitive functioning in children and adolescents diagnosed with ADHD. Lubar and Lubar (1984) refined the antiseizure protocols being used for neurofeedback training for addressing ADHD, by reinforcing not only the mid-beta range of frequencies (where SMR is found) but also the frequency range associated with greater engagement with the environment, while inhibiting theta range activity. Theta frequencies are associated with visualization and a more internal focus, such as that experienced during daydreaming. Lubar and his colleagues published a series of articles in the 1970s and 1980s (for a review of these articles, see Sherlin, Arns, Lubar, & Sokhadze, 2010) describing this expanded approach to neurofeedback and the results they were obtaining. Until his retirement from academics, Lubar, in his role as professor at the University of Tennessee in Knoxville, taught the theory and application of neurofeedback to graduate students enrolled in the psychology program. Currently, several of his students are in leadership positions in the field of neurofeedback and within its professional organizations.

Eugene Peniston developed another modification to neurofeedback training after he attended a workshop given by Elmer Green at the Menninger Clinic. As noted previously, Green had observed increased alpha production in adept meditators when they were not in a meditative state. However, when he examined their EEG during meditation, Green noticed that, as the session progressed, the practitioners' theta amplitude eventually became higher than the alpha amplitude. While attending the workshop with Green where this finding was presented, Peniston envisioned a treatment approach combining autogenic peripheral biofeedback training to facilitate improved arousal regulation, and visualization exercises enhanced by neurofeedback training encouraging increases in both alpha and theta. After the workshop at the Menninger Clinic, Peniston eagerly returned to the Veterans Administration facility in Colorado where he was working and implemented the program he had envisioned. Peniston has described the degree of positive response as surprising even to him. The population he chose for his experiment was Vietnam combat veterans admitted with PTSD and alcoholism. Many of these patients had several previous hospital admissions indicating the chronicity of their struggles. The response to his program was extremely positive, with subsequent randomized studies showing reduced symptomatology, marked changes on personality measures, reduced medication usage, reduced readmissions, and changes in blood chemistry (reduced beta endorphins) indicating reduced overall stress (Peniston & Kulkosky, 1989, 1991). Subsequent replications of Peniston's neurofeedback augmented approach to treating substance abuse problems in residential treatment indicate it continues to be the most effective approach to addictive disorders (for a review of these replications, see Trudeau, 2000).

Through the pioneering work of Sterman, Kamiya, Lubar, Peniston, and many others, the application of EEG biofeedback was extended into several areas of clinical practice. From its beginnings with epilepsy, neurofeedback has been employed with ADHD, PTSD, addiction and substance abuse, depression, anxiety, autism, sleep disturbances, and learning disabilities (for a review, see Brenninkmeijer, 2010). The use of largely the same technique in the treatment of such a wide array of issues and problems produced skepticism among many professionals regarding its reported outcomes. Nearly everyone has heard the saying that "if something sounds too good to be true, it probably is." Additionally, some of the claims being made in the popular media regarding biofeedback were both hyperbolic and premature based on the existing scientific evidence of the time. This skepticism, combined with methodological weaknesses for evidence (e.g., weak or absent sham training controls for double-blinding), contributed to difficulty in obtaining grant money to fund large scale, randomized-controlled research of neurofeedback's efficacy. Nevertheless, empirical support gradually began to accumulate for the utility of neurofeedback for several clinical conditions and for optimal performance (see, e.g., Hammond, 2011).

Empirical Evidence

A recent search of Google Scholar produced 7,700 entries for neurofeedback and EEG biofeedback, with 3,800 papers published within the past 5 years. The recent sharp increase in the number of publications regarding neurofeedback reflects a growing recognition of the approach among research groups. Where much of the early research on neurofeedback was produced by clinicians in private practice and generally had many methodological weaknesses (e.g., small group sizes, limited control comparison, absence of blinding, lack of objective outcome measures), higher quality studies are now being conducted in academic settings and recognized research facilities, particularly in European university centers and governmental facilities in the United States and Canada. Much of the current interest in neurofeedback is propelled by an increased professional and popular interest in the brain and neuroplasticity. Additionally, there is a broadening search for more effective nonpharmacologic approaches to mental health treatment as limitations of the commonly used medications become more widely recognized. To quote the then director of the National Institute for Mental Health (NIMH), Thomas Insel, "current medications help too few people to get better and very few people to get well" (Insel, 2009, p. 704). Greater recognition of the limitations and risks associated with psychoactive medications has prompted greater interest in alternative approaches to changing the brain's operations. Despite increased interest in alternative approaches to treatment, medications remain a primary intervention for addressing mental health problems due to convenience and, in many cases, lower expense. Approaches like psychotherapy and neurofeedback involve a time and financial commitment that continues to limit the number of people seeking and utilizing these techniques. However, the number of clinicians offering such services continues to grow as the demand is increasing.

META-ANALYTIC STUDIES OF NEUROFEEDBACK

Several reviews and meta-analyses have addressed the efficacy of neurofeedback. Sterman (2000) examined 18 peer-reviewed studies on neurofeedback for seizure control and found that the studies showed on average a greater than 50% reduction in both the frequency and severity of seizures in people largely determined to have intractable seizure conditions. Arns, de Ridder, Strehl, Breteler, and Coenen (2009) conducted a meta-analysis of 15 published studies of neurofeedback for ADHD and found "large effect sizes (ES) for neurofeedback on impulsivity and inattention and a medium ES for hyperactivity." A review of the literature regarding outcomes for neurofeedback for substance abuse disorders conducted by Sokhadze, Cannon, and Trudeau (2008) concluded that existing work demonstrated that neurofeedback, when used in combination with residential treatment, added significant improvement in outcome through reduced recidivism and met the established standards for probably efficacious (Level 3 evidence).

The American Academy of Child and Adolescent Psychiatry (AACAP) has established guidelines for recommending different levels of evidence-based treatments. The criteria for the level of "clinical guidelines" states the following:

> "clinical guidelines" [CG] are recommendations that are based on empirical evidence (such as open trials, case studies) and/or strong clinical consensus. Clinical guidelines apply approximately 75% of the time. These practices should always be considered by the clinician, but there are exceptions to their application. (Greenhill et al., 2002, p. 24S)

Using the AACAP criteria, after a review of the published studies of neurofeedback, Hirshberg, Chiu, and Frazier (2005), in a special edition of the *Journal of Child and Adolescent Psychiatric Clinics of North America* on emerging interventions, concluded that neurofeedback

> meets criteria for "clinical guidelines" for treatment of ADHD, seizure disorders, anxiety (e.g., obsessive-compulsive disorder, GAD, posttraumatic stress disorder, phobias), depression, reading disabilities, and addictive disorders. This finding suggests that EBF [EEG biofeedback] should always be considered as an intervention for these disorders by a clinician. (p. 12)

Despite the supportive evidence, virtually all the reviewers of neurofeedback studies have concluded that additional and better-designed studies using randomized controlled trials need to be conducted; several of those studies are currently underway.

In contrast to these positive reports, some recent studies have cast doubt on the earlier outcome findings. A meta-analysis of neurofeedback and ADHD, conducted by Cortese et al. (2016), concluded that "outcomes currently fail to support neurofeedback as an effective treatment for ADHD" (p. 444). Marzbani, Marateb, and Mansourian (2016) reviewed existing neurofeedback outcome studies and also concluded that "current research does not support conclusive results about its efficacy" (p. 143). Both reviews were criticized by those in the neurofeedback community for omitting studies that appeared to satisfy the inclusion criteria for analysis or review, for excluding evidence of physiological change, and for overgeneralization of null findings. Regardless of the merit of the criticisms, important issues regarding neurofeedback research methodology were raised.

There are a wide variety of approaches for conducting neurofeedback, including the aspect of the EEG targeted for training, schedule, number and length of training sessions, EEG frequencies trained, thresholds for delivering feedback, discrete or continuous delivery of feedback, and the number of channels of EEG utilized. Further, many published studies do not show objective functional or physiological changes following training, which would permit transfer beyond the training situation. It was even suggested by one group of researchers that most of the reported positive neurofeedback outcome findings can be explained by placebo responses that should be explored for their utility, as neurofeedback may be a particularly potent placebo (Thibault, Lifshitz, & Raz, 2017). Most critical reviewers, though, rather than advocating its abandonment, have concluded that better research methodologies should be employed in investigating neurofeedback.

PROMISING NEUROFEEDBACK RESEARCH OUTCOMES

Neurofeedback's greatest contribution may prove to be in areas where the existing treatments show significant limitations. Due to the prevalence of early abuse, neglect, and trauma, combined with the large number of men and women exposed to the traumas associated with military combat and the increasing exposure to violence and terrorism throughout the world, there are a great many people dealing with chronic and complex PTSD. Several neuroimaging studies have shown significant disruptions of neurobiological functioning from chronic traumatic exposure (for a recent review, see Teicher, Samson, Anderson, & Ohashi, 2016). Some recent publications show a positive response to neurofeedback training when combined with trauma-focused psychotherapy (Gapen et al., 2016; Nicholson et al., 2016; van der Kolk et al., 2016). The studies showed significant improvement through reduction of PTSD symptoms and improvement in affect regulation. The positive outcomes described in these recent studies on complex and chronic trauma have prompted further exploration and implementation of neurofeedback in settings specialized for trauma treatment, such as military and veterans' treatment facilities, and in residential treatment centers for adolescents who experienced trauma during their early development.

A second area garnering interest for additional benefit from the addition of neurofeedback to existing treatment approaches is autism spectrum disorder (ASD). According to statistics from the Centers for Disease Control and Prevention, the rate of diagnosis for ASD more than doubled between 2000 and 2012. Though some optimal outcomes have been reported where treated individuals no longer met criteria for an ASD diagnosis, the condition for most is generally considered to be lifelong, with relatively few people with moderate to severe symptoms ever attaining the ability to fully live independently. Studies involving the addition of neurofeedback to the treatment regimen for individuals with ASD have shown improvement in impulsivity, anxiety, neuropsychological functioning, and educational performance (e.g., Othmer, 2007; Thompson & Thompson, 2003; Thompson, Thompson, & Reid, 2010).

A third area of promise for the use of neurofeedback is schizophrenia, which is generally regarded as a severe and persistent mental disorder. In the Western nations, neuroleptic medications are typically considered to be the first-line choice of treatment for schizophrenia, but several studies over the years have shown some disturbing statistics regarding the efficacy of neuroleptic medications in the long-term outcomes for this population. As reported by Robert Whitaker (2005), a review of research beginning in the 1970s shows increased incidents of relapse in actively medicated patients with schizophrenia, compared with those receiving placebo, and negative side effects associated with the medications frequently led to noncompliance. Two outcome studies involving the use of neurofeedback for schizophrenia show very encouraging results. Bolea (2010) described the outcomes for 70 patients identified as "severe and chronic schizophrenic patients" showing changes in the EEG, along with improved test scores and functional ability with persistence at two-year follow-up. Additionally, Surmeli, Ertem, Eralp, and Kos (2012) reported the use of neurofeedback with 51 patients diagnosed with schizophrenia, showing improvement in both positive and negative symptoms of schizophrenia and improved cognitive functioning. Although there was no randomization and control group comparisons in either of these studies, the outcomes are sufficiently promising to warrant further investigation.

Expanding Approaches to Neurofeedback

In addition to the original neurofeedback protocols of alpha, beta/SMR, and alpha/theta training pioneered by Kamiya, Sterman, and Peniston, a variety of additional protocols for training the EEG have emerged over the past 2 decades. Current neurofeedback applications exist for training aspects of the EEG beyond frequency and amplitude—these include slow cortical potentials, evoked potentials, and variability of the EEG. Additionally, specific areas of the brain can be targeted by using protocols aimed at particular brain regions through source localization procedures and EEG measures obtained from a quantitative assessment of the EEG (where comparisons are made to a normative database). Many of the newer approaches involve the use of multiple channels of EEG data and higher order mathematics. There is less empirical support for these more recent approaches in terms of the number of studies conducted, and, currently, they have not been shown to be superior to the earlier applications. However, as we continue to learn more about the brain and its operations, it is likely that additional, more specialized, techniques will continue to be developed.

Even though there are many studies showing beneficial outcomes from the application of neurofeedback training for a variety of disorders, there is no consensus regarding the specific mechanisms for achieving beneficial changes. In the seizure studies reviewed by Sterman (2000), he concluded that although many of the subjects who showed a good clinical outcome had contingency-related EEG changes and the expected shift toward normalization, others who improved their seizure control did not show the expected changes. Still other studies showed a shift toward normalization of the EEG without a change in seizure frequency or intensity. However, still other studies for different conditions have shown that expected EEG changes positively correlated with symptom improvement (e.g., Gevensleben et al., 2009; Paquette, Beauregard, & Beaulieu-Prévost, 2009). To further complicate matters, more studies using functional imaging measures other than the EEG have shown brain changes in response to neurofeedback in regions not closely associated with the site of training (e.g., Lévesque, Beauregard, & Mensour, 2006; Nicholson et al., 2016). Given the recognized complexity of the brain's organization and operation, it should not be too surprising that many of the mechanisms for change have yet to be fully identified.

Regarding biofeedback procedures, though, the general rationale is that the feeding back of information regarding physiological functioning permits one to learn volitional control over the response. With neurofeedback, the information being fed back relates to the activity of the EEG, and the activity of the EEG is correlated with the arousal level of the brain. The frequency ranges of brain wave activity from 0 to 30 Hz form a continuum reflecting the spectrum of arousal. The slower speeds are associated with lower states of arousal (e.g., deep sleep), while the higher frequencies reflect progressively greater states of arousal reaching excitement or anxiety (in the faster beta ranges). It is this correlation between brain wave activity and arousal that has been most broadly employed in neurofeedback applications and accumulated the greatest amount of empirical support.

THE AROUSAL MODEL OF NEUROFEEDBACK

The Yerkes-Dodson Law, showing the familiar inverted U relationship between arousal and performance, was originally applied to learning via an intensity of punishment paradigm (see Yerkes & Dodson, 1908). The popular understanding of the original research indicates that performance will increase as arousal increases to a point, and then will begin to decrease as arousal continues to climb. This understanding led to the idea of a single optimal arousal level in the middle of the inverted U. Subsequent researchers, however, have developed a more nuanced view of arousal by indicating that optimal arousal is associated with the complexity level of the task. Simpler tasks require a higher level of arousal to be performed efficiently, while more complex tasks require a lower level. These findings may sound somewhat paradoxical initially, but we generally know that a boring task will require us to stay more aroused to complete it quickly and efficiently and, thus, we may tend to have some extra caffeine or resort to playing music with a more upbeat tempo. However, when engaged in a complex task, such as calculations or reading more challenging material, in order to reduce our arousal, we will tend to reduce external stimulation by seeking a quiet space and might choose no music or slower tempo instrumental sounds for our background. The conclusion is that there is no single level of arousal that is optimal for every task. Optimal functioning is associated with flexible arousal and the ability to adjust arousal according to task demands.

Many people struggle with problems associated with being "stuck" at one end or the other of the arousal continuum. Instead of having flexible arousal, they spend much of their day in a similar arousal condition. Excesses of the faster beta frequencies or a deficit of resting activity, such as alpha, as depicted in the EEG, represents overarousal. Problems typical of overarousal marked by elevated fast beta or deficient slower frequency activity, such as low alpha, include anxiety, sleep onset problems, anger and agitation, restlessness and hyperactivity, and pain associated with excess muscle tension. Underarousal is reflected in the brain by excesses of slower frequency activity, such as alpha or theta, especially when an individual is attempting to engage in a task. Issues associated with underarousal include depression, attention and concentration problems, early morning awakenings, low motivation, and excessive daydreaming. Difficulties achieving and maintaining appropriate levels of arousal are ubiquitous among clinical populations but can also be seen in the general public. Emotion regulation is closely associated with arousal regulation and is why many approaches to dealing with dysregulated emotions involve calming the physiology with relaxation techniques, or activation strategies (e.g., exercise, increased interpersonal engagement) are common in the treatment of anxiety or depression. Neurofeedback has primarily been a tool throughout its utilization as a means for training improved arousal regulation. Many of the positive results reported for neurofeedback may well rely on improved self-regulation.

EXECUTIVE FUNCTIONS AND EEG PROFILES

Another important cognitive function that has proven amenable to neurofeedback training is executive attention. Many, if not most, clinical problems have a negative impact on the functioning of executive attention. Certainly, it is an important feature of ADHD, but it is also impacted with depression and anxiety disorders. Humans possess two attention systems in the brain. The evolutionarily older attention system is closely associated with the reticular activating system, originating in the brain stem with nerve fibers primarily projecting to the posterior areas of the brain importantly involved in sensory input and integration. This older system's purpose is to aid in our basic survival by facilitating the orienting reflex responses, quickly recognizing danger, feeding, mating opportunities, and the identification and evaluation of novel stimuli. It appears to be largely instinctively programmed and develops early in life. The executive attention system, on the other hand, is largely mediated by the more recently evolved frontal lobes and helps form the basis of executive functioning. It involves the ability to choose our focus, ignore distractions, and allocate limited processing resources. Modern life places high demands on our attentional capacity, and executive attention is necessary for adaptive and efficient functioning in human societies. From the many outcome studies on the use of neurofeedback for ADHD, neurofeedback training can have a positive effect on executive attention.

Role of Neurofeedback in Clinical Practice

Since arousal dysregulation and attention problems are very common in a variety of clinical conditions, there appears to be a significant role for neurofeedback training in mental health practice given its history of good outcomes for these issues. However, many issues ultimately limit its adoption for use. In addition to still having to overcome lingering skepticism regarding a single technique having such broad applicability, another major factor has been the lack of reimbursement for neurofeedback services from third-party payors. Most insurance companies continue to consider neurofeedback an "experimental" approach or deem it "not medically necessary" given the availability of more recognized therapies (i.e., mainly medications and conventional psychotherapies). This lack of coverage results in many clients having to pay for the services out-of-pocket when their insurance will cover medication and/or psychotherapy services, but not neurofeedback. Another factor is that the training sessions in a practitioner's office are often recommended to occur more than once weekly, requiring the scheduling of multiple appointments. Further, the number of qualified providers of neurofeedback services is still relatively low, often making it difficult to find a conveniently located and experienced clinician. The costs of obtaining training in neurofeedback and purchasing the necessary equipment, as well as the rather steep learning curve for competent operation of the equipment, can pose a challenge to clinicians. The cost of equipment can quickly reach several thousand dollars. These associated costs can be a major deterrent for many clinicians, particularly early-career ones who may be confronting large college-loan debts.

RECENT TECHNOLOGICAL ADVANCES IN NEUROFEEDBACK EQUIPMENT

Fortunately, some recent technological advances provide solutions for many of the major barriers facing clinicians who would like to employ neurofeedback procedures in their practices. Several personal-use neurofeedback training devices have been produced that are affordable and require minimal training to use. As modern societies move to ever greater incorporation of technology in daily life, it seems inevitable that we will be including more of it to help foster improved health and greater well-being. Mass production of EEG measurement and training hardware has resulted in the availability of neurofeedback devices that cost under $300 (with some as low as $100) and are extremely easy for an individual to learn to use. Many established neurofeedback providers have been reluctant to utilize these devices, but others are starting to employ them as a means of providing EEG biofeedback or extending training beyond their offices.

The majority of personal neurofeedback training devices currently available are aimed at relaxation and/or improving focus. Although there are many specialized approaches or applications used in neurofeedback not currently available in personal-use devices, the ones now on the market employ aspects of neurofeedback protocols that have been used in research studies or clinical practice primarily oriented to helping people learn to regulate their arousal and strengthen their focus. The personal-use devices and programs generally provide a limited and fixed number of placement sites for sensing the EEG. The system typically used for EEG recording in both neurology and neurofeedback settings is called the International 10/20 system and involves a series of sites covering 19 standardized locations on the scalp, overlaying each of the major lobes and midline areas of the brain. With the typical approaches to neurofeedback, sites are individually selected on the basis of the therapist's assessment and prepared by using alcohol, a mild abrasive scrub, and the application of conductive gel on the sensors. Care is taken to move the hair, when necessary, to achieve good contact with the scalp in order to facilitate the recording of an electrical signal so small it is measured in microvolts. However, with most of the personal-use devices, placements primarily involve the locations on the forehead to avoid signal connection complications associated with hair and to reduce the need for extensive site preparation. Some equipment manufacturers have developed innovative sensor technologies that allow scalp placements beyond the forehead and still not requiring abrasion or gel. Sensor technology is advancing rapidly, and the current limitations for sensor placement will likely be obsolete in the very near future. However, for the purposes of general arousal and focus training, specific site locations become less critical as global changes for a particular frequency are seen when it is reinforced or inhibited at any particular location. Also, as mentioned previously, studies examining the changes in brain functioning in response to neurofeedback training show alterations in major governing networks that may be anatomically removed from the specific site of training.

There is growing recognition that our old system of diagnosing and treating psychological problems by employing medical model approaches based on specific treatments for specific diagnoses has not served mental health well. The NIMH has adopted a new Research Domain Criteria Initiative to help guide research and treatment initiatives in mental health (with descriptions of the domains posted on the NIMH website). The domains and constructs are transdiagnostic and not unique to a particular disorder. Research proposals submitted to NIMH are expected to reflect a focus on the identified domains and constructs reflecting the current perspectives on emotion, cognition, motivation, and social behavior. In this new model, five domains are currently identified as important for adaptive functioning. The domains include several aspects that have been shown to be responsive to neurofeedback training, including arousal/regulatory systems, anxiety, attention, and social communication.

Neuroscience evidence appears to support the new approach of NIMH for shifting the focus from discrete diagnoses to functional domains. A recently published meta-analysis of MRI studies showed significant overlap in the neuroanatomical abnormalities across a number of different diagnoses, such as major depressive disorder, bipolar disorder, social anxiety disorder, and obsessive–compulsive disorder (see Jenkins et al., 2016). The problem identified in the 37 studies reviewed reflects a common deficit of functional connectivity between the executive control centers of the brain (which helps plan and maintain task focus) and the so-called default mode network (the system responsible for our passive, self-focused thoughts). Since these networks work in alternation—activation of one suppresses the other—the findings indicate the common functional difficulty is excessive engagement of the default mode network. Activation of the central executive network, as happens when volitional attention is engaged, leads to suppression of the default mode network. Recent studies have shown the ability of neurofeedback to impact these critical networks (Lanius, Frewen, Tursich, Jetly, & McKinnon, 2015).

COMMON UNDERLYING NEUROPHYSIOLOGICAL FEATURES

The idea of common neurophysiological features underlying a variety of psychological problems facilitates an understanding of the broad clinical application of mindfulness meditation seen in the past several years. A review of the empirical literature on the effects of mindfulness on psychological health conducted at Duke University (Keng, Smoski, & Robins, 2011) concluded that the practice of "mindfulness brings about various positive psychological effects, including increased subjective well-being, reduced psychological symptoms and emotional reactivity, and improved behavioral regulation" (p. 1041). These are the outcomes most therapists generally seek to achieve in their practice of psychotherapy with clients, and meditation facilitates their development. However, despite the greater acceptance of meditation practices in the West since the work of Jon Kabat-Zinn, Daniel Goleman, and many others (Kabat-Zinn, 2013; Mindful Staff, 2011), they remain somewhat foreign to the Western culture and lifestyles, and many practitioners admit that it is difficult to get their clients to practice meditation on a regular schedule. Here is where inexpensive, convenient, and easy-to-use neurofeedback technology and training can be of particular benefit.

The low cost and low burden of expertise necessary for adoption of neurofeedback training in mental health practices provides an opportunity for professionals to begin to easily and confidently include applied neuroscience approaches in their work with clients. Most clients now are exposed to brain science information through popular media, creating a curiosity and interest that can be tapped by clinicians to help their clients. Clients are also hearing about the brain's plasticity and how this may be applied to develop new capacities or reduce the impact of stress and aging. Also, a large and growing number of people have heard about or even tried to engage in meditation practices and are aware of their potential benefits, but have failed to implement them in their daily routine or have tried but given up for a variety of reasons. All of this creates an unprecedented opportunity for clinicians to introduce applied neuroscience technology with their clients, and neurofeedback has the longest history of clinical application and the most empirical support for its use.

Getting Started—Incorporating Neurofeedback in Clinical Practice

The interested clinician should begin by exploring the personal-use neurofeedback equipment that is currently available. There are more devices and training programs being introduced on a regular basis. Some of the current devices include the Neurosky, BrainLink, Muse, Versus, and iFocusBand. These products come with instructions for their training programs, which generally target improving executive focus, arousal reduction, or both. Some connect with mobile devices, such as tablets and smart-phones, while others can connect with computers. The focus of the clinician's practice may influence the choice of a specific device as some, such as Versus or iFocusBand, are primarily aimed at sports and peak performance applications, while the Muse is marketed as an aid for stress reduction and meditation, and the Neurosky and Brain-Link have applications for improving and sustaining focus combined with programs for meditation and arousal reduction.

Once a decision is reached regarding the most advantageous available product for the patient, it will be important for the clinician to become thoroughly familiar with the device and the accompanying training protocols. Learning how to wear the device and attain a good connection will better position clinicians to instruct clients in how to get started with their own training. To describe the training experience to clients, the clinician will also need to be familiar with the training experience. Some of the programs use visual displays, some auditory, and some a combination. Some devices even have choices regarding modalities for feedback. Though most of the personal neurofeedback devices are intended for direct sale to consumers, clients will typically feel more confident if they are introduced to the device and its utilization by the therapist recommending its use.

FOCUS OF NEUROFEEDBACK

Further, it will be important for the clinician to be familiar with arousal techniques and their importance for self-regulation. Recognizing which problems are associated with over- and underarousal can help clinicians choose which applications to use for a client's training. Arousal reduction techniques are more often associated with relaxation, stress reduction, or meditation applications. Problems, which are often reduced by arousal reduction approaches, include anxiety, fear, anger, restlessness, impatience, tension, and difficulties falling asleep. Problems associated with under-arousal include depressed mood, inattentiveness, poor concentration, fogginess, lack of motivation, and sleep maintenance issues. These issues are often helped by training to increase focus, which tends to increase arousal. The clinician's ability to relate the client's complaints to problems with the regulation of arousal will help motivate the client to be more consistent with their utilization of the training technology.

Psychoeducation is also important when incorporating neurofeedback. It is important for the clinician to convey some of the basics regarding neuroplasticity, which is another concept that can be useful for clients. The increased availability of information regarding the brain's influence on our perceptions, emotions, thoughts, and behavior has not gone unnoticed. The most revolutionary findings from this body of knowledge, though, are those related to neuroplasticity. The fact that the structure and organization of the brain can be altered by experience provides a very realistically hopeful message for most clients. Many members of the general public may have understood that their life struggles may be related to problems in their brain, but fewer will have learned that at least some of these issues can be altered. There are many sources available for learning about neuroplasticity, but two particularly useful sources are Norman Doidge's (2010) *The Brain That Changes Itself: Stories of Personal Triumph From the Frontiers of Brain Science* and Jeffrey Schwartz and Sharon Begley's (2002) *The Mind and the Brain: Neuroplasticity and the Power of Mental Force.* Some books among those that are available do make claims that cannot be substantiated at this time. It is clear that the limits of neuroplasticity are not yet known, but it is important to relay information to clients that can be empirically demonstrated, in order to preserve credibility. Unrealistic expectations by either the clinician or the client are likely to lead to disappointment.

INDIVIDUALIZING TREATMENT

There is no established evidence for the frequency or the length of individual training sessions. However, the personal neurofeedback training devices allow for many more options than appointments with a provider would likely accommodate. One thing that is known regarding neuroplasticity, though, is that frequency, intensity, and duration are important for the process. There are likely individual differences in optimal levels with regard to the frequency of practice sessions, the difficulty of the challenge level, and the length of the training sessions. Most clinicians have to make similar decisions when making assignments for work outside of the office sessions when they are working with clients. The advantage when using neurofeedback is that most of the devices provide feedback on the frequency, duration, and outcome from the sessions to help clinicians with their decision making (see, e.g., Magnavita, 2016).

In clinical practice, most practitioners have found that daily practice of arousal reduction techniques are common, whether meditation, progressive muscle relaxation, diaphragmatic breathing, or other approaches are used. Having access to technology that can be used at home can effectively speed the response to neurofeedback by extending training beyond the therapist's office. For all general purposes, the more an overaroused person can practice reducing arousal, the quicker they are likely to realize relief. With focus training, however, more energy is involved in the training, and the length of training sessions can be graduated, beginning with short and frequent sessions progressing to longer, but less frequent, ones. Research on focus training in neurofeedback typically has involved two to three sessions per week. Again, the use of personal training equipment provides opportunities to use home practice between office visits, but the length of these sessions will need to be tailored to the age and stamina of the individual client.

EXPANDING EXPERTISE AND RANGE OF APPLICATION THROUGH FURTHER TRAINING

Many practitioners who begin to employ personal neurofeedback technology with their clients may decide to expand their neurofeedback capabilities and pursue additional training and equipment that allow for the use of more targeted placement of EEG sensors and protocols aimed at changing other features of the EEG beyond frequency amplitude. As we learn more about the brain and how it functions, more options for training by means of EEG biofeedback will be added. Approved training courses and certification in neurofeedback is available through the Biofeedback Certification International Alliance (http://www.bcia.org). With progressively more clinics and facilities beginning to offer neurofeedback services, options and exposure will likely continue expanding for the foreseeable future. However, the range and quality of the equipment available permits almost all clinicians to begin using this very promising approach in their practices immediately.

Summary

We are entering an era in which technology will be increasingly incorporated into mental health treatment, just as it has become inexorably interwoven in daily life. Advances in brain imaging technology have produced insights into the central nervous system's role in a variety of mental and behavioral disorders. These discoveries have helped to launch a variety of new interventions for use in mental health practice, including EEG biofeedback, transcranial direct current stimulation, cranial electrotherapy stimulation, vagal nerve stimulation, low-level laser therapy, and others. Of the technology-based approaches, EEG biofeedback, or neurofeedback as it is commonly known, has been employed by the largest number of clinicians for the longest time and has the most empirical support for its efficacy, despite continued controversy regarding its outcomes. Using brain–computer interface technology, neurofeedback provides moment-by-moment information to the trainee about EEG functions, which in turn helps patients learn to regulate these functions. Neurofeedback has been used to promote relaxation and stress reduction and in the treatment of epilepsy, ADHD, substance abuse, anxiety, PTSD and many other conditions. There are a large number of studies showing neurofeedback's efficacy. There are promising findings of neurofeedback's utility in some conditions considered difficult to treat, such as chronic PTSD, schizophrenia, and ASD. Many of these studies, though, have methodological weaknesses as they have been conducted primarily in clinical settings; but research using randomized clinical trials is currently underway at several universities and research facilities throughout the world.

Despite the amount of promising evidence for its efficacy, neurofeedback has not been as widely incorporated into typical mental health practices as might be expected. At least one of the limits to its broader utilization is financial. At present, few payors cover the cost of the clients' sessions, requiring them to pay out-of-pocket for neurofeedback sessions. There is also the cost of equipment and training in its use, which can easily reach several thousand dollars. Recently, though, better quality personal-use neurofeedback technology has become available at a much lower cost. These devices are easy to learn to use and can be incorporated into treatment without the need to schedule separate training sessions. Although the personal-use devices have a limited range of placement and training targets, they are generally aimed at reducing arousal, facilitating meditation-type states, or improving focus. Since these are often goals in typical mental health treatment plans, the personal-use devices can readily be used in the treatment of a broad array of presenting problems or for performance enhancement. More specific neurofeedback applications may be necessary for more severe or complicated problems, but personal-use devices may still help clients extend their self-regulation training beyond the office setting. Some of the personal-use applications even permit the clinician to monitor the client's frequency and duration of practice, along with their performance, when practicing at home. It appears very likely that the improved quality, relatively low cost, and ease of use of the new equipment will expand the incorporation of neurofeedback in mental health practices and eventually lead more clinicians to pursue additional training for its use in more specialized applications.

References

Arns, M., de Ridder, S., Strehl, U., Breteler, M., & Coenen, A. (2009). Efficacy of neuro-feedback treatment in ADHD: The effects on inattention, impulsivity and hyperactivity: A meta-analysis. *Clinical EEG and Neuroscience, 40*, 180–189. http://dx.doi.org/10.1177/155005940904000311

Behavior: Brain wave of the future. (1971, July 19). *Time*. Retrieved from http://content.time.com/time/subscriber/article/0,33009,905369,00.html

Ben-Ari, Y., Krnjevic, K., & Reinhardt, W. (1979). Hippocampal seizures and failure of inhibition. *Canadian Journal of Physiology and Pharmacology, 57*, 1462–1466. http://dx.doi.org/10.1139/y79-218

Bolea, A. S. (2010). Neurofeedback treatment of chronic inpatient schizophrenia. *Journal of Neurotherapy, 14*, 47–54. http://dx.doi.org/10.1080/10874200903543971

Brenninkmeijer, J. (2010). Taking care of one's brain: How manipulating the brain changes people's selves. *History of the Human Sciences, 23*, 107–126. http://dx.doi.org/10.1177/0952695109352824

Cortese, S., Ferrin, M., Brandeis, D., Holtmann, M., Aggensteiner, P., Daley, D., . . . European ADHD Guidelines Group. (2016). Neurofeedback for attention-deficit/

hyperactivity disorder: Meta-analysis of clinical and neuropsychological outcomes from randomized controlled trials. *Journal of the American Academy of Child & Adolescent Psychiatry*, 55, 444–455. http://dx.doi.org/10.1016/j.jaac.2016.03.007

Diamond, M., & Hopson, J. (1999). *Magic trees of the mind: How to nurture your child's intelligence, creativity, and healthy emotions*. New York, NY: Penguin Putnam.

Doidge, N. (2010). *The brain that changes itself: Stories of personal triumph from the frontiers of brain science*. Carlton North, Victoria, Australia: Scribe.

Gapen, M., van der Kolk, B. A., Hamlin, E., Hirshberg, L., Suvak, M., & Spinazzola, J. (2016). A pilot study of neurofeedback for chronic PTSD. *Applied Psychophysiology and Biofeedback*, 41, 251–261. http://dx.doi.org/10.1007/s10484-015-9326-5

Gevensleben, H., Holl, B., Albrecht, B., Schlamp, D., Kratz, O., Studer, P., . . . Heinrich, H. (2009). Distinct EEG effects related to neurofeedback training in children with ADHD: A randomized controlled trial. *International Journal of Psychophysiology*, 74, 149–157. http://dx.doi.org/10.1016/j.ijpsycho.2009.08.005

Greenhill, L. L., Pliszka, S., Dulcan, M. K., & the Work Group on Quality Issues. (2002). Practice parameter for the use of stimulant medication in the treatment of children, adolescents, and adults. *Journal of the American Academy of Child and Adolescent Psychiatry, 41*(2 Suppl.), 26S–49S.

Hammond, D. C. (2011). What is neurofeedback: An update. *Journal of Neurotherapy*, 15, 305–336. http://dx.doi.org/10.1080/10874208.2011.623090

Hebb, D. O. (1949). *The organization of behavior*. New York, NY: Wiley and Sons.

Hirshberg, L. M., Chiu, S., & Frazier, J. A. (2005). Emerging brain-based interventions for children and adolescents: Overview and clinical perspective. *Child and Adolescent Psychiatric Clinics of North America*, 14, 1–19. http://dx.doi.org/10.1016/j.chc.2004.07.011

Insel, T. R. (2009). Disruptive insights in psychiatry: Transforming a clinical discipline. *Journal of Clinical Investigation*, 119, 700–705. http://dx.doi.org/10.1172/JCI38832

Jenkins, L. M., Barba, A., Campbell, M., Lamar, M., Shankman, S. A., Leow, A. D., . . . Langenecker, S. A. (2016). Shared white matter alterations across emotional disorders: A voxel-based meta-analysis of fractional anisotropy. *NeuroImage: Clinical*, 12, 1022–1034. http://dx.doi.org/10.1016/j.nicl.2016.09.001

Kabat-Zinn, J. (2013). *Full catastrophe living* (Rev. ed.). New York, NY: Bantam Books.

Kamiya, J. (1968). Conscious control of brain waves. *Psychology Today*, 1, 56–60.

Kandel, E. R. (2006). *In search of memory: The emergence of a new science of mind*. New York, NY: W. W. Norton.

Keng, S.-L., Smoski, M. J., & Robins, C. J. (2011). Effects of mindfulness on psychological health: A review of empirical studies. *Clinical Psychology Review, 31*, 1041–1056. http://dx.doi.org/10.1016/j.cpr.2011.04.006

Lanius, R. A., Frewen, P. A., Tursich, M., Jetly, R., & McKinnon, M. C. (2015). Restoring large-scale brain networks in PTSD and related disorders: A proposal for neuroscientifically-informed treatment interventions. *European Journal of Psychotraumatology*, 6, 27313. http://dx.doi.org/10.3402/ejpt.v6.27313

Lévesque, J., Beauregard, M., & Mensour, B. (2006). Effect of neurofeedback training on the neural substrates of selective attention in children with attention-deficit/hyperactivity disorder: A functional magnetic resonance imaging study. *Neuroscience Letters, 394*(3), 216–221. http://dx.doi.org/10.1016/j.neulet.2005.10.100

Lubar, J. O., & Lubar, J. F. (1984). Electroencephalographic biofeedback of SMR and beta for treatment of attention deficit disorders in a clinical setting. *Biofeedback and Self-Regulation, 9,* 1–23. http://dx.doi.org/10.1007/BF00998842

Magnavita, J. J. (2016). *Clinical decision making in mental health practice.* Washington, DC: American Psychological Association. http://dx.doi.org/10.1037/14711-000

Marzbani, H., Marateb, H. R., & Mansourian, M. (2016). Neurofeedback: A comprehensive review on system design, methodology, and clinical applications. *Basic and Clinical Neuroscience, 7,* 143–158. http://dx.doi.org/10.15412/J.BCN.03070208

Merzenich, M. (2013). *Soft-wired: How the new science of brain plasticity can change your life.* San Francisco, CA: Parnassus.

Miller, N. E., & DiCara, L. (1967). Instrumental learning of heart rate changes in curarized rats: Shaping, and specificity to discriminative stimulus. *Journal of Comparative and Physiological Psychology, 63,* 12–19. http://dx.doi.org/10.1037/h0024160

Mindful Staff. (2011, April 20). Why we find it hard to meditate. *Mindful,* 51–52.

Mind over body, mind over mind. (1971, September 12). *The New York Times,* p. SM34. Retrieved from http://www.nytimes.com/1971/09/12/archives/mind-over-body-mind-over-mind-such-is-the-twin-promise-of.html

Nicholson, A. A., Ros, T., Frewen, P. A., Densmore, M., Théberge, J., Kluetsch, R. C., . . . Lanius, R. A. (2016). Alpha oscillation neurofeedback modulates amygdala complex connectivity and arousal in posttraumatic stress disorder. *NeuroImage: Clinical, 12,* 506–516. http://dx.doi.org/10.1016/j.nicl.2016.07.006

Nowlis, D. P., & Kamiya, J. (1970). The control of electroencephalographic alpha rhythms through auditory feedback and the associated mental activity. *Psychophysiology, 6,* 476–484. http://dx.doi.org/10.1111/j.1469-8986.1970.tb01756.x

Orndorff-Plunkett, F., Singh, F., Aragón, O. R., & Pineda, J. A. (2017). Assessing the effectiveness of neurofeedback training in the context of clinical and social neuroscience. *Brain Sciences, 7,* E95. http://dx.doi.org/10.3390/brainsci7080095

Othmer, S. (2007, February). *Progress in neurofeedback for the autism spectrum.* Paper presented at the 38th meeting of the Association for Applied Psychophysiology & Biofeedback, Monterey, CA.

Paquette, V., Beauregard, M., & Beaulieu-Prévost, D. (2009). Effect of a psychoneurotherapy on brain electromagnetic tomography in individuals with major depressive disorder. *Psychiatry Research: Neuroimaging, 174,* 231–239. http://dx.doi.org/10.1016/j.pscychresns.2009.06.002

Peniston, E. G., & Kulkosky, P. J. (1989). Alpha-theta brainwave training and beta-endorphin levels in alcoholics. *Alcoholism: Clinical and Experimental Research, 13,* 271–279. http://dx.doi.org/10.1111/j.1530-0277.1989.tb00325.x

Peniston, E. G., & Kulkosky, P. J. (1991). Alpha-theta brainwave neuro-feedback for Vietnam veterans with combat-related post-traumatic stress disorder. *Medical Psychotherapy, 4,* 47–60.

Robbins, J. (2008). *A symphony in the brain* (2nd ed.). New York, NY: Grove Press.

Rose, N., & Abi-Rached, J. M., (2013). *Neuro: The new brain sciences and the management of the mind.* Princeton, NJ: Princeton University Press.

Schirmann, F. (2014). "The wondrous eyes of a new technology"—A history of the early electroencephalography (EEG) of psychopathy, delinquency, and immorality. *Frontiers in Human Neuroscience, 8,* 232. http://dx.doi.org/10.3389/fnhum.2014.00232

Schwartz, J. M., & Begley, S. (2002). *The mind and the brain: Neuroplasticity and the power of mental force.* New York, NY: HarperCollins.

Sherlin, L., Arns, M., Lubar, J. F., & Sokhadze, E. (2010). A position paper on neuro-feedback for treatment of ADHD. *Journal of Neurotherapy, 14,* 66–78. http://dx.doi.org/10.1080/10874201003773880

Sokhadze, T. M., Cannon, R. L., & Trudeau, D. L. (2008). EEG biofeedback as a treatment for substance use disorders: Review, rating of efficacy, and recommendations for further research. *Applied Psychophysiology and Biofeedback, 33,* 1–28. http://dx.doi.org/10.1007/s10484-007-9047-5

Sterman, M. B. (2000). Basic concepts and clinical findings in the treatment of seizure disorders with EEG operant conditioning. *Clinical Electroencephalography, 31,* 45–55. http://dx.doi.org/10.1177/155005940003100111

Sterman, M. B., Macdonald, L. R., & Stone, R. K. (1974). Biofeedback training of the sensorimotor electroencephalogram rhythm in man: Effects on epilepsy. *Epilepsia, 15,* 395–416. http://dx.doi.org/10.1111/j.1528-1157.1974.tb04016.x

Surmeli, T., Ertem, A., Eralp, E., & Kos, I. H. (2012). Schizophrenia and the efficacy of qEEG-guided neurofeedback treatment. *Clinical EEG and Neuroscience, 43,* 133–144.

Teicher, M. H., Samson, J. A., Anderson, C. M., & Ohashi, K. (2016). The effects of childhood maltreatment on brain structure, function and connectivity. *Nature Reviews Neuroscience, 17,* 652–666. http://dx.doi.org/10.1038/nrn.2016.111

Thibault, R. T., Lifshitz, M., & Raz, A. (2017). Neurofeedback or neuroplacebo? *Brain: A Journal of Neurology, 140,* 862–864. http://dx.doi.org/10.1093/brain/awx033

Thompson, L., Thompson, M., & Reid, A. (2010). Neurofeedback outcomes in clients with Asperger's syndrome. *Applied Psychophysiology and Biofeedback, 35,* 63–81. http://dx.doi.org/10.1007/s10484-009-9120-3

Thompson, M., & Thompson, L. (2003). *The neurofeedback book: An introduction to basic concepts in applied psychophysiology.* Wheat Ridge, CO: Association of Applied Psychophysiology and Biofeedback.

Trudeau, D. L. (2000). The treatment of addictive disorders by brain wave biofeedback: A review and suggestions for future research. *Clinical EEG (Electroencephalography), 31,* 13–26. http://dx.doi.org/10.1177/155005940003100107

Ulrich, G. (2002). *Psychiatric electroencephalography* (Rev. ed.). New York, NY: Gustav Fischer Verlag.

van der Kolk, B. A., Hodgdon, H., Gapen, M. Musicaro, R., Suvak, M. K., Hamlin, E., & Spinazzola, J. (2016). A randomized controlled study of neurofeedback for chronic PTSD. *PLoS ONE, 11:* e0166752. http://dx.doi.org/10.1371/journal.pone.0166752

Whitaker, R. (2005). Anatomy of an epidemic: Psychiatric drugs and the astonishing rise of mental illness in America. *Ethical Human Psychology and Psychiatry, 7,* 23–35.

Wyrwicka, W., & Sterman, M. B. (1968). Instrumental conditioning of sensorimotor cortex EEG spindles in the waking cat. *Physiology & Behavior, 3,* 703–707. http://dx.doi.org/10.1016/0031-9384(68)90139-X

Yerkes, R. M., & Dodson, J. D. (1908). The relation of strength of stimulus to rapidity of habit-formation. *Journal of Comparative Neurology and Psychology, 18,* 459–482. http://dx.doi.org/10.1002/cne.920180503

Paul M. Lehrer and Richard Gevirtz

Heart Rate Variability Biofeedback
Current and Potential Applications

7

Heart rate variability (HRV) biofeedback offers clinicians an excellent and cost-effective technology for a number of mental health and behavioral conditions. Although it requires some training to administer, the technology has become very friendly and, for most psychologists, certification-level training can be obtained with the equivalent of one or two 3-credit university courses, plus some supervision (for details of training requirements for becoming a certified biofeedback therapist, see http://www.bcia.org). Technical equipment costs range from handheld devices costing a few hundred dollars through research-grade multichannel devices costing several thousand. Some smartphone apps also are available for a few dollars, although the requirements to hold warm hands very steady in a spot where pulse amplitude is high (often above heart level) sometimes cause difficulty in pulse detection, in our experience.

Google, PsycINFO, or Medline searches on HRV yield a large number of articles on the topic. They can be classified in two clusters: (a) papers showing the relationship between HRV and autonomic balance, and (b) those showing the relationship between HRV and adaptability (Berntson et al., 1997; Di Simplicio et al., 2012; Lehrer & Eddie, 2013). Both clusters are important for understanding how the body works and is regulated. Because HRV biofeedback is used primarily as a method for improving adaptability, we emphasize this interpretation here.

http://dx.doi.org/10.1037/0000085-008
Using Technology in Mental Health Practice, J. J. Magnavita (Editor)

A number of HRV indicators are related to health, including various measures of respiratory sinus arrhythmia (RSA), general HRV, baroreflex strength, and complexity of HRV. Is it possible, then, that an intervention that specifically targets these aspects of HRV might also help prevent and modulate various disease processes and improve human performance? This is the rationale for incorporating HRV biofeedback technology into the clinic.

Heart Rate Variability, Environmental Challenges, and Self-Regulation

HRV reflects the person's ability to respond to environmental demands and to self-regulate. During exercise, the heart needs to speed up in order to provide nourishment to the muscles. When the heart functions poorly, this response is attenuated, and, as a result, the person moves more slowly, gets out of breath, and has generally reduced exercise capacity (Cubbon et al., 2016; Vallebona, Gigli, Orlandi, & Reggiardo, 2005). Increased heart rate occurs even when the person mobilizes for mental functioning, such as in mental arithmetic tasks (Carr, Lehrer, Hochron, & Jackson, 1996). Many people mistakenly think that when faced with a challenge, a larger increase in heart rate reflects greater anxiety and dysfunction. The opposite is more often the case. In one study (Lehrer & Leiblum, 1981), we showed a film presenting short vignettes requiring an assertive response to some mild abuse or inconsiderate behavior to two groups of women. The women were instructed to respond appropriately to the characters in the vignette. One group of participants comprised a group of people known to the investigators to be assertive and socially competent. The other was a group of patients from a large mental health center, referred by their therapists as having difficulties asserting themselves. We found that the assertive women responded more assertively and also showed much greater increases in heart rate and respiration rate in response to the vignettes than did the unassertive women. In another study, we gave a set of cognitive tests to a group of patients with closed head injury and cognitive difficulties, as well as to a group of age-matched healthy people (Lehrer & Leiblum, 1981). Again, the healthy people showed much greater increases in heart and respiration rates. In both of these studies, we interpreted the attenuated response to indicate withdrawal from the situation and lack of engagement in coping behavior.

HRV also reflects the ability of the body to self-regulate. There are a number of rhythms in resting heart rate, each of which reflects a particular regulatory mechanism. When these rhythms are attenuated or absent, the person's ability to adapt is diminished. One such rhythm is RSA (i.e., the changes in heart rate associated with breathing). Usually, RSA occurs with a rhythm of between 0.15 and 0.4 Hz (9–24 cycles/minute), known as the high frequency (HF) rhythm in HRV (Berntson et al., 1997). Inhalation produces an increase in heart rate, exhalation produces a decrease. Thus, when the lung is richest in oxygen, the most blood is available to exchange oxygen and carbon dioxide (Eckberg, 2003; Hayano, Yasuma, Okada, Mukai, & Fujinami, 1996; Porges, 1991; Yasuma & Hayano, 2004). Additionally, because RSA is controlled by the parasympathetic system through the vagus nerve, the amplitude of this rhythm is proportional to the amount of parasympathetic control over the heart (Berntson et al., 1997). Without this "vagal brake," heart rate would rise to between 80 and 120 beats per minute (Jose & Collison, 1970), and the system would exhaust itself. RSA also allows us to use breathing to calm us down, through a large vagal discharge during a long slow exhalation. This helps emotional regulation.

BLOOD PRESSURE

Another rhythm in HRV reflects activity in the baroreflex system. The baroreflex is an important reflex that helps control blood pressure. When blood pressure rises, heart rate falls; and when blood pressure falls, heart rate rises. This produces a rhythm in heart rate in the neighborhood of 0.1 Hz (six/minute; Berntson et al., 1997; Moak et al., 2007; Vaschillo, Lehrer, Rishe, & Konstantinov, 2002). Baroreflex action keeps blood pressure changes from becoming too extreme. The baroreflex is controlled through a center in the brain stem (i.e, the nucleus tractus solitarius) that communicates directly with centers that control emotion: the insula and the amygdala (Henderson et al., 2004). It, therefore, seems to be involved in emotional regulation. This activity also appears mostly to be vagally mediated but at times also is reflective of sympathetic activity, perhaps primarily beta sympathetic (Chen & Mukkamala, 2008). Although there is some controversy about this, the ratio between HRV in the frequency band most influenced by the cardiac baroreflex, between 0.05 and 0.15 Hz, the low frequency (LF) band, and the HF band is sometimes taken as a measure of sympathetic: parasympathetic balance. This ratio is increased in anxiety and cardiovascular disease, and decreased in states of calmness and relaxation.

Activity at a very slow rate of 0.005 to 0.05 Hz is less well understood but is known to be primarily affected by vascular tone and perhaps by the vascular tone limb of the baroreflex (Vaschillo, Vaschillo, Buckman, Pandina, & Bates, 2012; Vaschillo, Vaschillo, & Lehrer, 2006), such that blood vessels dilate as blood pressure rises and constrict as it falls. It also appears to be related to thermal control (Fleisher et al., 1996; Kinugasa & Hirayanagi, 1999; Thayer, Nabors-Oberg, & Sollers, 1997) and may be under alpha sympathetic control.

Note that all three sources of HRV reflect feedback loops through which important functions are regulated—most directly, blood pressure (through the baroreflexes) and oxygen regulation. Is it any wonder, then, that both amplitude and complexity of HRV are associated with various aspects of health and adaptability? These include youth (Ogliari et al., 2015; Voss, Schroeder, Heitmann, Peters, & Perz, 2015), aerobic fitness (Carreira et al., 2015; Kaikkonen et al., 2014; Leite et al., 2015), and athletic performance (da Silva, de Oliveira, Silveira, Mello, & Deslandes, 2015; Plews, Laursen, Stanley, Kilding, & Buchheit, 2013). Conversely, amplitude and complexity of HRV are diminished by almost all forms of disease (Adlan, Lip, Paton, Kitas, & Fisher, 2014; Bär, 2015; La Rovere & Christensen, 2015; Reinsberger et al., 2015; Zhang & Wang, 2014).

These characteristics of HRV also have implications for many aspects of psychological, interpersonal, and physical functioning—from athletic performance (Aubert,

Seps, & Beckers, 2003; Paul & Garg, 2012) and socialization (Alvares et al., 2013; Geisler, Kubiak, Siewert, & Weber, 2013; Porges, Doussard-Roosevelt, Portales, & Greenspan, 1996; Smeekens, Didden, & Verhoeven, 2015), to cardiovascular function and health (Kop et al., 2010; Stapelberg, Hamilton-Craig, Neumann, Shum, & McConnell, 2012; Sunkaria, Kumar, Saxena, & Singhal, 2014), inflammation (Huston & Tracey, 2011; Scheff, Mavroudis, Calvano, Lowry, & Androulakis, 2011), and emotional stability (Agelink et al., 2001; Alvares et al., 2013; Gaebler, Daniels, Lamke, Fydrich, & Walter, 2013; Minassian et al., 2014; Tully, Cosh, & Baune, 2013). HRV reflects processes involved in both of the systems mentioned above and others, primarily because it reflects neural control of the cardiovascular system, and almost all other systems affect and/or are affected by at least one of these two systems.

Neural control of heart rate occurs through the sinoatrial node (Lombardi, 2002; Rocchetti, Malfatto, Lombardi, & Zaza, 2000; Tao, Paterson, & Smith, 2011; Yaniv et al., 2014), which, in turn, is affected by both sympathetic and parasympathetic activity, although primarily through the vagus nerve—a parasympathetic nerve carrying bidirectional messages from central nervous system (CNS) centers in the brain stem to visceral organs throughout the body (Inoue et al., 1991; Mark, 1987; Raybould et al., 1991). Thus, vagus nerve activity slows the heart, but changes in heart action feed back to the vagus nerve, which, in turn, influences all other vagus nerve functions and various CNS processes controlling various physiological, emotional, and social processes.

SOCIAL ACTIVITY

HRV also is correlated with social activity, probably though the vagus nerve's interaction with the trigeminal nerve (Eckberg, Mohanty, & Raczkowska, 1984), which affects facial expression in humans (i.e., a predominant pathway for social communication). Porges has pointed out that nonsocial animals have less vagally mediated HRV than social animals, just as do people with impaired socialization (e.g., those suffering from autism; Geisler et al., 2013; Porges, 1995b, 2001, 2007). We do not know yet whether inducing increased HRV in autistic individuals produces increases in vagally mediated HRV, but we do know this about depression. Effective cognitive behavior therapy (CBT) increases HRV in patients with comorbid depression and heart disease (Carney et al., 2000), and training to increase HRV through biofeedback decreases depression.

AUTONOMIC BALANCE

HRV is also related to autonomic balance. Parasympathetic activity is blocked during the fight-or-flight reaction and, in various emotional disorders (particularly those involving heightened vigilance and preparation for action, e.g., anxiety disorders). The activity is heightened, however, during relaxation and rest (Lehrer et al., 1997; Sakakibara, Takeuchi, & Hayano, 1994). Cardiac effects of such a central process also are mediated by the vagus nerve. Thus, procedures that stimulate parasympathetic activity usually are associated with feelings of calmness and relaxation (Grimonprez, Raedt, Baeken, Boon, & Vonck, 2015; Trevizol, Barros, Liquidato, Cordeiro, & Shiozawa, 2015), just as these emotions increase vagus nerve activity. Various conditions such as stress or anxiety decrease vagal activity (Porges, 1995a), and procedures that decrease them increase vagal activity (Bax, Robinson, Goedde, & Shaffer, 2007; Sakakibara et al., 1994). Thayer has introduced a neurovisceral theory showing the relationship between HRV and neural processes involved in emotional regulation (Thayer & Ruiz-Padial, 2006).

HRV is inherently complex, influenced not only by the vagus nerve but also by various sympathetic processes (particularly alpha sympathetic activity, which directly affects vascular tone and lower HRV frequencies; Berntson et al., 1997). Each function is mediated by a number of simultaneous negative feedback loops that modulate many of the processes affected by the autonomic nervous system (ANS; Lehrer & Eddie, 2013). As described above, these various processes tend to produce oscillations at different frequencies and, thus, a greater complexity in HRV.

Evidence Base for Heart Rate Variability Biofeedback

The effects of HRV biofeedback are mediated through effects of breathing on the baroreflex (Lehrer, 2013). When one breathes at the same frequency as the baroreflex, systematic changes occur in the phase relationships among breathing, HRV, and blood pressure variability (Vaschillo et al., 2002). Usually these three functions are not in phase with each other (Censi et al., 2000; Karavaev et al., 2013; Vaschillo et al., 2002). Thus, under conditions of normal rest, the baroreflex is only moderately stimulated, blood pressure is only moderately controlled, and gas exchange in the lung is only moderately efficient. However, the phase relationships change with the frequency of respiration. When one breathes slowly, at the baroreflex frequency (close to six times a minute), a remarkable phase event occurs: HRV is completely in phase with breathing (0 degrees), such that peak heart rate occurs when the lungs are maximally filled with air, while blood pressure and heart rate oscillate completely *out* of phase (180-degree phase relationship), such that peak heart rate occurs at the point of minimum blood pressure, and lowest heart rate occurs at the point of highest BP (Vaschillo et al., 2002). Therefore, breathing at this rate produces maximal blood pressure control (through maximal gain in the baroreflex; Vaschillo et al., 2002) and maximal gas exchange efficiency (Yasuma & Hayano, 2004). Put another way, breathing at this rate causes maximal stimulation of the baroreflex, maximal blood pressure modulation, and most efficient exchange between oxygen and carbon dioxide.

There is one more process that augments all of these effects: resonance (Lehrer, 2013; Vaschillo et al., 2002). Actually, the increases in HRV amplitude that occur when breathing at baroreflex frequency are much greater than the sum of RSA and the cardiac baroreflex amplitudes. This occurs because the structure of the baroreflex causes resonance characteristics in the cardiovascular system. The baroreflex system is a feedback system with a constant delay, and all such systems have the characteristic of resonance. Think of a resonating chamber. If you plucked a violin string not attached to a violin, you would hardly hear the sound. The violin is a resonating chamber that greatly amplifies the sound. Similarly, think of a child on a swing. The length of the cords determine frequency of back and forth oscillation on the swing. If you push the swing at the natural frequency of oscillation (i.e., frequency of resonance or resonance frequency), the child will swing higher and higher. When you push at a different frequency, you can even stop the swing. In the cases of HRV biofeedback, then, breathing is the push and the baroreflex is the cord and swing.

The length of the delay in the baroreflex appears to be caused by blood volume (Lehrer, 2013; Vaschillo et al., 2006). It is not functional and is not affected by HRV biofeedback. People with more blood (taller people and men) have slower resonance frequencies than shorter people and women. This is probably caused by inertia in the blood supply, but also may, at least theoretically, be affected by resistance in the blood vessels.

There is an additional factor that must be added to all this: neuroplasticity of the baroreflex (Lehrer et al., 2003). What happens in the CNS when the baroreflex is stimulated maximally with every breath? An important homeostatic reflex is exercised. What happens during repeated regular exercise of a reflex? It becomes more efficient. This is exactly what happens to the baroreflexes during HRV biofeedback. After several months of regular practice, the baroreflex is strengthened. Thus, even when people are not doing HRV biofeedback, greater changes in heart rate occur with given fluctuations in blood pressure (i.e., modulation of blood pressure is improved throughout the day). Presumably, the same thing happens with RSA, although this has not been completely documented. This appears to be why HRV biofeedback has such profound effects on so many aspects of human functioning.

Scope of Application

Although few large-scale multisite randomized controlled trials have been funded to assess HRV biofeedback, a number of smaller controlled trials have appeared in refereed publications. Gevirtz (2013) recently reviewed all available publications for the efficacy of HRV biofeedback. Studies were subdivided by probable mediational mechanisms. Thus, disorders thought to be related to autonomic dysfunction (e.g., asthma, irritable bowel syndrome, chronic muscle pain, hypertension) were evaluated. Twenty-three studies were found. Though sample sizes were often small, almost all of the studies reported superior outcomes for the HRV biofeedback group when compared with various comparison or wait-list groups. Effect sizes were moderate to large. Another group of disorders thought to be more associated with central processes (e.g., depression, anxiety, stress, sleep) were examined. Here, 19 studies were found. Again, HRV biofeedback was associated with greater improvements compared to treatment as usual, talk therapies, or relaxation training. Effect sizes were more variable, depending on the nature of the comparison group. A more complete description of the evidence base is presented in a chapter in *Biofeedback: A Practitioners*

Guide (Gevirtz, Lehrer, & Schwartz, in press). Because a good deal of the evidence above has come from the labs and clinics of the present authors, some caution is warranted. Overall, however, the evidence base for HRV biofeedback is very promising.

More recently, Goessl, Curtiss, and reviewed Hofmann (2017) 24 studies (484 patients) that examined HRV Biofeedback for Stress and anxiety. They found that

> The pre–post within-group effect size (Hedges' g) was 0.81. The between-groups analysis comparing biofeedback to a control condition yielded Hedges' $g = 0.83$. Moderator analyses revealed that treatment efficacy was not moderated by study year, risk of study bias, percentage of females, number of sessions, or presence of an anxiety disorder. (p. 1)

Although the effects of biofeedback on a variety of conditions are strong, the mechanism for the effects has not been definitively proven. We know that acute effects of HRV biofeedback on amplitude of HRV and baroreflex gain are very strong (Lehrer et al., 2003), the effects on baseline HRV are often marginal, as are the correlations between changes in HRV and improvement in various measures of resilience and symptom recovery (Wheat & Larkin, 2010). A possible explanation for this is the large acute effects on symptoms that might translate into chronic effects as people become more confident in controlling their bodies and improving symptoms and performance through HRV biofeedback. Further research on mechanisms for clinical effects of HRV biofeedback is needed.

Based on the premise that HRV biofeedback improves autonomic homeostasis and most probably affects central structures in a similar way to vagal nerve stimulation (see Lehrer & Gevirtz, 2014, for a full explication of this idea). Other therapies can be supplemented with HRV biofeedback, as well as with other biofeedback modalities. The most obvious use of HRV biofeedback is as a psychoeducational tool. Demonstrating and explaining physiological phenomena that are related to client problems (e.g., stress, anxiety) can have a powerful effect. We have observed that it lowers attrition, reduces stigmatization, and greatly increases the probability of client buy-in.

HRV biofeedback is often combined with therapies such as CBT or acceptance and commitment therapy (ACT) (or other mindfulness-based interventions). The therapist prescribes daily practice and, after mastery, "rescue techniques." The client is taught to identify anxiety, stress, or rumination episodes and use a very short version of the resonance frequency breathing to (a) be mindful and (b) watch the episodes fade away. This can be used with a variety of therapeutic techniques for many sorts of symptoms.

Benefits of Incorporating Heart Rate Variability Biofeedback Into Practice

There are many good reasons for the mental health clinician to incorporate HRV biofeedback and other physiological measures into their practice. Peter Lang, a pioneer in the psychophysiology of emotion, proposed that, along with behavior and self-reports of cognitive processes, physiological measures would give a more complete picture of the whole person (Lang, 1979). With the advent of inexpensive, non-invasive technologies, it is now possible for the clinician to be observing physiological processes during clinical sessions. The four most common and useful modalities are (a) skin conductance, (b) finger temperature (or pulse amplitude), (c) heart rate (both beat-to-beat patterns and average levels), and (d) respiration. These measures can give us a picture of autonomic processes (sympathetic: skin conductance and temperature [pulse amplitude], and parasympathetic: HRV) on an ongoing basis. For example, during CBT or ACT, the clinician might observe a dramatic increase in skin conductance during exposure of a feared stimulus. Along with observation and subjective verbal report, this would seem to guarantee enough arousal to produce extinction (or inhibition learning; Craske, Treanor, Conway, Zbozinek, & Vervliet, 2014). On the other hand, clients may report high levels of subjective discomfort (SUDS), without the accompanying physiological arousal. This might be important information, since the exposure may not be sufficient to produce reduced fear or avoidance.

Of particular relevance to HRV biofeedback are signs of vagal withdrawal in anxiety or stress related disorders (Agorastos et al., 2013; Porges, 1995a). Vagal withdrawal can be observed by watching beat-by-beat heart rate traces. A flatter, higher trace, even without signs of sympathetic arousal, is indicative of the loss of the "vagal brake" (Dale et al., 2009).

A 5-minute resting baseline, followed by an exercise or mental stressor, is often used to assess psychophysiological profiles. Using free online software, KUBIOS-HRV (Tarvainen, Niskanen, Lipponen, Ranta-Aho, & Karjalainen, 2014) or other commercially available HRV editing software, HRV parameters for baseline and recovery can easily be assessed. This can be a valuable tool in client assessment.

CASE EXAMPLE: SOCIAL PHOBIA

While treating a patient for a social phobia, a clinician developed a hierarchy of feared situations. Based on the psychophysiological profile developed in the initial sessions, the client showed marked vagal withdrawal and moderate sympathetic arousal during a social stimulus. The next session focused on determination of resonance frequency. After progressing through several breathing paces, 6.5 breaths per minute was chosen. At this pace, the heart rate graph showed coherence with respiration, produced the largest peak valley differences, and was smoothest. The client practiced 10 minutes, twice per day, with a free app on their smartphone; plus, the client did "rescue breathing" or a short version of resonance frequency breathing whenever any anxiety occurred.

After progressing through the least fear-producing situations (giving a short speech to the therapist), the sessions moved to in vivo exposures. Talking to a small group of colleagues seemed to produce an adequate level of sympathetic arousal and vagal withdrawal at first, but based on the physiology (but not the SUDS levels), a plateau was reached in a subsequent session. Using this added information, the therapist created a slightly more fearful situation and the client progressed nicely. After six sessions, the client joined Toastmasters, a social anxiety support group, and felt much more confident in social situations.

CASE EXAMPLE: SOMATIC SYMPTOMS

A patient with extreme sensitivity and overreaction to bodily sensations was referred because of the increasingly crippling nature of their symptoms. The fifth edition of the *Diagnostic and Statistical Manual of Mental Disorders* (American Psychiatric Association, 2013) calls these symptoms Somatic Symptom Disorder. The client knew, at some level, that his concerns were not completely rational (after many medical workups). After explaining the mechanisms of the ANS and checking for hyperventilation, the clinician determined resonance frequency and prescribed home practice. This client preferred using a musical breath pacer (BreathSync.com) to the many free apps available (e.g., MyCalmBeat, Breathe2Relax, BreathPacer). The initial stages of the HRV biofeedback reduced symptom severity by about one half. Using a strategy based on ACT (Harris, 2008), the clinician had the client mindfully observe the "attacks," begin rescue breathing as a strategy to help tolerate them, and record the results. This combination reduced symptoms dramatically and, more important, improved functional factors (e.g., less avoidance/constriction) almost completely. Since the client had mastered the biofeedback skills, subsequent sessions focused on ACT skills (e.g., defusion, values, commitment). By the 2-month mark, the client felt confident that he could tolerate his "somatic" attacks and terminated the therapy.

CASE EXAMPLE: PANIC ATTACKS

A woman in her early 20s decided to seek therapy because of panic attacks that were occurring with increasing frequency—now several times each week. Attacks consisted of a variety of sensations, including difficulty breathing, trembling, heart palpitations, derealization, sweating, and feelings that the symptoms were life threatening. Symptoms seemed to occur from "out of the blue," without a particular pattern—sometimes when she was tired or stressed, but sometimes when relaxing or even sleeping. In most cases, symptoms gradually worsened over a period of about 20 minutes and then gradually subsided of the course of about 1 hour. Although she had previously occasionally had such episodes, their frequency had increased over the past few weeks, following the end of a 3-year relationship in which she had been "dumped" by a high school sweetheart and a severe upper respiratory infection that was followed by some asthma-like symptoms. The patient had visited her primary care physician on several occasions, but no medical basis was found for her continuing symptoms. The physician had offered to prescribe tranquilizing medication, but the patient decided she would rather first try a nondrug treatment.

In the first session, the therapist gathered symptom information and a brief history and also, given her hyperventilation-like symptoms, measured her end-tidal CO_2, which was moderately low (32 mm Hg). The therapist briefly explained how hyperventilation can decrease blood flow to the brain, heart, and muscles, which could completely explain all of her symptoms. The therapist then offered to teach the patient a breathing technique that would help her control them. The patient agreed, and, in the same session, the therapist determined her resonance frequency. The therapist instructed her to breathe at that rate for 20 minutes twice/day and to repeat this regimen when she experienced symptoms.

The patient returned the next week, saying that she found the technique moderately helpful, but that sometimes the slow breathing would itself trigger some of the hyperventilation symptoms. She was then instructed to breathe more shallowly at her resonance frequency and was trained in relaxed abdominal breathing, while observing her HRV and end tidal CO_2. The resonance frequency was rechecked to determine if it was correct, and this was verified.

The following week, the patient reported that she had experienced the beginning of three panic attacks, and each time was able to abort them using resonance frequency breathing. At this session, the therapist instructed her to hyperventilate deliberately and then to abort symptoms using resonance frequency breathing. Symptoms of lightheadedness and palpitations aborted within 2 minutes. The patient reported that she felt more confident in her ability to control the symptoms. In the following two sessions, she reported decreasing frequency of attacks, all quickly resolved by resonance frequency breathing. Throughout the therapy, the patient also discussed her anger and sadness about rejection by her boyfriend and found herself ruminating about it much less frequently. Within 2 months, her symptoms had completely resolved, and the patient reported that she was confident in her ability to control them, indicating that her therapy goals had been met. The therapist met with her monthly for 2 additional months, and then, with agreement from the patient, terminated therapy.

Steps and Requirements for Incorporating Heart Rate Variability Biofeedback in Mental Health Practice

HRV equipment has become increasingly inexpensive and easy to use, with biofeedback units ranging from $5 smartphone applications to research-grade multisystem devices costing thousands of dollars. A barrier to use of almost all biofeedback technology, however, can be insurance regulations. Although HRV technology is easy to access and to use, some specialized training on the part of the clinician is desirable. The Biofeedback Certification International Alliance (http://www.bcia.org) lists training requirements that are generally recognized in the biofeedback field for independent practice. In some localities and for some disorders, biofeedback can be incorporated as psychotherapy techniques, in others, biofeedback alone can be billed for particular problems; in still others there, is no compensation given for biofeedback services.

Here is an overview of procedures for doing HRV biofeedback. In the first session, we usually determine the individual's resonance frequency. We do this by having the individual do paced breathing for several minutes at frequencies between 4.5 and 7 breaths per minute, while recording HRV, ideally while monitoring the following variables: instantaneous heart rate, a respiration tracing, updating spectral analyses, an index of average peak-trough amplitudes in heart rate, and an updating measure of average low-frequency HRV. Some units also provide a measure of internal coherence or normalized LF HRV. These also can be useful. Resonance frequency can be determined with fewer variables, with some loss in accuracy. We usually have respiratory frequencies done in fairly random order, and the therapist should note that changes in the individual's level of stress or relaxation could affect some measures, so that a repeat process (at least of a few frequencies near the resonance frequency) is recommended, usually at a second session. The following criteria usually all yield the same conclusion, although, occasionally, the various criteria diverge from each other, in which case a judgment call is needed. The criteria for resonance frequency are (in order of importance): (a) height of the highest peak in the low frequency range on the spectral graph; (b) highest peak-to-trough amplitude; (c) highest low-frequency HRV; (d) greatest smoothness of the HRV pattern, without "ripples," best approximating a simple sine wave; and (e) perfect phase relationship with breathing, such that the beginning of increases, peak, and decreases in heart rate exactly coincide with the beginning of inhalation, the point of maximum tidal volume, and the end of exhalation. Where the various indices diverge, we suggest emphasizing the first three criteria applications involving autonomic and emotional control, but using the last criterion for various respiratory diseases.

For homework, we calculate the individual's resonance frequency in terms of seconds per breath (e.g., 10 seconds for 6/minute, 11 seconds for 5.5/minute) and instruct the client to breathe at this frequency using the second hand of a clock or watch, or to download various respiration pacers available from the Internet and to set the stimulus rate at the individual's resonance frequency. We ask clients to practice, ideally, for 20 minutes twice daily, and to use the technique when symptomatic. Although this goal is rarely achieved, most research studies on HRV biofeedback efficacy have used this frequency of home practice.

A caution is in order. Despite the fact that HRV biofeedback, when properly done, tends to elevate blood levels of carbon dioxide slightly and to decrease vulnerability to hyperventilation, some people do tend to hyperventilate during initial training sessions. Slow breathing necessarily requires an increase in tidal volume in order to maintain homeostatic levels of oxygen and carbon dioxide, and some individuals tend to overcompensate for slow breathing by breathing too deeply. Thus, we instruct clients not to breathe too deeply, and we query them about hyperventilation symptoms during resonance frequency testing and subsequent practice sessions. Such symptoms typically include lightheadedness, a pounding heart, tingling sensations, and, occasionally, increases in anxiety. When these occur, the client is told that they are normal and simply reflect too great an increase in tidal volume; they are then advised to breathe more shallowly. Paced breathing does sometimes initially produce some anxiety and discomfort, particularly among people with body anxiety, concern about breathing, and hyperventilation symptomatology. The therapist must be aware of this possibility, and both reassure and instruct the client accordingly. Also, a few people may show evidence of irregular heartbeat while doing slow breathing (e.g., a systematic increase in preventricular contractions). We usually stop training when this occurs.

In subsequent sessions, we gradually shift from paced breathing to biofeedback, where the individual follows the instantaneous heart rate tracing, and tries to produce the highest possible increases during inhalation, and the greatest possible decreases during exhalation, while breathing close to resonance frequency. Some individuals are not comfortable doing slow-paced breathing but find it much easier to follow the heart rate and do HRV biofeedback from the first session onwards. For these folks, it is important to have access to a home biofeedback trainer, which can be obtained in various forms for between $5 and $200. Research tends to show that approximately four sessions of training are necessary to learn how to do HRV biofeedback effectively (Vaschillo et al., 2006).

Essential Resources

For clinical use of HRV biofeedback, little is needed other than a machine that reliably records HRV. It should have the capability of displaying a spectral analysis of HRV rhythms, as well as a tracing of instantaneous heart rate (or cardiac interbeat interval). It is desirable that the display also includes a respiratory tracing. Although a recording from a finger pulse is adequate, recording from an electrocardiogram is more accurate. For accuracy in reporting results and finding resonance frequency, it also is desirable that HRV data be edited to delete artifact, which can occur from various sources (e.g., movement of electrodes on the skin, interference from electromyography or line signals, various cardiac arrhythmias). A number of programs are commercially available that facilitate HRV editing.

Knowledge of procedures for determining resonance frequency for each individual also is necessary, as well as of a protocol for the procedure. These materials were published recently (Lehrer et al., 2013) and included in a compilation of papers about the nature, procedures, and uses of HRV biofeedback (Moss & Shaffer, 2016). Similarly, a background course in psychophysiology is desirable, and some laboratory experience that includes detection and elimination of artifact is helpful.

References

Adlan, A. M., Lip, G. Y. H., Paton, J. F. R., Kitas, G. D., & Fisher, J. P. (2014). Autonomic function and rheumatoid arthritis—A systematic review. *Seminars in Arthritis and Rheumatism, 44*, 283–304. http://dx.doi.org/10.1016/j.semarthrit.2014.06.003

Agelink, M. W., Majewski, T., Wurthmann, C., Postert, T., Linka, T., Rotterdam, S., & Klieser, E. (2001). Autonomic neurocardiac function in patients with major depression and effects of antidepressive treatment with nefazodone. *Journal of Affective Disorders, 62*, 187–198. http://dx.doi.org/10.1016/S0165-0327(99)00202-5

Agorastos, A., Boel, J. A., Heppner, P. S., Hager, T., Moeller-Bertram, T., Haji, U., . . . Stiedl, O. (2013). Diminished vagal activity and blunted diurnal variation of heart rate dynamics in posttraumatic stress disorder. *Stress, 16*, 300–310. http://dx.doi.org/10.3109/10253890.2012.751369

Alvares, G. A., Quintana, D. S., Kemp, A. H., Van Zwieten, A., Balleine, B. W., Hickie, I. B., & Guastella, A. J. (2013). Reduced heart rate variability in social anxiety disorder: Associations with gender and symptom severity. *PLoS One, 8,* e70468. http://dx.doi.org/10.1371/journal.pone.0070468

American Psychiatric Association. (2013). *Diagnostic and statistical manual of mental disorders* (5th ed.). Arlington, VA: Author.

Aubert, A. E., Seps, B., & Beckers, F. (2003). Heart rate variability in athletes. *Sports Medicine, 33,* 889–919. http://dx.doi.org/10.2165/00007256-200333120-00003

Bär, K.-J. (2015). Cardiac autonomic dysfunction in patients with schizophrenia and their healthy relatives—A small review. *Frontiers in Neurology, 6,* 139. http://dx.doi.org/10.3389/fneur.2015.00139

Bax, A., Robinson, T., Goedde, J., & Shaffer, F. (2007). The Cousins relaxation exercise increases heart rate variability [Abstract]. *Applied Psychophysiology and Biofeedback, 32*(1), 52.

Berntson, G. G., Bigger, J. T., Jr., Eckberg, D. L., Grossman, P., Kaufmann, P. G., Malik, M., . . . van der Molen, M. W. (1997). Heart rate variability: Origins, methods, and interpretive caveats. *Psychophysiology, 34,* 623–648. http://dx.doi.org/10.1111/j.1469-8986.1997.tb02140.x

Carney, R. M., Freedland, K. E., Stein, P. K., Skala, J. A., Hoffman, P., & Jaffe, A. S. (2000). Change in heart rate and heart rate variability during treatment for depression in patients with coronary heart disease. *Psychosomatic Medicine, 62,* 639–647. http://dx.doi.org/10.1097/00006842-200009000-00007

Carr, R. E., Lehrer, P. M., Hochron, S. M., & Jackson, A. (1996). Effect of psychological stress on airway impedance in individuals with asthma and panic disorder. *Journal of Abnormal Psychology, 105,* 137–141. http://dx.doi.org/10.1037/0021-843X.105.1.137

Carreira, M. A., Nogueira, A. B., Pena, F. M., Kiuchi, M. G., Rodrigues, R. C., Rodrigues, R. R., . . . Lugon, J. R. (2015). Heart rate variability correlates to functional aerobic impairment in hemodialysis patients. *Arquivos Brasileiros de Cardiologia, 104,* 493–500.

Censi, F., Calcagnini, G., Lino, S., Seydnejad, S. R., Kitney, R. I., & Cerutti, S. (2000). Transient phase locking patterns among respiration, heart rate and blood pressure during cardiorespiratory synchronisation in humans. *Medical & Biological Engineering & Computing, 38,* 416–426. http://dx.doi.org/10.1007/BF02345011

Chen, X., & Mukkamala, R. (2008). Selective quantification of the cardiac sympathetic and parasympathetic nervous systems by multisignal analysis of cardiorespiratory variability. *American Journal of Physiology: Heart and Circulatory Physiology, 294,* H362–H371. http://dx.doi.org/10.1152/ajpheart.01061.2007

Craske, M. G., Treanor, M., Conway, C. C., Zbozinek, T., & Vervliet, B. (2014). Maximizing exposure therapy: an inhibitory learning approach. *Behaviour Research and Therapy, 58,* 10–23. http://dx.doi.org/10.1016/j.brat.2014.04.006

Cubbon, R. M., Ruff, N., Groves, D., Eleuteri, A., Denby, C., Kearney, L., . . . Kearney, M. T. (2016). Ambulatory heart rate range predicts mode-specific mortality and hospitalisation in chronic heart failure. *Heart, 102,* 223–229. http://dx.doi.org/10.1136/heartjnl-2015-308428

Dale, L. P., Carroll, L. E., Galen, G., Hayes, J. A., Webb, K. W., & Porges, S. W. (2009). Abuse history is related to autonomic regulation to mild exercise and psychological wellbeing. *Applied Psychophysiology and Biofeedback, 34,* 299–308. http://dx.doi.org/10.1007/s10484-009-9111-4

da Silva, V. P., de Oliveira, N. A., Silveira, H., Mello, R. G. T., & Deslandes, A. C. (2015). Heart rate variability indexes as a marker of chronic adaptation in athletes: A systematic review. *Annals of Noninvasive Electrocardiology, 20,* 108–118. http://dx.doi.org/10.1111/anec.12237

Di Simplicio, M., Costoloni, G., Western, D., Hanson, B., Taggart, P., & Harmer, C. J. (2012). Decreased heart rate variability during emotion regulation in subjects at risk for psychopathology. *Psychological Medicine, 42,* 1775–1783. http://dx.doi.org/10.1017/S0033291711002479

Eckberg, D. L. (2003). The human respiratory gate. *The Journal of Physiology, 548,* 339–352.

Eckberg, D. L., Mohanty, S. K., & Raczkowska, M. (1984). Trigeminal-baroreceptor reflex interactions modulate human cardiac vagal efferent activity. *The Journal of Physiology, 347,* 75–83. http://dx.doi.org/10.1113/jphysiol.1984.sp015054

Fleisher, L. A., Frank, S. M., Sessler, D. I., Cheng, C., Matsukawa, T., & Vannier, C. A. (1996). Thermoregulation and heart rate variability. *Clinical Science, 90,* 97–103.

Gaebler, M., Daniels, J. K., Lamke, J.-P., Fydrich, T., & Walter, H. (2013). Heart rate variability and its neural correlates during emotional face processing in social anxiety disorder. *Biological Psychology, 94,* 319–330. http://dx.doi.org/10.1016/j.biopsycho.2013.06.009

Geisler, F. C. M., Kubiak, T., Siewert, K., & Weber, H. (2013). Cardiac vagal tone is associated with social engagement and self-regulation. *Biological Psychology, 93,* 279–286. http://dx.doi.org/10.1016/j.biopsycho.2013.02.013

Gevirtz, R. (2013). The promise of heart rate variability biofeedback: Evidence-based applications. *Biofeedback, 41,* 110–120. http://dx.doi.org/10.5298/1081-5937-41.3.01

Gevirtz, R., Lehrer, P., & Schwartz, M. S. (in press). Cardiorespiratory biofeedback. In M. S. Schwartz & F. Andrasik (Eds.), *Biofeedback: A practitioner's handbook* (4th ed.). New York, NY: Guilford Press.

Goessl, V. C., Curtiss, J. E., & Hofmann, S. G. (2017). The effect of heart rate variability biofeedback training on stress and anxiety: A meta-analysis. *Psychological Medicine, 47,* 2578–2586.

Grimonprez, A., Raedt, R., Baeken, C., Boon, P., & Vonck, K. (2015). The anti-depressant mechanism of action of vagus nerve stimulation: Evidence from pre-clinical studies. *Neuroscience and Biobehavioral Reviews, 56,* 26–34. http://dx.doi.org/10.1016/j.neubiorev.2015.06.019

Harris, R. E. (2008). *The happiness trap: How to stop struggling and start living.* Boston, MA: Trumpeter.

Hayano, J., Yasuma, F., Okada, A., Mukai, S., & Fujinami, T. (1996). Respiratory sinus arrhythmia. A phenomenon improving pulmonary gas exchange and circulatory efficiency. *Circulation, 94,* 842–847. http://dx.doi.org/10.1161/01.CIR.94.4.842

Henderson, L. A., Richard, C. A., Macey, P. M., Runquist, M. L., Yu, P. L., Galons, J.-P., & Harper, R. M. (2004). Functional magnetic resonance signal changes in neural structures to baroreceptor reflex activation. *Journal of Applied Physiology, 96,* 693–703. http://dx.doi.org/10.1152/japplphysiol.00852.2003

Huston, J. M., & Tracey, K. J. (2011). The pulse of inflammation: Heart rate variability, the cholinergic anti-inflammatory pathway and implications for therapy. *Journal of Internal Medicine, 269,* 45–53. http://dx.doi.org/10.1111/j.1365-2796.2010.02321.x

Inoue, S., Nagase, H., Satom, S., Saito, M., Egawa, M., Tanaka, K., & Takamura, Y. (1991). Role of the efferent and afferent vagus nerve in the development of ventromedial hypothalamic (VMH) obesity. *Brain Research Bulletin, 27,* 511–515. http://dx.doi.org/10.1016/0361-9230(91)90151-9

Jose, A. D., & Collison, D. (1970). The normal range and determinants of the intrinsic heart rate in man. *Cardiovascular Research, 4,* 160–167. http://dx.doi.org/10.1093/cvr/4.2.160

Kaikkonen, K. M., Korpelainen, R. I., Tulppo, M. P., Kaikkonen, H. S., Vanhala, M. L., Kallio, M. A., . . . Korpelainen, J. T. (2014). Physical activity and aerobic fitness are positively associated with heart rate variability in obese adults. *Journal of Physical Activity & Health, 11,* 1614–1621. http://dx.doi.org/10.1123/jpah.2012-0405

Karavaev, A. S., Kiselev, A. R., Gridnev, V. I., Borovkova, E. I., Prokhorov, M. D., Posnenkova, O. M., . . . Shvartz, V. A. (2013). Phase and frequency locking of 0.1-Hz oscillations in heart rate and baroreflex control of blood pressure by breathing of linearly varying frequency as determined in healthy subjects. *Human Physiology, 39,* 416–425. http://dx.doi.org/10.1134/S0362119713010040

Kinugasa, H., & Hirayanagi, K. (1999). Effects of skin surface cooling and heating on autonomic nervous activity and baroreflex sensitivity in humans. *Experimental Physiology, 84,* 369–377. http://dx.doi.org/10.1111/j.1469-445X.1999.01839.x

Kop, W. J., Stein, P. K., Tracy, R. P., Barzilay, J. I., Schulz, R., & Gottdiener, J. S. (2010). Autonomic nervous system dysfunction and inflammation contribute to the increased cardiovascular mortality risk associated with depression. *Psychosomatic Medicine, 72,* 626–635. http://dx.doi.org/10.1097/PSY.0b013e3181eadd2b

Lang, P. J. (1979). A bio-informational theory of emotional imagery. *Psychophysiology, 16,* 495–512. http://dx.doi.org/10.1111/j.1469-8986.1979.tb01511.x

La Rovere, M. T., & Christensen, J. H. (2015). The autonomic nervous system and cardiovascular disease: Role of n-3 PUFAs. *Vascular Pharmacology, 71,* 1–10. http://dx.doi.org/10.1016/j.vph.2015.02.005

Lehrer, P. (2013). How does heart rate variability biofeedback work? Resonance, the baroreflex, and other mechanisms. *Biofeedback, 41,* 26–31. http://dx.doi.org/10.5298/1081-5937-41.1.02

Lehrer, P., & Eddie, D. (2013). Dynamic processes in regulation and some implications for biofeedback and biobehavioral interventions. *Applied Psychophysiology and Biofeedback, 38,* 143–155. http://dx.doi.org/10.1007/s10484-013-9217-6

Lehrer, P. M., & Gevirtz, R. (2014). Heart rate variability biofeedback: How and why does it work? *Frontiers in Psychology, 5,* 756. http://dx.doi.org/10.3389/fpsyg.2014.00756

Lehrer, P. M., Hochron, S. M., Mayne, T., Isenberg, S., Lasoski, A. M., Carlson, V., . . . Porges, S. (1997). Relationship between changes in EMG and respiratory sinus arrhythmia in a study of relaxation therapy for asthma. *Applied Psychophysiology and Biofeedback, 22*, 183–191. http://dx.doi.org/10.1023/A:1026263826106

Lehrer, P. M., & Leiblum, S. R. (1981). Physiological, behavioral, and cognitive measures of assertiveness and assertion anxiety. *Behavioral Counseling Quarterly, 1*, 261–274.

Lehrer, P. M., Vaschillo, B., Zucker, T., Graves, J., Katsamanis, M., Aviles, M., & Wamboldt, F. (2013). Protocol for heart rate variability biofeedback training. *Biofeedback, 41*, 98–109. http://dx.doi.org/10.5298/1081-5937-41.3.08

Lehrer, P. M., Vaschillo, E., Vaschillo, B., Lu, S.-E., Eckberg, D. L., Edelberg, R., . . . Hamer, R. M. (2003). Heart rate variability biofeedback increases baroreflex gain and peak expiratory flow. *Psychosomatic Medicine, 65*, 796–805. http://dx.doi.org/10.1097/01.PSY.0000089200.81962.19

Leite, M. R., Ramos, E. M. C., Kalva-Filho, C. A., Rodrigues, F. M. M., Freire, A. P. C. F., Tacao, G. Y., . . . Ramos, D. (2015). Correlation between heart rate variability indexes and aerobic physiological variables in patients with COPD. *Respirology, 20*, 273–278. http://dx.doi.org/10.1111/resp.12424

Lombardi, F. (2002). Clinical implications of present physiological understanding of HRV components. *Cardiac Electrophysiology Review, 6*, 245–249. http://dx.doi.org/10.1023/A:1016329008921

Mark, A. L. (1987). Sensitization of cardiac vagal afferent reflexes at the sensory receptor level: An overview. *Federation Proceedings, 46*, 36–40.

Minassian, A., Geyer, M. A., Baker, D. G., Nievergelt, C. M., O'Connor, D. T., & Risbrough, V. B., for the Marine Resiliency Study Team. (2014). Heart rate variability characteristics in a large group of active-duty marines and relationship to post-traumatic stress. *Psychosomatic Medicine, 76*, 292–301. http://dx.doi.org/10.1097/PSY.0000000000000056

Moak, J. P., Goldstein, D. S., Eldadah, B. A., Saleem, A., Holmes, C., Pechnik, S., & Sharabi, Y. (2007). Supine low-frequency power of heart rate variability reflects baroreflex function, not cardiac sympathetic innervation. *Heart Rhythm, 4*, 1523–1529. http://dx.doi.org/10.1016/j.hrthm.2007.07.019

Moss, D., & Shaffer, F. (2016). *Foundations of heart rate variability biofeedback: A book of readings*. Wheat Ridge, CO: Association for Applied Psychophysiology and Biofeedback.

Ogliari, G., Mahinrad, S., Stott, D. J., Jukema, J. W., Mooijaart, S. P., Macfarlane, P. W., . . . Sabayan, B. (2015). Resting heart rate, heart rate variability and functional decline in old age. *Canadian Medical Association Journal, 187*, E442–E449. http://dx.doi.org/10.1503/cmaj.150462

Paul, M., & Garg, K. (2012). The effect of heart rate variability biofeedback on performance psychology of basketball players. *Applied Psychophysiology and Biofeedback, 37*, 131–144. http://dx.doi.org/10.1007/s10484-012-9185-2

Plews, D. J., Laursen, P. B., Stanley, J., Kilding, A. E., & Buchheit, M. (2013). Training adaptation and heart rate variability in elite endurance athletes: Opening the door to effective monitoring. *Sports Medicine, 43*, 773–781. http://dx.doi.org/10.1007/s40279-013-0071-8

Porges, S. W. (1991). Vagal mediation of respiratory sinus arrhythmia. Implications for drug delivery. *Annals of the New York Academy of Sciences, 618,* 57–66. http://dx.doi.org/10.1111/j.1749-6632.1991.tb27237.x

Porges, S. W. (1995a). Cardiac vagal tone: A physiological index of stress. *Neuroscience and Biobehavioral Reviews, 19,* 225–233. http://dx.doi.org/10.1016/0149-7634(94)00066-A

Porges, S. W. (1995b). Orienting in a defensive world: Mammalian modifications of our evolutionary heritage. A polyvagal theory. *Psychophysiology, 32,* 301–318. http://dx.doi.org/10.1111/j.1469-8986.1995.tb01213.x

Porges, S. W. (2001). The polyvagal theory: Phylogenetic substrates of a social nervous system. *International Journal of Psychophysiology, 42,* 123–146. http://dx.doi.org/10.1016/S0167-8760(01)00162-3

Porges, S. W. (2007). The polyvagal perspective. *Biological Psychology, 74,* 116–143. http://dx.doi.org/10.1016/j.biopsycho.2006.06.009

Porges, S. W., Doussard-Roosevelt, J. A., Portales, A. L., & Greenspan, S. I. (1996). Infant regulation of the vagal "brake" predicts child behavior problems: A psychobiological model of social behavior. *Developmental Psychobiology, 29,* 697–712. http://dx.doi.org/10.1002/(SICI)1098-2302(199612)29:8<697::AID-DEV5>3.0.CO;2-O

Raybould, H. E., Holzer, P., Thiefin, G., Holzer, H. H., Yoneda, M., & Tache, Y. F. (1991). Vagal afferent innervation and regulation of gastric function. *Advances in Experimental Medicine and Biology, 298,* 109–127. http://dx.doi.org/10.1007/978-1-4899-0744-8_10

Reinsberger, C., Sarkis, R., Papadelis, C., Doshi, C., Perez, D. L., Baslet, G., . . . Dworetzky, B. A. (2015). Autonomic changes in psychogenic nonepileptic seizures: Toward a potential diagnostic biomarker? *Clinical EEG & Neuroscience, 46,* 16–25. http://dx.doi.org/10.1177/1550059414567739

Rocchetti, M., Malfatto, G., Lombardi, F., & Zaza, A. (2000). Role of the input/output relation of sinoatrial myocytes in cholinergic modulation of heart rate variability. *Journal of Cardiovascular Electrophysiology, 11,* 522–530. http://dx.doi.org/10.1111/j.1540-8167.2000.tb00005.x

Sakakibara, M., Takeuchi, S., & Hayano, J. (1994). Effect of relaxation training on cardiac parasympathetic tone. *Psychophysiology, 31,* 223–228. http://dx.doi.org/10.1111/j.1469-8986.1994.tb02210.x

Scheff, J. D., Mavroudis, P. D., Calvano, S. E., Lowry, S. F., & Androulakis, I. P. (2011). Modeling autonomic regulation of cardiac function and heart rate variability in human endotoxemia. *Physiological Genomics, 43,* 951–964. http://dx.doi.org/10.1152/physiolgenomics.00040.2011

Smeekens, I., Didden, R., & Verhoeven, E. W. M. (2015). Exploring the relationship of autonomic and endocrine activity with social functioning in adults with autism spectrum disorders. *Journal of Autism and Developmental Disorders, 45,* 495–505. http://dx.doi.org/10.1007/s10803-013-1947-z

Stapelberg, N. J., Hamilton-Craig, I., Neumann, D. L., Shum, D. H. K., & McConnell, H. (2012). Mind and heart: Heart rate variability in major depressive disorder and coronary heart disease–a review and recommendations. *Australian and New Zealand Journal of Psychiatry, 46,* 946–957. http://dx.doi.org/10.1177/0004867412444624

Sunkaria, R. K., Kumar, V., Saxena, S. C., & Singhal, A. M. (2014). An ANN-based HRV classifier for cardiac health prognosis. *International Journal of Electronic Healthcare, 7*, 315–330. http://dx.doi.org/10.1504/IJEH.2014.064332

Tao, T., Paterson, D. J., & Smith, N. P. (2011). A model of cellular cardiac-neural coupling that captures the sympathetic control of sinoatrial node excitability in normotensive and hypertensive rats. *Biophysical Journal, 101*, 594–602. http://dx.doi.org/10.1016/j.bpj.2011.05.069

Tarvainen, M. P., Niskanen, J. P., Lipponen, J. A., Ranta-Aho, P. O., & Karjalainen, P. A. (2014). Kubios HRV—heart rate variability analysis software. *Computer Methods and Programs in Biomedicine, 113*, 210–220. http://dx.doi.org/10.1016/j.cmpb.2013.07.024

Thayer, J. F., Nabors-Oberg, R., & Sollers, J. J., III. (1997). Thermoregulation and cardiac variability: A time-frequency analysis. *Biomedical Sciences Instrumentation, 34*, 252–256.

Thayer, J. F., & Ruiz-Padial, E. (2006, August). Neurovisceral integration, emotions and health: An update. In C. Kubo and T. Kuboki (Eds.), *Psychosomatic medicine: Proceedings of the 18th World Congress on Psychosomatic Medicine* (pp. 122–127). http://dx.doi.org/10.1016/j.ics.2005.12.018

Trevizol, A., Barros, M. D., Liquidato, B., Cordeiro, Q., & Shiozawa, P. (2015). Vagus nerve stimulation in neuropsychiatry: Targeting anatomy-based stimulation sites. *Epilepsy & Behavior, 51*, 18. http://dx.doi.org/10.1016/j.yebeh.2015.07.009

Tully, P. J., Cosh, S. M., & Baune, B. T. (2013). A review of the effects of worry and generalized anxiety disorder upon cardiovascular health and coronary heart disease. *Psychology, Health and Medicine, 18*, 627–644. http://dx.doi.org/10.1080/13548506.2012.749355

Vallebona, A., Gigli, G., Orlandi, S., & Reggiardo, G. (2005). Heart rate response to graded exercise correlates with aerobic and ventilatory capacity in patients with heart failure. *Clinical Cardiology, 28*, 25–29. http://dx.doi.org/10.1002/clc.4960280107

Vaschillo, E., Lehrer, P., Rishe, N., & Konstantinov, M. (2002). Heart rate variability biofeedback as a method for assessing baroreflex function: A preliminary study of resonance in the cardiovascular system. *Applied Psychophysiology and Biofeedback, 27*, 1–27. http://dx.doi.org/10.1023/A:1014587304314

Vaschillo, E. G., Vaschillo, B., Buckman, J. F., Pandina, R. J., & Bates, M. E. (2012). Measurement of vascular tone and stroke volume baroreflex gain. *Psychophysiology, 49*, 193–197. http://dx.doi.org/10.1111/j.1469-8986.2011.01305.x

Vaschillo, E. G., Vaschillo, B., & Lehrer, P. M. (2006). Characteristics of resonance in heart rate variability stimulated by biofeedback. *Applied Psychophysiology and Biofeedback, 31*, 129–142. http://dx.doi.org/10.1007/s10484-006-9009-3

Voss, A., Schroeder, R., Heitmann, A., Peters, A., & Perz, S. (2015). Short-term heart rate variability—Influence of gender and age in healthy subjects. *PLoS One, 10*, e0118308. http://dx.doi.org/10.1371/journal.pone.0118308

Wheat, A. L., & Larkin, K. T. (2010). Biofeedback of heart rate variability and related physiology: A critical review. *Applied Psychophysiology and Biofeedback, 35*, 229–242. http://dx.doi.org/10.1007/s10484-010-9133-y

Yaniv, Y., Ahmet, I., Liu, J., Lyashkov, A. E., Guiriba, T.-R., Okamoto, Y., . . . Lakatta, E. G. (2014). Synchronization of sinoatrial node pacemaker cell clocks and its autonomic modulation impart complexity to heart beating intervals. *Heart Rhythm, 11,* 1210–1219. http://dx.doi.org/10.1016/j.hrthm.2014.03.049

Yasuma, F., & Hayano, J. (2004). Respiratory sinus arrhythmia: Why does the heartbeat synchronize with respiratory rhythm? *Chest, 125,* 683–690. http://dx.doi.org/10.1378/chest.125.2.683

Zhang, J., & Wang, N. (2014). Prognostic significance and therapeutic option of heart rate variability in chronic kidney disease. *International Urology and Nephrology, 46,* 19–25. http://dx.doi.org/10.1007/s11255-013-0421-3

PROFESSIONAL DEVELOPMENT  III

Michael J. Lambert

Clinical Measurement and Patient Feedback Systems

8

Although many clinicians view empirical research as irrelevant and alien to their work (Castonguay, Locke, & Hayes, 2011), certain data-driven practices lend themselves to facilitating positive treatment outcomes in routine care. This chapter describes one such approach and provides evidence for its value. First, I briefly describe an approach to outcome monitoring based on the Outcome Questionnaire-Analyst (OQ-A), a data-tracking system for clinicians that has been in use for years. I describe some of our experiences in implementing it and what we have learned. Finally, I provide examples of the way we have collaborated with providers to use the data collected to help make clinical decisions and enhance the outcomes of patients.

The OQ-Analyst System for Monitoring and Enhancing Patient Treatment Response

The OQ-A is a computer-assisted feedback and progress-tracking system designed to help increase psychotherapy treatment effectiveness. Similar tools exist; Drapeau (2012) identified 10 such systems, and more are sure to

Michael J. Lambert is a partner of OQ Measures, a company that owns, markets, and distributes the OQ-Analyst, which includes the measures discussed in this chapter.

http://dx.doi.org/10.1037/0000085-009
Using Technology in Mental Health Practice, J. J. Magnavita (Editor)

come. It cannot be said that each of these rests on a sound (or any) evidence base; thus, the emphasis on the OQ-A in this chapter.

By assessing the attainment of expected progress during therapy, the OQ-A system provides feedback to therapists on whether patients are staying on track toward positive treatment outcomes. This information may be shared with the patient at the therapist's discretion. In addition, the OQ-A can provide decision support to the therapist to maximize the likelihood of a positive outcome for the client. Prior to therapy sessions, patients complete the Outcome Questionnaire 45 (OQ-45), a 45-item self-report measure, or the Youth Outcome Questionnaire–30 (Y-OQ-30), a parent or youth self-report instrument. The OQ-45 and Y-OQ-30 (Lambert et al., 2013) were created specifically to measure and assess real-time change in adult and youth psychotherapy, and therapist can then use the results to identify deteriorating cases and ultimately improve patient outcome prior to treatment termination.

The OQ-45 is designed for repeated administration throughout the course of treatment and at termination. In accordance with several reviews of the literature, the OQ-45 was conceptualized and designed to assess three domains of patient functioning: symptoms of psychological disturbance (particularly anxiety and depression), interpersonal problems, and social role functioning. Consistent with this conceptualization of outcome, the OQ-45 provides a Total Score, based on all 45 items, as well as Symptom Distress, Interpersonal Relations, and Social Role subscale scores. Each of these subscales also contains some items related to the positive quality of life of the individual. Research has indicated that the OQ-45 is a psychometrically sound instrument, with strong internal consistency, adequate test–retest reliability, and strong concurrent validity (Lambert et al., 2013).

Furthermore, the items that make up the OQ-45 have been shown to be sensitive to changes in multiple client populations over short periods of time while remaining relatively stable in untreated individuals (Vermeersch et al., 2004). Evidence from factor analytic studies suggests it measures an overall psychological distress factor, as well as factors consistent with the three subscales (e.g., de Jong et al., 2007). There is also a shortened version of the OQ-45—the Outcome Questionnaire-30—that is in general use with adult patients. Similar measures have been developed for use with children (see http://www.oqmeasures.com).

The Y-OQ (Burlingame et al., 2004) is a 64-item parent/guardian report measure of treatment progress for children and adolescents (ages 4–17) receiving mental health intervention. Similar in its intent to the OQ-45, the Y-OQ is meant to track actual change in functioning as opposed to treatment planning and diagnosis. The Y-OQ is composed of 64 items in six separate subscales designed to tap diverse elements of healthy and unhealthy youth functioning: are Interpersonal Distress (ID), Somatic Complaints (S), Intrapersonal Relations (IP), Critical Items (CI), Social Problems (SP), and Behavioral Dysfunction (BD). The Youth Outcome Questionnaire Self-Report (Y-OQ-SR) is the equivalent self-report measure completed by youth ages 12 to 17 years. In addition, a shorter form, the Y-OQ-30, is available for parents, clinicians, and youth.

In short, the OQ and Y-OQ are brief measures of psychological disturbance that are reliable, valid, and sensitive to changes patients make during psychotherapy.

They are well suited for tracking patient status during and following treatment, and they provide clinicians with a mental health vital sign. The measures have been extensively reviewed elsewhere (Burlingame et al., 2004; Lambert et al., 2013; see also http://www.oqmeasures.com).

Responses to the questions are entered into a computer with the OQ-A via hand-held devices, computer kiosk, online, or by hardcopy, and a report is generated for use by the therapist. The OQ-A also uses responses to a 40-item measure (Assessment for Signal Clients) to measure the quality of the therapeutic alliance, client motivation/expectation, quality of social supports, negative life events, and possible need for change in treatment (e.g., medication referral). A similar clinical support tool is available for children. The OQ-A then suggests possible courses of action. The OQ-A is designed to detect treatment effectiveness regardless of treatment modality, diagnosis, or therapy type. Questions are answered in relation to the last week of the patient's life.

The OQ-A software system is available for $200 per clinician per year. This is based on an average of 200 clients per year per clinician, at $1 per client per year. The cost includes unlimited administrations for each client, along with scoring, alerts, and progress profiling. A fully hosted web-based system is available using a prorated cost model for organizations that serve more than 1,000 patients per year and employ more than 50 clinicians. The initial start-up costs for the hosted system average about $3 per patient per year, which includes software and hardware, and yearly costs thereafter are under $1 per patient per year. Both cost models deliver an unlimited number of administrations per patient providing an incentive to repeatedly track patients at no additional cost (i.e., there are no per-administration charges), with technical assistance/installation support available for about $150.

Why Would Clinicians Want to Include the Use of the OQ-Analyst in Routine Care?

Hansen, Lambert, and Forman (2002) examined a representative sample of randomized clinical trial outcomes based on 89 treatment comparisons (mostly cognitive–behavioral therapy) and reported an average of 57% to 67% recovered or improved after receiving an average of 12 to 13 sessions of treatment. These outcomes were contrasted with those found in over 6,000 clients who participated in routine care that lasted an average of four sessions, with patients ranging from those treated in community mental health centers to those being seen in employee assistance programs. Rates of improvement/recovery averaged 35%, and deterioration varied from a low of 3.2% to a high of 14%, with an average rate of 8%. Even when an empirically supported treatment is offered to individuals who have the same disorder and see therapists who have been carefully selected, monitored, and supervised, 30% to 50% of patients fail to respond to treatment. This means that, even if there were a right treatment or best practice for an individual, we would need to identify patients who are failing to respond to this treatment—feeding this information back to clinicians who can then take appropriate actions before these clients departed from their care. The major assumption of this practice is that clinicians can, in fact, identify poorly responding patients in a timely fashion and then take timely actions that will benefit them.

The situation for child and adolescent outcomes in routine care is even more sobering than that for adult populations. The small body of outcome studies in community-based usual care settings has yielded an overall mean effect size near zero (e.g., Weiss, Catron, Harris, & Phung, 1999), yet millions of youth are served each year in these systems of care (National Advisory Mental Health Council, 2001). In a comparison of children being treated in community mental health ($n = 936$) or through managed care ($n = 3,075$), estimates of deterioration were 24% and 14%, respectively (Warren, Nelson, Mondragon, Baldwin, & Burlingame, 2010). Furthermore, increased attention to deterioration in treatment may be warranted given the high rates of treatment dropout observed in clinical practice. It is estimated that 40% to 60% of children and adolescents discontinue treatment prematurely (Kazdin, 1996; Wierzbicki & Pekarik, 1993); many of these dropouts are likely due to perceived lack of benefit from treatment. With regard to measuring treatment response in child and adolescent psychotherapy, Kazdin (2005) noted that "such information would be enormously helpful if used to monitor and evaluate treatment in clinical practice" (p. 555).

Unfortunately, clinicians' views of their own clients' outcomes are much more positive than measured outcomes using self-report scales. Walfish et al.'s (2012) survey of clinicians suggests that such practitioners estimate that about 85% of their clients are improving or recovering. In addition, they have the common impression that they are unusually successful with their own patients—90% rate themselves in the upper quartile and none see themselves as below average (50th percentile) in providing services. Another serious problem in practice is that doubts exist about the ability of clinicians to identify clients during the course of therapy who ultimately deteriorate and to note worsening during treatment as a warning sign of deterioration and treatment failure (Hannan et al., 2005; Hatfield et al., 2010). Clinicians could benefit from using the tracking systems because of their likely overly optimistic estimates of their patients' outcome and their inability to predict treatment failure, specifically negative change. At relatively little cost, therapists can formally measure, monitor, and track patient well-being and change, as well as predict treatment response, especially with patients who worsen during the course of treatment.

Sapyta, Riemer, and Bickman (2005) reviewed the effects of feedback on human performance and indicated that its effectiveness is likely to vary as a function of the degree of discrepancy between therapists' views of progress and measured progress, and that the greater the discrepancy, the more likely such feedback will be helpful. A key element of effective feedback is bringing into the recipient's awareness the discrepancy between what the clinician thinks is happening and what the client or patient actually feels, thereby prompting corrective action. In general, this research supports the conclusion that feedback in clinical practice improves patient outcome.

This finding is consistent with feedback theories (e.g., Riemer & Bickman, 2004) that suggest feedback will only change behavior when the information provided indicates the individual is not meeting an established standard. Riemer and colleagues (Riemer & Bickman, 2004; Riemer, Rosof-Williams, & Bickman, 2005) have developed a contextual feedback intervention theory to explain how feedback is interpreted and made useful. Basic tenets of this theory are that clinicians (and professionals, generally) will benefit from feedback if (a) they are committed to the goal of improving their performance; (b) they are aware of a discrepancy between the goal and reality (particularly if the goal is attractive and the clinician believes it can be accomplished); (c) the feedback source is credible; (d) feedback is immediate, frequent, systematic, cognitively simple (e.g., graphic in nature) and unambiguous; and (e) it provides clinicians with concrete suggestions for how to improve.

If clinicians do not consider feedback as credible, valid, informative, or useful, they are more likely to dismiss it whenever it does not fit their own observations. As research on cognitive dissonance shows, people can change attitudes rather than persevering toward a goal, thus regarding the goal as less important, or clinicians can see a client as too resistant or injured to benefit from treatment (e.g., disown personal responsibility for meeting the goal of positive functioning; Riemer, Rosof-Williams, & Bickman, 2005). As feedback research suggests, the value of monitoring and systematic feedback through psychological assessments hinges on the degree to which the information provided goes beyond what a clinician can observe and understand about patient progress without such information. It is important for the information to add something to the psychotherapist's view of patient well-being and future actions. Unfortunately, clinicians may have an overly optimistic view of their patients' progress (Walfish et al., 2012). Clinicians may also overlook negative changes and have a limited capacity to make accurate predictions of the final benefit clients will receive during treatment, particularly when clients are failing to improve. One study, for example, found that even when therapists were provided with the base rate of deterioration in the clinic where they worked (8%), and were asked to rate each client that they saw at the end of each session (i.e., with regard to the likelihood of treatment failure and the current condition of the patient compared with their intake level of functioning), they rated only three of 550 clients as predicted failures and seriously underestimated worsened functioning for a significant portion of clients (Hannan et al., 2005). Further, a retrospective review of case notes of clients who had deteriorated during treatment found infrequent mention of worsening (perhaps 20%–30% of clients), even when its degree was dramatic (Hatfield et al., 2010).

Such results are not surprising given psychotherapist optimism about their ability to help; the complexity of persons; and a treatment context that calls for considerable commitment and determination on the part of the therapist, who actually has little control over the patient's life circumstances and personal characteristics. Patients' response to treatment is, especially in the case of a worsening state, a likely place where outside feedback might have the greatest chance of impact. Helping the therapist become aware of negative change and discussing such progress in the therapeutic encounter are much more likely when formal feedback is provided to therapists. Such feedback helps the client communicate and helps the therapist to become aware of the possible need to adjust treatment—alter or address problems in the therapeutic relationship or in the implementation of treatment goals.

A core element of these feedback systems is the prediction of treatment failure. To improve outcomes for clients who are responding poorly to treatment, therapists must identify such clients before termination and, ideally, as early as possible in the course of treatment. The OQ system plots a statistically generated expected recovery curve for differing levels of pretreatment distress and uses this as a basis for identifying clients who are not making expected treatment gains and are at risk of having a poor outcome. The accuracy of this signal-alarm system has been evaluated in a number of empirical investigations (e.g., Ellsworth, Lambert, & Johnson, 2006; Lambert, Whipple, Bishop, et al., 2002; Lutz et al., 2006; Spielmans, Masters, & Lambert, 2006). This research shows that 85% to 100% of clients who deteriorate in treatment can be accurately identified prior to departing from treatment. A sample feedback report for the OQ-45 is provided in Figure 8.1.

Clients can complete a brief measure of their psychological function by using standardized rating scales, and then this information can be delivered to psychotherapists in real time. In addition to alerting therapists to deviations from expected treatment response, the material gathered from patients provides novel information. Collecting this information from the client on a session-by-session basis provides the clinician with a systematic way of monitoring life functioning from the client's point of view. A brief formal assessment can provide a summary of life functioning that is not otherwise available to the therapist, unless the therapist uses time in the treatment hour to systematically inquire about all the areas of functioning covered by the self-report scale, an activity that detracts from service delivery.

The use of outcome monitoring is akin to physicians' use of lab tests and vital sign measurement and tracking in the management of physical disease. But consider the tortured history of physicians' relationship with technological advances in measuring body temperature as an example of resistance to the adoption of useful innovations in practice. The thermometer was invented 250 years before German physician Carl Wunderlich published *The Course of Temperature in Diseases in 1668*. Despite the ability to objectively and reliably measure temperature, clinicians were not employing this technological advancement in routine care but were content instead to rely on the touching of various parts of the patient's body. Wunderlich presented temperature data he had systematically collected from more than 25,000 patients, finding that the average normal temperature of a healthy person was 98.6 degrees Fahrenheit, with an upper limit of 100.4 degrees. These findings became the first objective and quantitative definition of a fever, eventually replacing physicians' diagnosis of fever from their personal blend of intuition and clinical experience based on touching the patient.

In his book, Wunderlich went further and proposed a radical idea: Physicians could determine the course of an illness by reading their patients' temperature at regular intervals. Physicians were instructed to record the temperature readings by making dots on a chart. Drawing a line through the dots created a graph that would show the course of a disease. This proposal, termed *clinical thermometry*, suggested that a fever is a symptom of an illness, rather than the illness itself as had been assumed during the previous millennia of medical practice.

Physicians of the day did not receive clinical thermometry with eager acceptance. The thermometers were difficult to use. They were cumbersome—almost a foot long—and it took 20 to 25 minutes to register a patient's temperature. The

FIGURE 8.1

Name:	C-OQ45, GEORGE, R	ID:	MRN0101
Session Date:	12/25/2006	Session:	1
Clinician:	Clinician, Bob	Clinic:	TX Dallas Clinic
Diagnosis:	Unknown Diagnosis		
Instrument:	ASC		

Subscales	Current Scores	Alerts
Therapeutic Alliance:	39	RED
Social Support:	36	
Motivation:	30	RED
Life Events:	29	

`Display Interventions Handout`

Therapeutic Alliance: RED
It is advisable that you address your relationship with the client. Please click 'Display Interventions Handout' button for more information.

1. I felt cared for and respected as a person.	Neutral
2. I felt my therapist understood me.	Neutral
3. I thought the suggestions my therapist made were useful.	Neutral
4. I felt like I could trust my therapist completely.	Slightly Agree
9. My therapist seemed to be glad to see me.	Neutral
10. My therapist and I seemed to work well together to accomplish what I want.	Slightly Disagree
11. My therapist and I had a similar understanding of my problems.	Strongly Disagree

Social Support:

15. I got the emotional help and support I needed from someone in my family.	Strongly Disagree
16. There was a special person who was around when I was in need.	Neutral
21. I felt connected to a higher power.	Strongly Disagree

Motivation: RED
It is advisable that you address your client's motivation in therapy. Please click 'Display Interventions Handout' button for more information.

23. I wonder what I am doing in therapy; actually I find it boring.	Slightly Agree
26. I had thoughts about quitting therapy; it's just not for me.	Slightly Agree
27. I don't think therapy will help me feel any better.	Neutral
28. I have no desire to work out my problems.	Strongly Agree
31. I am in therapy because someone is requiring it of me.	Neutral

Life Events:

32. I had an interaction with another person that I found upsetting.	Strongly Agree
38. I had health problems (such as physical pain).	Strongly Agree

REMINDER: THE USER IS SOLELY RESPONSIBLE FOR ANY AND ALL DECISIONS AFFECTING PATIENT CARE. THE OQ®-A IS NOT A DIAGNOSTIC TOOL AND SHOULD NOT BE USED AS SUCH. IT IS NOT A SUBSTITUTE FOR A MEDICAL OR PROFESSIONAL EVALUATION. RELIANCE ON THE OQ®-A IS AT USER'S SOLE RISK AND RESPONSIBILITY. (SEE LICENSE FOR FULL STATEMENT OF RIGHTS, RESPONSIBILITIES & DISCLAIMERS)

Sample feedback report for the OQ-45. Copyright 2017 by OQ Measures. Reprinted with permission.

thermometers had reliability problems, and medical staff weren't sure about the best ways to use them.

Quite aside from the inconvenience, many physicians were affronted by the suggestion that they should consider data from medical instruments to inform their diagnosis, rather than relying on their trained senses and the clinical wisdom that had been accrued from years of experience. Some even worried that the use of thermometers would lead to the loss of important clinical skills. Some 150 years later, psychotherapy metrics delivered via computer have received the same reaction. When feedback systems are made available, half or fewer of therapists actually use them (that rate is even lower among private practitioners), despite mounting evidence that proper use of outcome measures and normative data can enhance treatment outcome. In my experience the routine adoption of progress and outcome data is very low because of the belief that clinical intuition is superior to quantitative data and a computer—which cannot possibly capture the subtle, nuanced texture of psychotherapy. Thus, many clinicians feel the whole idea can be rejected at face value.

The first part of this argument is probably correct: Psychotherapy measurements can't capture the full range of psychological functioning any more than a thermometer can detect cancer, diabetes, or heart disease. Furthermore, collecting psychotherapy data can't cure mental illness any more than sticking a thermometer in a patient's mouth can cure the flu. Feedback data itself are not helpful unless clinicians know how to use the data to improve treatment.

Medical historian A. J. Youngson (1979) wrote, "It is probably true that one of the commonest features of new ideas—certainly of practical new ideas—is their imperfection" (p. 225). Although the thermometer was invented in the early 17th century, it took two and a half more centuries of experimentation by prominent scientists (including German engineer Daniel Fahrenheit and Swedish astronomer Anders Celsius) before Wunderlich developed a reliable system for clinical thermometry. The development of feedback-assisted treatment using standardized scales is similarly new to routine care and also limited in value, yet, as I will document, it has substantial value in routine care.

In conjunction with identifying alarm status, the Assessment for Signal Cases (ASC; Lambert, Bailey, White, Tingey, & Stevens, 2015) was developed to assist clinicians in problem solving with clients who backslide during treatment (i.e., when a therapist receives a warning message predicting deterioration). This 40-item measure does not produce a total score but instead provides subscale score feedback and item feedback for therapists to consider in problem solving. For example, the first 11 items of the ASC require the client to reflect on the therapeutic relationship and report his or her perceptions. The ASC is central to the Clinical Support Tool (CST), which is composed of a problem-solving decision tree designed to systematically direct therapists' attention to subscales and the following items: the therapeutic alliance, social support, readiness to change, diagnostic formulation, life events, and need for medication referral. A sample feedback report for the ASC is provided in Figure 8.2.

FIGURE 8.2

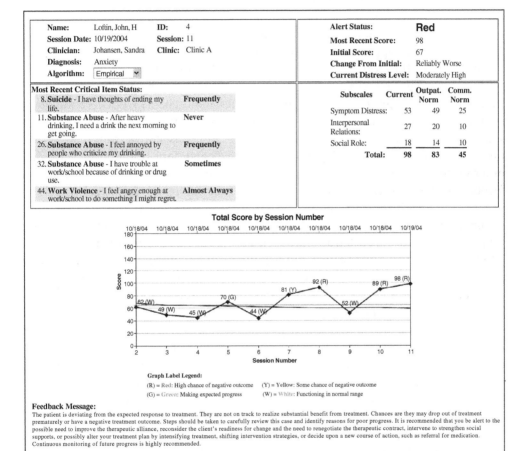

Sample feedback report for the ASC. Copyright 2017 by OQ Measures.
Reprinted with permission.

Review of the Evidence Base

Methods incorporated in the OQ-A are clearly helpful to patients (Shimokawa, Lambert, & Smart, 2010). The Shimokawa meta/mega-analysis sums the effects of monitoring patients on a weekly basis by looking across six clinical trials. In these published studies, each therapist was asked to practice as they routinely do with half their caseload while using the OQ-A information with the other half of their caseload. In this recent meta-analytic review of the OQ system, Shimokawa et al. (2010) reanalyzed the combined data set ($N = 6,151$) from all six OQ feedback studies published up to that date (Harmon et al., 2007; Hawkins, Lambert, Vermeersch, Slade, & Tuttle, 2004; Lambert, Whipple, et al., 2001; Lambert, Whipple, Vermeersch, et al., 2002; Slade, Lambert, Harmon, Smart, & Bailey, 2008; Whipple et al., 2003). Each of the studies evaluated the effects of providing feedback about each client's improvement through the use of progress graphs and warnings about clients who were not demonstrating expected treatment responses (i.e., signal-alarm cases). The six studies shared many design and methodological features: (a) consecutive cases seen in routine care regardless of client diagnosis or comorbid conditions (rather than being disorder specific); (b) random assignment of clients to experimental conditions (various feedback interventions) and treatment-as-usual conditions (no feedback) was made in four of the six studies, while reasonable measures were taken in the two other studies to ensure equivalence in experimental and control conditions at pretreatment; (c) psychotherapists provided a variety of theoretically guided treatments, with most adhering to cognitive behavioral and eclectic orientations and fewer representing psychodynamic and experiential orientations; (d) a variety of therapist experience— postgraduate therapists and graduate students each accounted for about 50% of clients seen; (e) all therapists saw both experimental (feedback) and no feedback cases, thus limiting the likelihood that outcome differences between conditions could be due to therapist effects; (f) the outcome measure as well as the methodology rules/ standards for identifying signal-alarm clients (failing cases) remained constant; and (g) the length of therapy (dosage) was determined by client and therapist, rather than by research design or arbitrary insurance limits. The meta-analysis involved both intent-to-treat and efficacy analyses on the effects of various feedback interventions relative to TAU. Here, only those clients who received and completed the treatments were compared to treatment-as-usual. The summary of effect sizes is presented in Table 8.1.

Clients whose therapist did and did not receive feedback were randomly assigned to the treatment condition and followed until they left therapy, whenever that occurred. Thus, the research question was: Do therapists who get the feedback have patients who have better outcomes (relative to the outcomes they achieve without such feedback), and if so, how much better?

A key element in psychotherapy research is operationalizing the concepts of positive and negative outcome for the individual client. Jacobson and Truax (1991) offered a methodology by which client changes on an outcome measure can be classified into the following categories: recovered, reliably improved, no change, deteriorated. Two

TABLE 8.1

Clinical Significance Classification of Not-On-Track Clients by Treatment Conditions

Clinical significance	Treatment conditions (efficacy sample)			
	CST Fb	NOT P/T Fb	NOT Fb	NOT TAU
Worsened/deteriorated	5.5%	14.7%	9.1%	20.1%
No change	41.9%	40.1%	53.2%	57.5%
Improved/recovered	52.5%	45.2%	37.6%	22.3%

Note. CST Fb = Clinical Support Tool Feedback and progress feedback with alarm signals; NOT P/T = not-on-track clients whose therapists provided them with written feedback; NOT = not-on-track clients whose therapist was provided with progress feedback with alarm signals; NOT TAU = treatment-as-usual with not-on-track clients.

pieces of information are necessary to make these client-outcome classifications: A Reliable Change Index (RCI) and a normal functioning cutoff score. Clinical and normative data were analyzed by Lambert et al. (2013) to establish an RCI and a cutoff score for normal functioning. These two cutoffs when combined denote clinically significant change (recovery).

The first discovery suggested by the findings of the studies was that feedback was not especially helpful for all clients. Clients who make relatively steady progress continue to do so even when their therapists are notified that the progress from week-to-week is typical and nonproblematic. This holds true for the majority of patients in a typical clinician's caseload, and reflects the fact that therapy as it is routinely practiced is helping many individuals. The feedback did make a marked difference for clients who went significantly off-track (about 20%–40% of treated individuals, depending on the study sample). So an important finding from our studies is that a clinician cannot expect every client to benefit from feedback. We believe this is because the novel information that the clinician needs is that the client is not responding as expected.

EFFECTS OF OQ PROGRESS FEEDBACK (Fb) ON AT-RISK CLIENTS

These results suggest that the average client whose therapist received feedback was better off than approximately 70% of clients in the no feedback condition (i.e., with just routine care). In terms of the clinical significance at termination, 9% of those receiving feedback deteriorated and 38% achieved clinically significant improvement. In contrast, among clients whose therapists did not receive feedback, 20% deteriorated and 22% achieved clinically significant improvement. When the odds of deterioration and clinically significant improvement were compared, results indicated those in the feedback group had less than half the odds of experiencing deterioration, while having approximately 2.6 times higher odds of experiencing reliable improvement.

EFFECTS OF PATIENT/THERAPIST FEEDBACK (P/T Fb) ON AT-RISK CLIENTS

The effect size of the posttreatment OQ score averaged $g = .55$, $r = .25$, $p < .001$—effects very similar to that of the therapist-only feedback group. The rates of deterioration and clinically significant improvement, when both participants received written feedback, were 15% and 45%, respectively. The results suggest that clients who received feedback along with their therapist had approximately 0.7 times the odds of deterioration, while having approximately 3 times higher odds of achieving clinically significant improvement. These results suggest that although the average client who received feedback along with their therapist was better off than 71% of clients in treatment-as-usual, there may have been moderators that facilitated outcome enhancement in some clients while failing to prevent, or possibly contributing to, worsening.

EFFECTS OF CST Fb ON AT-RISK CLIENTS

When the outcomes of clients whose therapist received the CST feedback were compared with those of the treatment-as-usual clients, the effect size for the difference in mean posttreatment OQ scores was $g = 0.70$, $r = .33$, $p < .001$. These results indicate that the average client in the CST feedback group, who stayed in treatment to experience the benefit of this intervention, is better off than 76% of clients in treatment-as-usual. The rates of deterioration and clinically significant improvement among those receiving CST were 6% and 53%, respectively. The results suggest that clients whose therapists used CST have less than one fourth the odds of deterioration, while having approximately 3.9 times higher odds of achieving clinically significant improvement compared with treatment-as-usual provided by the same therapists. In the case of the off-track clients, notifying therapists that the client was in trouble allowed them to change the future course of therapy progress and outcome—therapists and clients found a way to turn the treatment course around.

Unfortunately, today most formal monitoring of patient mental health is being imposed on clinicians by systems of care that have come to realize that such practices can enhance patient outcomes or because they believe that the gathered data can be used to increase the quality of care offered to patients through accountability measures, which provides clinicians with further reasons to resist monitoring—we do not like external control and management. Nevertheless, it appears that this research-based innovation (formal monitoring and problem-solving) has little downside for clinicians (it is cheap and effective) and large upsides for patients.

There is no doubt that all of the deterioration that occurs during the time a patient is in treatment cannot be causally linked to therapist activities. Certainly, a portion of patients are on a negative trajectory at the time they enter treatment and the deteriorating course cannot be stopped. However, a portion of patients are prevented from taking their own lives as a result of effective practices, even if they do not show overall progress. Just as positive psychotherapy outcomes depend largely on patient characteristics, so do the negative changes that occur in patients who are undergoing psychological treatments.

Scope of Application

Since the meta/mega analysis of feedback studies was published, additional studies have been completed. These studies have demonstrated that feedback effects have a broad scope that reaches across clinical samples, treatment settings, and different nations. Table 8.2 provides an overview of the original, as well as the newer, studies. One of the newer published studies (Crits-Christoph et al., 2012) considered the effects of progress feedback and CSTs on substance abusing individuals in Philadelphia, New York, and Utah. In this study, the patients were, for the most part, from urban clinics and had chronic problems with high levels of comorbidity. Their treatment was subsidized by government agencies.

Simon et al. (2013) studied these methods with female eating-disordered patients treated in an inpatient setting. These individuals had chronic courses and high levels of co-morbidity. Of considerable interest for the effects of feedback was the high level of intensive treatment that all patients received over an approximately 30-day stay in the hospital. The treatment included individual therapy twice weekly, group psycho-therapy twice weekly, psychoeducation, numerous and varied recreational activities, nutritional counseling, with 90% of patients taking psychoactive medication. With such comprehensive and intense treatment, we had our doubts about the likelihood

TABLE 8.2

Published Clinical Trials Examining the Effects of Progress Monitoring With Alarm Signals and Clerical Support, Total Feedback Using the OQ-45

Study	N total/NOT[a]	Setting/ sample[b]	Significant effect	CST	Effect size (d)
Lambert et al., 2001	*609/66*	CC	Yes	No	.44
Lambert et al., 2002	1,422/240	CC	Yes	No	.40
Whipple et al., 2003	1,339/278	CC	Yes	Yes	.70
Hawkins et al., 2004	306/101	OP	Yes	No	.28
Harmon et al., 2007	1,374/369	CC	Yes	Yes	.73
Slade et al., 2008	1,101/328	CC	Yes	Yes	.75
Crits-Christoph et al., 2012	*304/116*	SA	Yes	Yes	.48
Simon et al., 2012	370/207	OP	Yes	Yes	.12/.34
Simon et al., 2013	133/59	ED/IP	Yes	Yes	.36
de Jong et al., 2012[c]	413/67	OP	No/Yes	No	?
Amble et al., 2015[d]	259/?	OP	Yes	No	.32
Probst et al., 2014[e]	252/66	IP/Som	Yes	Yes	.54

[a]The study *N* = the total sample; NOT = NOT Cases = Predicted treatment failure; [b]CC= college counseling center clients; OP = outpatient clinics; SA = substance abuse clinics; ED = eating disorder patients; IP = inpatient treatment setting; Som = psychosomatic patients; [c]Study conducted in the Netherlands; [d]Study conducted in Norway; [e]Study conducted in Germany.

that the effects of the feedback interventions could be detected. It was also true that the clinical staff (as is typical in our research studies) saw no need for formal tracking and feedback, and so were not eager adaptors of the methodology. Nevertheless, treatment effects were apparent and substantial, much to the surprise of all.

The final three studies in Table 8.2 were conducted outside the United States—in multiple clinics within the Netherlands and Norway and in an inpatient psychosomatic hospital in Germany. Data from these studies suggest that the effects of progress feedback are robust enough to translate cross-culturally in both in- and out-patient settings. In the Dutch study (de Jong et al., 2012) and in Simon et al. (2012) we came across our first evidence that feedback effects are absent if clinicians do not examine the feedback reports.

Major limitations of feedback research are the moderate number of studies evaluating effectiveness, the limited number of researchers responsible for the findings reviewed here, and the sole reliance on self-report measures as a method of identifying patients at risk for deterioration, as well as identifying final treatment status. It is likely that future research will be done across a wider range of treatment settings and patient populations, thus illuminating the limits of these procedures and clarifying the factors that maximize patient gains. The research reviewed here utilized two self-report measures and just two different methods of providing feedback and, therefore, presented a limited view of the impact of therapy and the effects of feedback. Another important limitation is the degree to which there exists unpublished studies that did not find an effect for feedback. This is commonly known as the *file-drawer problem*, which reflects the tendency of authors to submit articles with no significant findings and the hesitancy of journals to publish such studies if they are submitted.

As noted earlier in the chapter, similar tools to the OQ-A are emerging. When considering adoption of a progress monitoring system, consider the following as essential components: the ability to track on a weekly basis, published evidence of predictive accuracy for identifying likely treatment failures, and reliance on information technology such as online administration that allows for immediate, timely feedback.

Recommended Therapeutic Practices

- Use real-time client feedback to monitor patients' response to psychotherapy and satisfaction with the therapy relationship and other hindering forces. Such feedback probably improves psychotherapy outcomes and certainly does so for clients at risk for deterioration or dropout.
- Employ real-time client feedback to compensate for therapists' limited ability to accurately detect client worsening in psychotherapy. Despite considerable evidence that psychotherapists are not alert to treatment failure (e.g., Hannan et al., 2005; Hatfield et al., 2010), and strong evidence that clinical judgments are usually inferior to actuarial methods, therapists' confidence in their clinical judgment stands as a barrier to implementation of monitoring and feedback systems.

▪ Beware of those situations in which clients feel it may be in their interest to understate (or overstate) their problems and produce inaccurate ratings on feedback systems. The systems are predicated on accurate self-reporting of levels of disturbance and corresponding changes.

▪ Supplement with clinical support tools. As suggested by the general literature on feedback and the evidence presented here, problem-solving and decision-enhancement tools prove helpful to clinicians and, most importantly, to clients whose treatment response is in doubt.

▪ As yet, we are uncertain of the necessity of sharing progress feedback directly with clients. The OQ system has examined therapist feedback and direct client feedback separately with inconclusive results about additive effectiveness of direct client feedback.

▪ Consider using electronic versions of feedback systems that expedite and ease practical difficulties. Fortunately, the recent software for the OQ can provide instantaneous feedback to clinicians. If the client takes the OQ immediately before the scheduled psychotherapy session, electronic feedback is available to the therapist prior to beginning that session.

Benefits of Incorporating Client Feedback in Clinical Practice

In addition to the obvious benefits to clients of incorporating progress feedback methods, the OQ-A allows one to accumulate data on therapist effects, as well as effects within diagnostic and other groupings. Basic statistical summaries that characterize outcomes within individual and clinic caseloads are maintained that describe outcomes, which are immediately updated each time a new patient is treated (e.g., the percentage of patients who complete treatment as reliably improved or recovered).

Essential Resources

Clinicians and administrators can go to http://www.oqmeasures.com for further information about the OQ-A, including the opportunity to demo the software, obtain test manuals, and read about technical requirements, and so on. An annotated bibliography of research studies is also available at this site.

References

Amble, I., Gude, T., Stubdal, S., Andersen, B. J., & Wampold, B. E. (2015). The effect of implementing the Outcome Questionnaire-45.2 feedback system in Norway: A multisite randomized clinical trial in a naturalistic setting. *Psychotherapy Research, 25*, 669–677. http://dx.doi.org/10.1080/10503307.2014.928756

Burlingame, G. M., Wells, M. G., Lambert, M. J., & Cox, J. C. (2004). Youth Outcome Questionnaire (Y-OQ). In M. E. Maruish (Ed.), *The use of psychological testing for treatment planning and outcome assessment: Instruments for children and adolescents* (3rd ed., Vol. 2, pp. 235–274). Mahwah, NJ: Lawrence Erlbaum Associates.

Castonguay, L. G., Locke, B. D., & Hayes, J. A. (2011). The Center for Collegiate Mental Health: An example of a practice-research network in university counseling centers. *Journal of College Student Psychotherapy, 25*, 105–119. http://dx.doi.org/10.1080/87568225.2011.556929

Crits-Christoph, P., Ring-Kurtz, S., Hamilton, J. L., Lambert, M. J., Gallop, R., McClure, B., . . . Rotrosen, J. (2012). A preliminary study of the effects of individual patient-level feedback in outpatient substance abuse treatment programs. *Journal of Substance Abuse Treatment, 42*, 301–309. http://dx.doi.org/10.1016/j.jsat.2011.09.003

de Jong, K., Nugter, M. A., Polak, M. G., Wagenborg, J. E. A., Spinhoven, P., & Heiser, W. J. (2007). The Outcome Questionnaire (OQ-45) in a Dutch population: A cross-cultural validation. *Clinical Psychology & Psychotherapy, 14*, 288–301. http://dx.doi.org/10.1002/cpp.529

de Jong, K., Van Sluis, P., Nutger, A., Heiser, W. J., & Spinhoven, P. (2012). Understanding the differential impact of outcome monitoring: Therapist variables that moderate feedback effects in a randomized clinical trial. *Psychotherapy Research, 22*, 464–474. http://dx.doi.org/10.1080/10503307.2012.673023

Drapeau, M. (2012). The value of progress tracking in psychotherapy. *Integrating Science and Practice, 2*(2), 5–43.

Ellsworth, J. R., Lambert, M. J., & Johnson, J. (2006). A comparison of the Outcome Questionnaire-45 and Outcome Questionnaire-30 in classification and prediction of treatment outcome. *Clinical Psychology & Psychotherapy, 13*, 380–391. http://dx.doi.org/10.1002/cpp.503

Hannan, C., Lambert, M. J., Harmon, C., Nielsen, S. L., Smart, D. W., Shimokawa, K., & Sutton, S. W. (2005). A lab test and algorithms for identifying clients at risk for treatment failure. *Journal of Clinical Psychology, 61*, 155–163. http://dx.doi.org/10.1002/jclp.20108

Hansen, N. B., Lambert, M. J., & Forman, E. M. (2002). The psychotherapy dose-response effect and its implications for treatment delivery services. *Clinical Psychology: Science and Practice, 9*, 329–343. http://dx.doi.org/10.1093/clipsy.9.3.329

Harmon, S. C., Lambert, M. J., Smart, D. M., Hawkins, E., Nielsen, S. L., Slade, K., & Lutz, W. (2007). Enhancing outcome for potential treatment failures: Therapist–client feedback and clinical support tools. *Psychotherapy Research, 17*, 379–392. http://dx.doi.org/10.1080/10503300600702331

Hatfield, D., McCullough, L., Frantz, S. H. B., & Krieger, K. (2010). Do we know when our clients get worse? An investigation of therapists' ability to detect negative client change. *Clinical Psychology & Psychotherapy, 17*, 25–32. http://dx.doi.org/10.1002/cpp.656

Hawkins, E. J., Lambert, M. J., Vermeersch, D. A., Slade, K. L., & Tuttle, K. C. (2004). The therapeutic effects of providing patient progress information to therapists and patients. *Psychotherapy Research, 14*, 308–327. http://dx.doi.org/10.1093/ptr/kph027

Jacobson, N. S., & Truax, P. (1991). Clinical significance: A statistical approach to defining meaningful change in psychotherapy research. *Journal of Consulting and Clinical Psychology, 59*, 12–19. http://dx.doi.org/10.1037/0022-006X.59.1.12

Kazdin, A. E. (1996). Dropping out of child psychotherapy: Issues for research and implications for practice. *Clinical Child Psychology and Psychiatry, 1*, 133–156. http://dx.doi.org/10.1177/1359104596011012

Kazdin, A. E. (2005). Evidence-based assessment for children and adolescents: Issues in measurement development and clinical application. *Journal of Clinical Child and Adolescent Psychology, 34*, 548–558. http://dx.doi.org/10.1207/s15374424jccp3403_10

Lambert, M. J., Bailey, R. J., White, M., Tingey, K. M., & Stevens, E. (2015). *Clinical Support Tool Manual—Brief Version-40*. Salt Lake City, UT: OQ Measures.

Lambert, M. J., Kahler, M., Harmon, C., Burlingame, G. M., Shimokawa, K., & White, M. M. (2013). *Administration and Scoring Manual: Outcome Questionnaire OQ®-45.2*. Salt Lake City, UT: OQ Measures.

Lambert, M. J., Whipple, J. L., Bishop, M. J., Vermeersch, D. A., Gray, G. V., & Finch, A. E. (2002). Comparison of empirically-derived and rationally-derived methods for identifying clients at risk for treatment failure. *Clinical Psychology & Psychotherapy, 9*, 149–164. http://dx.doi.org/10.1002/cpp.333

Lambert, M. J., Whipple, J. L., Smart, D. W., Vermeersch, D. A., Nielsen, S. L., & Hawkins, E. J. (2001). The effects of providing therapists with feedback on patient progress during psychotherapy: Are outcomes enhanced? *Psychotherapy Research, 11*, 49–68. http://dx.doi.org/10.1080/713663852

Lambert, M. J., Whipple, J. L., Vermeersch, D. A., Smart, D. W., Hawkins, E. J., Nielsen, S. L., & Goates, M. (2002). Enhancing psychotherapy outcomes via providing feedback on client progress: A replication. *Clinical Psychology & Psychotherapy, 9*, 91–103. http://dx.doi.org/10.1002/cpp.324

Lutz, W., Lambert, M. J., Harmon, S. C., Stulz, N., Tschitsaz, A., Schürch, E., & Stulz, N. (2006). The probability of treatment success, failure and duration—what can be learned from empirical data to support decision making in clinical practice? *Clinical Psychology & Psychotherapy, 13*, 223–232. http://dx.doi.org/10.1002/cpp.496

National Advisory Mental Health Council. (2001). *Blueprint for change: Research on child and adolescent mental health: Report of the National Advisory Mental Health Council's Workgroup on Child and Adolescent Mental Health Intervention Development and Deployment*. Bethesda, MD: National Institute of Mental Health.

Probst, T., Lambert, M. J., Dahlbender, R. W., Loew, T. W., & Tritt, K. (2014). Providing patient progress feedback and clinical support tools to therapists: Is the therapeutic process of patients on-track to recovery enhanced in psychosomatic in-patient therapy under the conditions of routine practice? *Journal of Psychosomatic Research, 76*, 477–484. http://dx.doi.org/10.1016/j.jpsychores.2014.03.010

Riemer, M., & Bickman, L. (2004). *The contextualized feedback intervention theory: A theory of guided behavior change*. Unpublished manuscript, Center for Evaluation and Program Improvement, Peabody College, Vanderbilt University.

Riemer, M., Rosof-Williams, J., & Bickman, L. (2005). Theories related to changing clinician practice. *Child and Adolescent Psychiatric Clinics of North America, 14*, 241–254. http://dx.doi.org/10.1016/j.chc.2004.05.002

Sapyta, J., Riemer, M., & Bickman, L. (2005). Feedback to clinicians: Theory, research, and practice. *Journal of Clinical Psychology, 61*, 145–153. http://dx.doi.org/10.1002/jclp.20107

Shimokawa, K., Lambert, M. J., & Smart, D. W. (2010). Enhancing treatment outcome of patients at risk of treatment failure: Meta-analytic and mega-analytic review of a psychotherapy quality assurance system. *Journal of Consulting and Clinical Psychology, 78*, 298–311. http://dx.doi.org/10.1037/a0019247

Simon, W., Lambert, M. J., Busath, G., Vazquez, A., Berkeljon, A., Hyer, K., . . . Berrett, M. (2013). Effects of providing patient progress feedback and clinical support tools to psychotherapists in an inpatient eating disorders treatment program: A randomized controlled study. *Psychotherapy Research, 23*, 287–300. http://dx.doi.org/10.1080/10503307.2013.787497

Simon, W., Lambert, M. J., Harris, M. W., Busath, G., & Vazquez, A. (2012). Providing patient progress information and clinical support tools to therapists: Effects on patients at risk of treatment failure. *Psychotherapy Research, 22*, 638–647. http://dx.doi.org/10.1080/10503307.2012.698918

Slade, K., Lambert, M. J., Harmon, S. C., Smart, D. W., & Bailey, R. (2008). Improving psychotherapy outcome: The use of immediate electronic feedback and revised clinical support tools. *Clinical Psychology & Psychotherapy, 15*, 287–303. http://dx.doi.org/10.1002/cpp.594

Spielmans, G. I., Masters, K. S., & Lambert, M. J. (2006). A comparison of rational versus empirical methods in the prediction of psychotherapy outcome. *Clinical Psychology & Psychotherapy, 13*, 202–214. http://dx.doi.org/10.1002/cpp.491

Vermeersch, D. A., Whipple, J. L., Lambert, M. J., Hawkins, E. J., Burchfield, C. M., & Okiishi, J. C. (2004). Outcome Questionnaire: Is it sensitive to changes in counseling center clients? *Journal of Counseling Psychology, 51*, 38–49. http://dx.doi.org/10.1037/0022-0167.51.1.38

Walfish, S., McAlister, B., O'Donnell, P., & Lambert, M. J. (2012). An investigation of self-assessment bias in mental health providers. *Psychological Reports, 110*, 639–644. http://dx.doi.org/10.2466/02.07.17.PR0.110.2.639-644

Warren, J. S., Nelson, P. L., Mondragon, S. A., Baldwin, S. A., & Burlingame, G. M. (2010). Youth psychotherapy change trajectories and outcomes in usual care: Community mental health versus managed care settings. *Journal of Clinical and Consulting Psychology, 78*, 144–155. http://dx.doi.org/10.1037/a0018544

Weiss, B., Catron, T., Harris, V., & Phung, T. M. (1999). The effectiveness of traditional child psychotherapy. *Journal of Consulting and Clinical Psychology, 67*, 82–94. http://dx.doi.org/10.1037/0022-006X.67.1.82

Whipple, J. L., Lambert, M. J., Vermeersch, D. A., Smart, D. W., Nielsen, S. L., & Hawkins, E. J. (2003). Improving the effects of psychotherapy: The use of early identification of treatment and problem-solving strategies in routine practice. *Journal of Counseling Psychology, 50*, 59–68. http://dx.doi.org/10.1037/0022-0167.50.1.59

Wierzbicki, M., & Pekarik, G. (1993). A meta-analysis of psychotherapy dropout. *Professional Psychology Research and Practice, 24*, 190–195. http://dx.doi.org/10.1037/0735-7028.24.2.190

Youngson, A. J. (1979). *The scientific revolution in Victorian medicine.* New York, NY: Holmes & Meier.

Jasen Elliott, Allan Abbass, and Tony Rousmaniere

Technology-Assisted Deliberate Practice for Improving Psychotherapy Effectiveness

9

I n this chapter we describe several ways of incorporating audiovisual and videoconference technology as a deliberate practice (DP) platform (see Ericsson, 2014b) for improving clinicians' performance of psychotherapy. With rapid advances in audiovisual and videoconferencing technology, clinicians have increasingly affordable, user-friendly, and accessible means of obtaining supervision and advanced training in psychotherapy without leaving their office (Abbass et al., 2011; Elliott, Abbass, & Cooper, 2015; Rousmaniere, 2014). After reviewing relevant research on technology-based supervision and training, we describe how to use this technology in a training format aimed at improving psychotherapy practice in typical mental health settings. Finally, we describe the benefits of this technology-based DP method and offer case examples, guidelines, and resources for implementing this approach in independent practices.

Context for Using Deliberate Practice

The authors elaborated our technology-assisted model for clinical supervision and continuing professional development in a private practice context. All three chapter authors study an advanced psychotherapy method and

http://dx.doi.org/10.1037/0000085-010
Using Technology in Mental Health Practice, J. J. Magnavita (Editor)

metapsychology, intensive short-term dynamic psychotherapy (ISTDP; Abbass, 2015; Davanloo, 2001), in which common somatic, psychological, and relational problems are viewed as stemming from unprocessed complex feelings secondary to early attachment trauma. The complex feelings are activated in close relationships, including therapy relationships, and trigger somatic anxiety, avoidance mechanisms, and related symptoms. A series of specific and timed interventions are used to mobilize these previous unconscious processes, so the client can notice, evaluate, and actively override the emotional avoidance processes in order to resolve the complex underlying feelings. Learning and practicing ISTDP hinges on the moment-to-moment examination of the client's response to intervention, including the somatic experience of emotions, patterns of unconscious anxiety, and related avoidance responses. Video recording was not only instrumental in development of the therapy model but is standard procedure for research, training, and ISTDP practice to permit objective evaluation of diagnostic findings, client–therapist exchanges, response to intervention, and treatment progress after each session (Abbass, 2004; Abbass, Kisely, Rasic, & Katzman, 2013).

Why Deliberate Practice?

Although video recording and DP may be integral for therapists practicing ISTDP, why should other therapists be concerned with such practices in light of well-established evidence that most clients benefit from psychotherapy (e.g., Wampold & Imel, 2015) and estimates that up to 60% of clients achieve "recovery" in clinical trials (Lambert, 2013)? Part of the rationale for this investment comes from research findings that overall psychotherapy outcomes have not improved over the last 40 years (Miller, Hubble, Chow, & Seidel, 2013). As well, there is clearly room for improvement given conservative estimates that at least 40% of clients are not recovering, including partial treatment responses, premature termination, and a small proportion of clients who deteriorate (e.g., Lambert, 2013; Swift, Greenberg, Whipple, & Kominiak, 2012). Although therapists and professional groups have attempted to advance the field in various ways, including the dissemination of empirically based treatments (McHugh & Barlow, 2010), continuing education (Wise et al., 2010), training and supervision (American Psychological Association, 2015), and the incorporation of routine clinical feedback (Miller et al., 2013), these efforts have not produced improved overall psychotherapy outcomes in the field.

Emerging research on DP and expertise in psychotherapy offers a useful framework for studying and improving therapist performance beyond routine practice outcomes (Chow et al., 2015). DP involves individualized training activities designed to improve specific aspects of a person's performance through repetition and successive refinement over extended periods of time (Ericsson & Lehmann, 1996). Expertise research from other areas (e.g., musicians, athletes, chess players) indicates that experience with the routine execution of skills associated with a particular performance domain is not enough to lead to improvement (Ericsson, 2014a). Similarly, in a large longitudinal study investigating whether or not therapists' outcomes improved over time with experience, Goldberg et al. (2016) actually found evidence for a slight decrease in overall therapist outcomes over time and number of cases. Importantly, therapists did vary significantly across time, with some therapists demonstrating improvement over time despite the general tendency for outcomes to decline slightly.

In contrast to more passive accumulation of clinical experience (e.g., time providing therapy as usual), DP involves a highly specialized process that requires individuals to tolerate the discomfort of identifying areas for improvement while persisting to achieve specific performance targets just beyond their current capacity or skill level. Chow et al. (2015) recently surveyed a group of therapists about the amount of time and effort they dedicated to DP and found that, in a typical week, the most highly effective therapists (i.e., top quartile of therapy outcomes) spent almost three times the amount of time, on average, on DP outside of therapy sessions than did less effective therapists.

The particular focus of DP will naturally vary across therapy models and therapists depending on their level of performance or expertise, as well as the complexity of client difficulties before them. Actual performance monitoring is a central feature of DP that permits opportunity for immediate informative feedback to guide intensive self-study, planning, and rehearsal efforts for specific performance targets. We argue that audiovisual and videoconferencing technologies provide very accessible and cost-effective platforms for monitoring DP efforts, as well as facilitating peer and expert training feedback aimed at improving psychotherapy performance.

Evidence Base for Technology-Assisted Supervision and Performance Improvement

A growing body of research suggests that incorporating Internet and audiovisual technology into mental health practice can contribute to supervision, advanced training, and DP efforts for clinicians (Rousmaniere, 2014). A literature review of 63 publications focusing on Internet-based supervision or training between the years 2000 and 2015 included 33 research studies and 30 descriptive studies of new technologies, case examples, or reviews of the current literature. Of the research studies, 11 used qualitative methods, 19 used quantitative methods, and three used mixed methods. The vast majority of studies took place in the United States, although several studies were conducted in Australia, Germany, Norway, and the United Kingdom. A range of topics was investigated, including rural supervision, peer group supervision, substance abuse counseling, school and youth counseling, and rehabilitation counseling. Therapy modalities included a range of established approaches, such as cognitive behavioural therapy, motivational interviewing, and psychodynamic therapy. The number of participants in these studies ranged from three to 373. Ten studies involved licensed clinicians, 30 studies included prelicensure clinicians (e.g., trainees, interns), and three studies had a mixture of both groups. The quantitative studies assessed a wide range of outcomes, such as supervision process (e.g., measures of supervisory working alliance), supervisee satisfaction, and skill acquisition (e.g., measures of adherence after training). At least six of the studies focused on the use of Internet-based supervision in rural settings.

One concern repeatedly raised about videoconference- and technology-based supervision is the potential risk of undermining the supervisory working alliance due to the diminished capacity for subtle nonverbal communication while using video-conference, e-mail, or text chat formats (e.g., Rousmaniere, 2014; Sørlie, Gammon, Bergvik, & Sexton, 1999; Vaccaro & Lambie, 2007). Similar concerns involve the potential exacerbation of gender, race, or cultural misunderstandings in the supervisory relationship (Panos, Panos, Cox, Roby, & Matheson, 2002). In contrast to these concerns, preliminary research has suggested that technology-assisted supervision may facilitate a supervisory working alliance equivalent to in-person supervision (e.g., Abbass et al., 2011; Coker & Schooley, 2012; Conn, Roberts, & Powell, 2009; Reese et al., 2009; Rousmaniere & Frederickson, 2013). Dickens (2010) found that, regardless of supervisee experience level, "the supervisory working alliance can be satisfactory in distance formats of supervision similar to that of face-to-face formats of supervision" (p. 84). Research also indicates that supervisees have equivalent (or more) satisfaction with technology-assisted supervision and training as they do with traditional in-person formats (Rousmaniere, 2014). The previous finding has been observed with counselor trainees (e.g., Chapman, Baker, Nassar-McMillan, & Gerler, 2011) and licensed practitioners (e.g., Xavier, Shepherd, & Goldstein, 2007).

Regarding skill development and acquisition, Weingardt, Villafranca, and Levin (2006) conducted a controlled study comparing web-based training (WBT), in-person training, and a control group with 166 substance abuse counselors. They found the two training methods to be equivalent in knowledge transfer. In another study of 147 substance abuse counselors, Weingardt, Cucciare, Bellotti, and Lai (2009) found that two methods of WBT were both effective at increasing cognitive behavioural therapy knowledge and counselor self-efficacy. However, in a study with 78 substance abuse counselors, Sholomskas et al. (2005) found that adding a WBT component to traditional treatment manuals improved training outcomes, but not as much as in-person supervision. Weingardt et al. (2006) noted that WBT can be highly cost-efficient for delivering training to large populations and that, after the initial costs of putting a training program online are paid, the costs of allowing access to extra clinicians are relatively minor. The authors proposed that the "most effective clinical training applications may use a 'blended delivery' format that leverages the strengths of both WBT and face-to-face training" (Weingardt et al., 2006, p. 23).

Most of the previous studies were conducted by researchers who were pioneers or early adopters in the use of their respective technologies, which may contribute to potential allegiance effects. Additional research is warranted on optimal technology formats for enhancing routine clinical performance, supervision and training practices, and client outcomes. It is noteworthy that although recording therapy sessions for supervision was once considered a controversial practice in the 1960s, it is now commonplace in professional training programs for establishing clinical proficiency (e.g., Bernard & Goodyear, 2014; Gelso, 1974; Haggerty & Hilsenroth, 2011; Huhra, Yamokoski-Maynhart, & Prieto, 2008). As well, recent research suggests that the majority of clients are comfortable with recording therapy sessions (Briggie, Hilsenroth, Conway, Muran, & Jackson, 2016) and that such procedures may even benefit therapy outcome (e.g., Town et al., 2012). With rapid advances in the quality, user-friendliness, and affordability of videoconference programs, the growing acceptance of this technology enables clinicians to participate in advanced training and supervision with experts from the convenience of independent practice settings. The previous technology offers a DP practice platform for lifelong professional development and improved clinical performance beyond routine practice. For a more detailed literature review of technology assisted training, see Rousmaniere (2014).

Scope of Application

The way to incorporate audiovisual and videoconference technology for DP, training, and supervision purposes begins with video recording therapy sessions in a manner that enables viewers to see both therapist and client during the work of therapy. It is strongly recommended that video recording setups emphasize secure storage of recordings and ease of use for busy practice settings. For practices in the United States, if the clinician plans to use cloud storage for therapy session videos (or for any of the practice's private health information), make sure to choose a service that provides a Business Associate Agreement (BAA) and that encrypts data at rest and data in transit, according to criteria put in place by the National Institute of Standards and Technology (2001).

Recordings are used for DP with highly focused study of selected performance areas, rather than unstructured reviews of recordings that are impractical in busy practices and unlikely to improve psychotherapy performance alone (see Ericsson, 2014a).

In addition to solo DP efforts (e.g., performance evaluation, reflection, rehearsal) (Rousmaniere, 2016), the authors use inexpensive, secure videoconferencing applications to facilitate peer or expert performance feedback in the convenience of one's office setting. In the authors' case, videoconference members observe each other and the psychotherapy recordings together along with instant messaging feedback and queries regarding the unfolding clinical material. Members can also pause the psychotherapy video as needed for longer verbal discussion or clarification of content, process, or performance matters of interest. Videoconference sessions can also be recorded so that participants can review and study the video and performance feedback repeatedly. More detailed sources of information and guidelines about videoconference applications are presented in the Essential Resources section near the end of the chapter.

The technology and DP platform has been incorporated into various training programs for the treatment model (Abbass, 2015; Davanloo, 2001). In the authors' particular case, this technology has been used with over 100 mental health professionals from 11 countries, with members speaking eight languages (e.g., Elliott et al., 2015). Several webconferencing formats are available, including supervisors working with individual clinicians, small groups (e.g., three to four clinicians), or larger class formats (e.g., 12 psychiatric residents) lasting between 30 minutes and 2 hours, depending on format. Group formats either involve clinicians gathering at a common location to webconference with the supervisor (e.g., Abbass et al., 2011) or clinicians from multiple locations meeting online with the supervisor via videoconferencing applications that allow for multiple participants (e.g., Elliott et al., 2015). The video-conference focus can range from specific areas of clinical performance on recordings, all the way to formal courses on the ISTDP model covering basic theory, evidence base, and application across the spectrum of suitable clients. More specifically, course material can be conveyed with slide presentations, discussion, and instructor videos demonstrating key aspects of the therapeutic model across increasingly complex clinical presentations (e.g., from complicated grief to borderline personality organization; Katzman, Abbass, Coughlin, & Arora, 2015). Similarly, role playing and rehearsal of key performance areas within a DP framework are easily accommodated with this technology (Rousmaniere, 2016; Rousmaniere, Goodyear, Miller, & Wampold, 2017).

In Elliott, Abbass, and Cooper's (2015) description of this ISTDP training platform, participants in videoconference sessions were regulated psychologists as well as psychiatrists and other mental health professionals with a mixture of academic affiliations and private practice, as well as training in multiple psychotherapy modalities. Most trainees participated in online supervision for a year or more, including core-training groups involving about 20 sessions per year over 3 or more years. About one third of trainees met on a monthly basis or as-needed for a year. Typically, the WBT acted as an adjunct to 3-day, in-person training workshops conducted on an annual or quarterly basis, although the webconferencing platform has been used as a first point of contact for some clinicians.

DP requires persistent effort to reach just beyond one's comfort zone to improve performance, including efforts to acquire peer and expert feedback (Ericsson, 2014a). Accordingly, trainee anxiety about improving performance and simply opening up to others is also commonplace and important to monitor in order to optimize learning. The opportunity to visualize trainee anxiety during supervision and in the recorded psychotherapy session is a major advantage for supervisors in order to adjust feedback effectively. Supervisors can assist by maintaining a collaborative and encouraging stance aimed at improved performance while modeling openness to self-reflection and feedback. Some trainees with severe levels of anxiety may benefit from graded training exposure to improve their anxiety tolerance over time, including progressive exposure to conceptual materials, observing supervisor and/or peers' video recordings, observing their own recordings, and eventually presenting recordings to others (Abbass, 2004).

A more graded approach can also be useful for supervision with unlicensed or more junior supervisees, and for initiating online supervision with individuals who have not met in person. As with in-person supervision or training, it is important to have sufficient opportunity to clarify respective roles, expectations, and supervision goals in order to promote a collaborative working alliance for online formats. Beyond providing a technical orientation and an encouraging rationale for the use of recordings to help advance clinician performance, it is key for supervisors to assess each supervisee's developmental level, anxiety tolerance, self-awareness, and openness to feedback in order to respond effectively.

Some helpful prerequisites for using this technology and DP platform with groups of trainees include meeting everyone in person beforehand, if possible, at a workshop on the specific psychotherapy model in order to provide the basic conceptual footing and shared terminology. Alternatively, scheduling an online introductory orientation with group members can be helpful in this regard. Group members should possess similar competence and confidence levels regarding the psychotherapy model to prevent the supervision focus being either too basic or too complex for some members. Similarly, group members should have adequate computer skills and Internet access in order to optimize the training experience. More heterogeneous supervision groups require closer monitoring and intervention by supervisors regarding any differences that impede the overall intent of the group to advance self and clinical understanding while improving performance. Those issues can also be addressed by the supervisor's use of didactic materials, general discussion, and video samples demonstrating relevant clinical interventions, while modeling openness to carefully studying one's work with others.

Although the technology and DP platform described here is used specifically with ISTDP training, the same methods can be applied to other psychotherapy approaches (e.g., cognitive, humanistic, and somatic therapies) for the sake of improving psychotherapy performance beyond proficiency. Similarly, this platform is applicable to most client populations, including children and adults with a spectrum of difficulties from unresolved grief to complex trauma and related personality disorders. Some notable exceptions include clients involved in litigation, experiencing severe anxiety, marked shame, or acute suspicion who may not consent to recording or online consultation. In the latter cases, clients may reconsider recording options following some success mitigating anxiety, shame, and suspicion in therapy. However, we generally find that most clients consent to this platform when informed about the rationale for improving their therapy and the related security measures designed to maintain confidentiality.

Benefits of Incorporating Technology-Assisted Deliberate Practice

The increasing availability of accredited online educational seminars regarding a broad spectrum of client difficulties and related interventions brings a wealth of information to clinicians in their practices. A growing body of research on videoconferencing technology also suggests it can provide a platform at least comparable to in-person psychotherapy training and supervision, especially as this technology rapidly improves in user-friendliness and in the quality of the audio-visual medium. There is evidence for trainee satisfaction, skills acquisition, and adequate supervisory working alliance with supervisees using this technology. However, the translation of the formal training programs and widely available clinical seminars and more accessible supervision or training into improved psychotherapy performance and outcomes has lagged behind in the overall field (e.g., Goldberg et al., 2016; Miller et al., 2013; Owen, Wampold, Kopta, Rousmaniere, & Miller, 2016).

As mentioned above, the primary rationale for incorporating a technology-based DP platform into clinical work stems from the specific psychotherapy model (ISTDP; Abbass, 2015) that requires extremely close and continual monitoring of client verbal and non-verbal responses to evaluate and guide successive therapy interventions during session. Audiovisual recordings allow for structured self-study and expert feedback regarding specific performance areas depending on the practitioner's level of expertise, ranging from relatively basic inquiry to identify the client's presenting problems to more complex interventions targeting automatic emotional avoidance mechanisms that maintain symptoms.

For example, Exhibit 9.1 includes typical instant messaging regarding about 10 minutes of a therapy session recording during online supervision with a small group of therapists from across North America. The supervisor generally helps the supervisee perform continuous assessment of key parameters in the client's nonverbal and verbal responses to interventions throughout the segment. The supervisee identified concerns with the client's affect mobilization beforehand. In response, the supervisor uses shared shorthand terminology (UTA < R, where UTA = unconscious therapeutic alliance, R = resistance) to give general feedback that complex unconscious affect and therapeutic alliance are being blocked by avoidance or defensive processes (e.g., passive, smile, helpless, thinking) associated with symptoms (e.g., somatic anxiety, tension). The supervisor also suggests interventions in quotations specifically aimed at addressing the defensive processes ("Notice you smile to cover up tension," "If you don't think, what do you feel?") as corrective feedback for the supervisee. The supervisee asks for more feedback about improving performance ("How to get out of this?") and the supervisor responds with a general principle in shorthand (P plus C) that emphasizes the need for challenge ("If you don't . . .") directed at defenses ("X, Y, and Z . . ."), combined with pressure to complex affect ("What's in your body, now, that you call anger?").

Pausing the recording is helpful for lengthier verbal discussions of process and conceptual topics, as well as for clarifying different perspectives about the clinical material under review. The supervisee in this case is equipped with specific feedback regarding missing defensive work with this particular client that is available for further self-study and preparation prior to the next session with the individual client.

This platform also facilitates the development of a productive supervisory working alliance, including the emotional bond and shared tasks of supervision aimed at improved performance. For example, Exhibit 9.2 follows the lead-up to a significant exposure of complex affect associated with therapeutic effects in a client–therapist pair working closely to override somatization involving gastrointestinal distress (i.e., gastrointestinal symptoms, repression). The supervisory working alliance is evident in the shared enthusiasm regarding an impending breakthrough of complex affect and direct encouragement regarding the client and therapist efforts.

There is considerable complexity in the client and session represented in the Exhibit, including well over 100 interventions progressing to therapeutic efforts near a threshold or window of tolerance involving somatization. The supervisee acquired feedback regarding the specific indicators (Negation) of the degree of affect mobilization (1/3), the importance of intervention timing, and the recognition of blocked positive feelings in facilitating mobilization. The previous feedback is conceptually and theoretically quite

EXHIBIT 9.1

Sample of Instant Messages From 11 Minutes of Video Recording Case Review

[12:22:02 PM] Sup: Zero fragility here [diagnostic impression]

[12:22:33 PM] Sup: Somatic pathway is going up now [affect increase]

[12:22:38 PM] Sup: Some heat [affect]

[12:22:46 PM] Sup: Smile [defense]

[12:23:04 PM] Sup: Ok [response to verbal question]

[12:23:09 PM] Sup: "If you don't think . . ." [suggested challenge to defense of rumination]

[12:23:24 PM] Sup: No, but anxiety and ruminating [identifying anxiety and related defense]

[12:23:37 PM] Ther1: Rise? [query re: degree of affect mobilization]

[12:23:38 PM] Sup: Crystallizing now [high affect mobilization triggering defenses with Ther1]

[12:23:42 PM] Ther1: Ok

[12:23:42 PM] Sup: She wants challenge [encouraging challenge of defenses]

[12:23:53 PM] Ther2: UTA? [query if therapeutic alliance is emerging]

[12:23:58 PM] Sup: Need challenge to show you hate her resistance [emphasis on avoidance]

[12:24:06 PM] Sup: Almost

[12:24:08 PM] Ther2: "Something I'm needing that I'm not getting" = UTA?

[12:24:09 PM] Sup: Tony . . .

[12:24:16 PM] Sup: Sort of

[12:24:33 PM] Sup: UTA < R [therapeutic alliance still impeded by resistance]

[12:24:46 PM] Sup: Passive [defense]

[12:25:03 PM] Sup: Smile [defense]

[12:25:16 PM] Sup: "Notice you smile to cover up tension" [suggests clarify defense]

[12:25:27 PM] Sup: "If you don't think-what do you feel?" [suggests challenge defense with pressure to affect]

[12:26:37 PM] Sup: All that's missing is work on the defenses

[12:27:12 PM] Ther1: So this is puffing up defense? [intervention assessment]

[12:27:28 PM] Sup: Not so much, just delaying breakthrough [defenses limiting affect experience]

[12:27:32 PM] Ther1: Ok

[12:28:21 PM] Sup: Helpless, regressed mostly now [defenses]

[12:28:29 PM] Ther1: How to get out of this?

[12:28:35 PM] Sup: P plus C [pressure to affect plus challenge to defense]

[12:28:40 PM] Sup: "If you don't . . ." [challenge]

[12:28:45 PM] Sup: "X, Y, and Z . . ." [defenses]

[12:28:59 PM] Sup: "What's in your body, now, that you call anger?" [pressure to immediate experience of affect]

[12:29:04 PM] Ther1: Ok

[12:29:08 PM] Sup: "If you don't choke back" [challenge]

[12:29:43 PM] Ther1: I started recapping . . .

[12:29:48 PM] Ther1: Pause

[12:33:12 PM] Ther2: Cool!

Note. Supervisee has this as record to reflect on later if desired. R = resistance; Sup = supervisor; Ther = therapist 1, 2, or 3; UTA = unconscious therapeutic alliance. Clarifying comments in brackets are added for the reader.

EXHIBIT 9.2

Sample of Instant Messages From a Video Recording Case Review

[10:51:26 am] Sup: Coming up again [client affect increasing]

[10:51:36 am] Sup: Mid chest [location of client affect experience]

[10:51:39 am] Ther: Yes [agrees]

[10:52:10 am] Ther: I'm low balling/underestimating for some reason [reduced pressure to affect]

[10:52:15 am] Sup: GI symptoms [affect somatization]

[10:52:20 am] Sup: Repression trying to happen [IDENTIFIES defense]

[10:52:32 am] Sup: Maybe that is why [repression to gut as basis for low affect]

[10:53:03 am] Sup: Negation!!! Tiny uta [increased therapeutic alliance]

[10:53:09 am] Ther: I think so

[10:53:18 am] Ther: She's going [affect mobilizing]

[10:54:08 am] Sup: Some here, maybe 1/3 [degree of complex affect mobilized]

[10:54:19 am] Sup: Good enough for some guilt to come if you don't hang here too long [emphasizing intervention timing]

[10:54:34 am] Sup: Very good

[10:56:42 am] Sup: Negation [indicator of alliance increasing]

[10:57:00 am] Sup: Guilt! [complex affect]

[10:57:50 am] Sup: "It's a very painful feeling in you" [suggested pressure to affect]

[10:58:11 am] Ther: Unblocks + [removal of defense on positive affect]

[10:59:01 am] Sup: Guilt

[10:59:08 am] Sup: Bravo you two

[10:59:39 am] Sup: I suspect that's the end of significant fragility [predicted treatment effect—improved anxiety and complex affect tolerance]

Note. Sup = Supervisor, Ther = therapist. Clarifying comments in brackets for reader.

consistent with the ISTDP model in literature and expert training videos. However, there is an added benefit to having feedback that is grounded in one's real-world therapy efforts that include stylistic differences, blind spots, technical errors, and important client differences. This feedback provides individualized data for further self-study, anticipation, and preparation aimed at improved performance (e.g., 2/3 mobilization of complex affect) in subsequent sessions. In addition to supervision feedback and the client's immediate report of significant relief at the end of the session, symptom and functional outcome monitoring between sessions also provide important sources of feedback for improving psychotherapy performance.

The DP and technology platform used here is applicable to any psychotherapy model and varying levels of client complexity and therapist expertise. Rather than simply acquiring more conceptual or technical information about client difficulties and related interventions, we attempt to study the moment-to-moment client response to intervention during and after the session as the clearest pathway to improved psychotherapy performance. Although still an emerging practice, therapy progress measures can also be completed by clients each session to study of how therapist deliberate practice efforts and client-therapist work in session relate to important outcomes, including therapeutic alliance, symptoms, functioning, and well-being (see Chapter 8, this volume; Overington, Fitzpatrick, Drapeau, & Hunsley, 2016).

Incorporating technology-based DP into one's daily routine undoubtedly requires significant time and effort aimed at improving psychotherapy outcomes. Our DP platform may offer a healthy countermeasure to research findings that therapists generally overestimate their therapy performance, often do not identify deterioration in clients, and tend not to have improved therapy outcomes over time (e.g., Goldberg et al., 2016; Lambert, 2013). Similarly, like clients, therapists have anxiety, defenses, and limits that are important to recognize and understand to avoid compassion fatigue and clinical blind spots so that we can engage most effectively with the people sitting across from us and help them address their difficulties. The platform enables therapists to study and build upon their emotional capacities through repeated exposure to their own challenging emotional processes that interfere with therapy tasks. For example, a therapist whose anxiety results in overactivity and controlling behavior in session can repeatedly observe the session segment to build anxiety awareness and tolerance without engaging in the overactive or controlling responses that interfere with therapeutic tasks. As well, the therapist can use solo practice to rehearse and implement appropriate interventions, such as noticing his or her emotional processes while helping clients to recognize rises in their anxiety (e.g., Do you notice that you have some anxiety or tension right now as you engage with me?).

The convenience, cost-effectiveness, and accessibility of this supervision and training format are major advantages for clinicians in independent practice, isolated locations, or those seeking advanced training from abroad. The small group videoconference format we use affords members opportunities to observe a broader spectrum of client difficulties, clinician interventions, and supervision practices during training, along with efforts to promote self-awareness, address common learning obstacles, and a shared sense of camaraderie.

Adopting a technology-based DP platform approaches the development and maintenance of psychotherapy expertise as a lifelong enterprise. Borrowing from the field of music, an étude is a short instrumental composition of considerable difficulty that is designed to provide practice material for mastering a particular musical skill. With persistence and DP over time, advanced musicians develop mastery over a repertoire of basic skills so they can move on to more complex and challenging compositions and performances. Similarly, DP for improved psychotherapy performance involves intensive study of a specific therapy model, combined with persistent study and refinement of therapist performance based on ongoing feedback from client response to intervention, progress measures, and expert feedback. Over time, DP and immediate feedback can contribute to mastery of a growing repertoire of relevant therapy techniques, methods, and capacity to tolerate anxiety and emotional experiences, thereby freeing up valuable cognitive and emotional resources for more complex and challenging work during session. Given that a considerable proportion of clients do not respond well to different research-based psychotherapies (Lambert, 2013), DP and ongoing feedback can help therapists get out of the rut of continuing to intervene in ways that do not help some clients. Finally, the technology-based DP approach also provides support for therapists attempting to innovate therapy techniques and methods in order to reach challenging clients more effectively, much like Davanloo's (2001) use of video analysis in the 1970s.

Basic Steps for Incorporating Technology-Assisted Deliberate Practice Into Mental Health Practice

In this section we emphasize technology with minimal cost and technical demands for maximum accessibility, particularly for use in independent practice settings. We also recommend recording and videoconference technology that is user-friendly with minimal time constraints.

AUDIOVISUAL RECORDINGS

An affordable recording setup can capture the client–therapist interaction by simply positioning a mirror behind or beside the client, who sits facing the therapist and the video camera. The camera captures the image of the client and the therapist as reflected in the mirror. Consumer-grade digital cameras appropriate for this purpose are available for less than $150. Split-screen software that combines images from two cameras, costing about $500, or a single camera with a second lens that captures the therapist, costing about $1,000, are more expensive options to record therapist and client interactions. External microphones may improve audio quality on some cameras, but basic recording devices are more than adequate for training and DP purposes. Recordings can be stored on encrypted external hard drives, DVDs, or other file storage meeting the most up-to-date computer security standards, such as the Federal Information Processing Standard (FIPS) Publication 140-2 (FIPS PUB 140-2).

VIDEOCONFERENCE APPLICATIONS

Numerous videoconferencing applications are currently available at no or minimal cost. Webconference software requires a computer with a microphone, speakers, web-camera, and broadband Internet access. Most of these videoconferencing applications use the participants' computer web browser (e.g., Safari, Firefox, Chrome) to present content, including options to share slides, audio and video files, instant messaging, and desktop screens, if necessary. Additionally, headsets can be used to enhance audio quality during discussion, if necessary. Further, inexpensive computer programs for recording videoconference calls are available for capturing online supervision sessions for subsequent DP purposes (e.g., Call Recorder).

VIDEO FILE STREAMING OR SHARING

Two methods are used in the authors' practices to share the actual recordings of psychotherapy sessions for videoconference training and supervision. First, the live streaming method uses the share screen function in the videoconference application that permits webconference members to view the display of the supervisee's computer, including a DVD or video file that is being played. The live streaming approach is very straightforward, but is still vulnerable to slower data transmission speeds during peak usage periods on the Internet. The second method that involves playing a video file at each member's location during the webconference in a synchronized manner is typically used. This requires a temporary link to the psychotherapy video file to be sent ahead of time to the group members using secure cloud-based file-sharing applications, such as the Google Drive business application. Cloud-based applications allow group members to access and play video files in a shared file folder for the purposes of supervision. After supervision, the video file is removed from the shared folder and is no longer accessible. One-hour video files can typically be uploaded into the shared file folder in less than 1 hour. For sessions recorded directly onto DVD, the DVD will need to be converted to a video file with relevant conversion software (e.g., AVS Video Converter) before the file can be uploaded to the shared folder. Finally, VLC Video Player is a free accessible program that is recommended for playing videos on both Macs and PCs.

CONFIDENTIALITY, CONSENT, AND SECURITY ISSUES

All supervisors and trainees using videoconferencing technology must conduct themselves in accordance with their respective ethical codes, practice guidelines, and relevant legislation, just as they would during conventional face-to-face supervision. Informed written consent is required from clients to record and share psychotherapy recordings for the purposes of supervision, including a detailed release form outlining the webconference process in plain language. It is important that clients understand that their consent is completely voluntary and will not affect their access to psychotherapy. Finally, we recommend use of the overarching principles of respecting the client's dignity and the integrity of the psychotherapy relationship, in addition to protecting the confidentiality of any client information that is stored or transmitted through an online means.

Storing and viewing recordings in secure physical and electronic settings, including the use of appropriate security protocols and user authentication procedures (e.g., strong password-protected files), is also necessary to protect the security and confidentiality of client information. It is important to make sure videoconferencing applications use encryption for the security of the information being transmitted and are HIPAA compliant, as described above. Similarly, it is important to maintain the security of video-recorded sessions that are shared or stored on a HIPAA-compliant cloud service, such as the Google Drive business application.

Essential Resources

In the authors' case, major technical difficulties interfering with a videoconference session were not experienced. Minor difficulties occurred in about 20% of sessions but were usually resolved in a few minutes. The authors had no formal technical training, certification, or support while implementing the videoconference supervision approach and found the following strategies sufficient for their purposes.

Given the rapid developments in technology, the use of contemporary application review websites (e.g., http://www.personcenteredtech.com, http://www. telementalhealthcomparisons.com) is recommended for general information about

EXHIBIT 9.3

Maximizing Internet Connection During Supervision Sessions

Preventative Measures

Use computer with adequate processing capacity.
Turn off other computer programs.
Turn off other computers if on a network.
Use broadband Internet connection (preferably 2–8 Mbps or more).
Use cloud sharing to send video rather than screen sharing.
Use cable versus wireless Internet connection.
Schedule webconference outside of peak Internet usage times.

Ameliorating Transmission Problems

Shut off video feature of application.
Ensure other programs are shut off.
Call over the Internet.
Call by telephone: always have numbers available.

---

various applications available online, including HIPAA compliance. Application tutorials, help or support sections, and user discussion forums are recommended as the primary sources of basic instruction overviews and specific troubleshooting information. YouTube often has instructional videos that are useful for familiarizing oneself with different applications. Trial runs are strongly recommended individually and with all webconference participants aimed at troubleshooting any technical or procedural issues that may undermine the overall quality of the supervision session. Similarly, Exhibit 9.3 outlines suggestions for maximizing Internet connection during trial runs and supervision sessions. More generally, Rousmaniere and Renfro-Michel's (2016) edited volume on using technology to enhance clinical supervision is a comprehensive resource, and supervisors may find it useful to review the telepsychology practice guidelines regarding videoconference applications from the American Telemedicine Association (2013) and the American Psychological Association (2013).

Conclusion

Psychotherapy is generally quite effective for most distressed clients, although there is still considerable room for improvement for a significant proportion of clients who do not respond well to therapy (Lambert, 2013; Wampold & Imel, 2015). Incorporating the authors' technology-based DP platform into clinical settings provides an invaluable resource for objectively studying, refining, and promoting improved performance and expertise in psychotherapy over time compared to supervision that is not based on recordings of client-therapist work, therapist solo practice efforts, and important therapy progress measures. The methodology is pantheoretical and can help bridge the scientist–practitioner divide by facilitating advanced training for research-based treatments, on the one hand, while offering objective feedback for frontline treatment innovations necessary for clients who do not respond well to established therapy protocols, on the other hand. Moreover, the platform allows for objective study and monitoring of the complex interplay of client and therapist factors involved in change processes within treatments, which may inform future research aimed at optimizing outcomes and advancing the psychotherapy field. Finally, the DP platform is inexpensive and very accessible for clinicians, and ties supervision and training efforts more closely to actual therapist performance and client improvement (see Watkins, 2011).

References

Abbass, A. (2004). Small-group videotape training for psychotherapy skills development. *Academic Psychiatry, 28*, 151–155. http://dx.doi.org/10.1176/appi.ap.28.2.151

Abbass, A. (2015). *Reaching through resistance: Advanced psychotherapy techniques.* Kansas City, MO: Seven Leaves Press.

Abbass, A., Arthey, S., Elliott, J., Fedak, T., Nowoweiski, D., Markovski, J., & Nowoweiski, S. (2011). Web-conference supervision for advanced psychotherapy training: A practical guide. *Psychotherapy, 48*, 109–118. http://dx.doi.org/10.1037/a0022427

Abbass, A., Kisely, S., Rasic, D., & Katzman, J. W. (2013). Residency training in intensive short-term dynamic psychotherapy: Methods and cost-effectiveness. *Psychiatric Annals, 43*, 508–512. http://dx.doi.org/10.3928/00485713-20131105-06

American Psychological Association. (2013). Guidelines for the practice of telepsychology. *American Psychologist, 68*, 791–800. http://dx.doi.org/10.1037/a0035001

American Psychological Association. (2015). Guidelines for clinical supervision in health service psychology. *American Psychologist, 70*, 33–46. http://dx.doi.org/10.1037/a0038112

American Telemedicine Association. (2013). *Practice guidelines for video-based online mental health services.* Retrieved from https://www.integration.samhsa.gov/operations-administration/practice-guidelines-for-video-based-online-mental-health-services_ATA_5_29_13.pdf

Bernard, J. M., & Goodyear, R. K. (2014). *Fundamentals of clinical supervision* (5th ed.). Needham Heights, MA: Allyn & Bacon.

Briggie, A. M., Hilsenroth, M. J., Conway, F., Muran, J. C., & Jackson, J. M. (2016). Patient comfort with audio or video recording of their psychotherapy sessions: Relation to symptomatology, treatment refusal, duration, and outcome. *Professional Psychology: Research and Practice, 47*, 66–76. http://dx.doi.org/10.1037/a0040063

Chapman, R. A., Baker, S. B., Nassar-McMillan, S. C., & Gerler, E. R. (2011). Cybersupervision: Further examination of synchronous and asynchronous modalities in counseling practicum supervision. *Counselor Education and Supervision, 50*, 298–314. http://dx.doi.org/10.1002/j.1556-6978.2011.tb01917.x

Chow, D. L., Miller, S. D., Seidel, J. A., Kane, R. T., Thornton, J. A., & Andrews, W. P. (2015). The role of deliberate practice in the development of highly effective psychotherapists. *Psychotherapy, 52*, 337–345. http://dx.doi.org/10.1037/pst0000015

Coker, J. K., & Schooley, A. L. (2012). *Investigating the effectiveness of clinical supervision in a CACREP accredited online counseling program*. Paper based on a program presented at the 2009 ACES Conference, San Diego, CA.

Conn, S. R., Roberts, R. L., & Powell, B. M. (2009). Attitudes and satisfaction with a hybrid model of counseling supervision. *Journal of Educational Technology & Society*, *12*, 298–306.

Davanloo, H. (2001). *Intensive short-term dynamic psychotherapy: Selected papers of Habib Davanloo, MD*. Chichester, England: John Wiley & Sons.

Dickens, A. D. H. (2010). *Satisfaction of supervisory working alliance: Distance versus face-to-face* (Doctoral dissertation). Retrieved from UMI Dissertation Publishing (UMI No. 3400640).

Elliott, J., Abbass, A., & Cooper, J. (2015). International group supervision using videoconferencing technology. In T. Rousmaniere & E. Renfro-Michel (Eds.), *Using technology to enhance clinical supervision* (pp. 191–202). Alexandria, VA: American Counseling Association.

Ericsson, K. A. (2014a). The acquisition of expert performance: An introduction to some of the issues. In K. A. Ericsson (Ed.), *The road to excellence: The acquisition of expert performance in the arts and sciences, sports, and games* (pp. 1–50). New York, NY: Psychology Press.

Ericsson, K. A. (2014b). Enhancing the development of professional performance: Implications from the study of deliberate practice. In K. A. Ericsson (Ed.), *Development of professional expertise: Toward measurement of expert performance and design of optimal learning environments* (pp. 405–431). New York, NY: Cambridge University Press.

Ericsson, K. A., & Lehmann, A. C. (1996). Expert and exceptional performance: Evidence of maximal adaptation to task constraints. *Annual Review of Psychology*, *47*, 273–305. http://dx.doi.org/10.1146/annurev.psych.47.1.273

Gelso, C. J. (1974). Effects of recording on counsellors and clients. *Counselor Education and Supervision*, *14*, 5–12. http://dx.doi.org/10.1002/j.1556-6978.1974.tb01987.x

Goldberg, S. B., Rousmaniere, T., Miller, S. D., Whipple, J., Nielsen, S. L., Hoyt, W. T., & Wampold, B. E. (2016). Do psychotherapists improve with time and experience? A longitudinal analysis of outcomes in a clinical setting. *Journal of Counseling Psychology*, *63*(1), 1–11. http://dx.doi.org/10.1037/cou0000131

Haggerty, G., & Hilsenroth, M. J. (2011). The use of video in psychotherapy supervision. *British Journal of Psychotherapy*, *27*, 193–210. http://dx.doi.org/10.1111/j.1752-0118.2011.01232.x

Huhra, R. L., Yamokoski-Maynhart, C. A., & Prieto, L. R. (2008). Reviewing videotape in supervision: A developmental approach. *Journal of Counseling and Development*, *86*, 412–418. http://dx.doi.org/10.1002/j.1556-6678.2008.tb00529.x

Katzman, J., Abbass, A., Coughlin, P., & Arora, S. (2015). Building connections through teletechnologies to augment resident training in psychodynamic psychotherapy. *Academic Psychiatry*, *39*, 110–113. http://dx.doi.org/10.1007/s40596-014-0108-9

Lambert, M. J. (2013). The efficacy and effectiveness of psychotherapy. In M. J. Lambert (Ed.), *Bergin and Garfield's handbook of psychotherapy and behavior change* (6th ed., pp. 169–218). New York, NY: John Wiley & Sons.

McHugh, R. K., & Barlow, D. H. (2010). The dissemination and implementation of evidence-based psychological treatments. A review of current efforts. *American Psychologist, 65*, 73–84. http://dx.doi.org/10.1037/a0018121

Miller, S. D., Hubble, M. A., Chow, D. L., & Seidel, J. A. (2013). The outcome of psychotherapy: Yesterday, today, and tomorrow. *Psychotherapy, 50*, 88–97. http://dx.doi.org/10.1037/a0031097

National Institute of Standards and Technology, U.S. Department of Commerce. (2001). *Federal information publication standards (FIPS PUB 140-2).* Retrieved from http://www.nist.gov

Overington, L., Fitzpatrick, M., Drapeau, M., & Hunsley, J. (2016). Perspectives on internship training directors on the use of progress monitoring measures. *Canadian Psychology, 57*(2), 120–129.

Owen, J., Wampold, B. E., Kopta, M., Rousmaniere, T., & Miller, S. D. (2016). As good as it gets? Therapy outcomes of trainees over time. *Journal of Counseling Psychology, 63*, 12–19. http://dx.doi.org/10.1037/cou0000112

Panos, P. T., Panos, A., Cox, S. E., Roby, J. L., & Matheson, K. W. (2002). Ethical issues concerning the use of videoconferencing to supervise international social work field practicum students. *Journal of Social Work Education, 38*, 421–437.

Reese, R. J., Aldarondo, F., Anderson, C. R., Lee, S.-J., Miller, T. W., & Burton, D. (2009). Telehealth in clinical supervision: A comparison of supervision formats. *Journal of Telemedicine and Telecare, 15*, 356–361. http://dx.doi.org/10.1258/jtt.2009.090401

Rousmaniere, T. (2014). Using technology to enhance clinical supervision and training. In C. E. Watkins & D. Milne (Eds.), *The Wiley international handbook of clinical supervision* (pp. 204–237). New York, NY: John Wiley & Sons. http://dx.doi.org/10.1002/9781118846360.ch9

Rousmaniere, T. (2016). *Deliberate practice for psychotherapists: A guide to improving clinical effectiveness.* New York, NY: Routledge.

Rousmaniere, T., & Frederickson, J. (2013). Internet-based one-way-mirror supervision for advanced psychotherapy training. *The Clinical Supervisor, 32*, 40–55. http://dx.doi.org/10.1080/07325223.2013.778683

Rousmaniere, T., Goodyear, R. K., Miller, S. D., & Wampold, B. E. (2017). *The cycle of excellence: Using deliberate practice to improve supervision and training.* London, England: Wiley Press. http://dx.doi.org/10.1002/9781119165590

Rousmaniere, T., & Renfro-Michel, E. (Eds.). (2016). *Using technology to enhance clinical supervision.* Alexandria, VA: American Counseling Association. http://dx.doi.org/10.1002/9781119268499

Sholomskas, D. E., Syracuse-Siewert, G., Rounsaville, B. J., Ball, S. A., Nuro, K. F., & Carroll, K. M. (2005). We don't train in vain: A dissemination trial of three strategies of training clinicians in cognitive-behavioral therapy. *Journal of Consulting and Clinical Psychology, 73*, 106–115. http://dx.doi.org/10.1037/0022-006X.73.1.106

Sørlie, T., Gammon, D., Bergvik, S., & Sexton, H. (1999). Psychotherapy supervision face-to-face and by videoconferencing: A comparative study. *British Journal of Psychotherapy, 15*, 452–462. http://dx.doi.org/10.1111/j.1752-0118.1999.tb00475.x

Swift, J. K., Greenberg, R. P., Whipple, J. L., & Kominiak, N. (2012). Practice recommendations for reducing premature termination in therapy. *Professional Psychology: Research and Practice*, *43*, 379–387. http://dx.doi.org/10.1037/a0028291

Town, J. M., Diener, M. J., Abbass, A., Leichsenring, F., Driessen, E., & Rabung, S. (2012). A meta-analysis of psychodynamic psychotherapy outcomes: Evaluating the effects of research-specific procedures. *Psychotherapy*, *49*, 276–290. http://dx.doi.org/10.1037/a0029564

Vaccaro, N., & Lambie, G. W. (2007). Computer-based counselor-in-training supervision: Ethical and practical implications for counselor educators and supervisors. *Counselor Education and Supervision*, *47*, 46–57. http://dx.doi.org/10.1002/j.1556-6978.2007.tb00037.x

Wampold, B., & Imel, Z. (2015). *The great psychotherapy debate: The evidence for what makes psychotherapy work* (2nd ed.). New York, NY: Routledge.

Watkins, C. E., Jr. (2011). Does psychotherapy supervision contribute to patient outcomes? Considering thirty years of research. *The Clinical Supervisor*, *30*, 235–256. http://dx.doi.org/10.1080/07325223.2011.619417

Weingardt, K. R., Cucciare, M. A., Bellotti, C., & Lai, W. P. (2009). A randomized trial comparing two models of web-based training in cognitive-behavioral therapy for substance abuse counselors. *Journal of Substance Abuse Treatment*, *37*, 219–227. http://dx.doi.org/10.1016/j.jsat.2009.01.002

Weingardt, K. R., Villafranca, S. W., & Levin, C. (2006). Technology-based training in cognitive behavioral therapy for substance abuse counselors. *Substance Abuse*, *27*, 19–25. http://dx.doi.org/10.1300/J465v27n03_04

Wise, E. H., Sturm, C. A., Nutt, R. L., Rodolfa, E., Schaffer, J. B., & Webb, C. (2010). Life-long learning for psychologists: Current status and a vision for the future. *Professional Psychology: Research and Practice*, *41*, 288–297. http://dx.doi.org/10.1037/a0020424

Xavier, K., Shepherd, L., & Goldstein, D. (2007). Clinical supervision and education via videoconference: A feasibility project. *Journal of Telemedicine and Telecare*, *13*, 206–209. http://dx.doi.org/10.1258/135763307780907996

Jon Frederickson and Tony Rousmaniere

Using Technology for Therapist Self-Development

10

lthough psychotherapy is a young field as a science, it shares with crafts the ancient teaching model of apprenticeship with a master as the primary model of professional development. Many, if not most, skills require apprenticeship with a master clinician in order for the therapist to reach the highest levels of skill. But Ellis et al. (2013) showed that over 90% of psychotherapy supervision is inadequate and 35% is actually harmful! In the past, therapists were limited in their supervision and training options by virtue of the requirements of their training organizations or by limits of geography.

Today, with the rise of the Internet and the numerous options for training with master clinicians, many avenues for self-development are becoming available around the world. This chapter reviews new tools for professional development that have emerged in only the past few years. To review the role of technology in self-development, the chapter examines how technology is influencing three domains of therapist self-development: supervision, teaching, and skill development.

Supervision

Just as online technology has changed psychotherapy (see Chapter 2), it has revolutionized supervision. This section looks at three forms of online supervision: individual, group, and remote live supervision.

http://dx.doi.org/10.1037/0000085-011
Using Technology in Mental Health Practice, J. J. Magnavita (Editor)

INDIVIDUAL SUPERVISION

Via the Internet, therapists can seek supervision from any supervisor in the world. Here, we examine online supervision of videotaped sessions, since this is the cutting edge of supervision practice today. For a review of the ethical and legal issues regarding online supervision, see Rousmaniere, Renfro-Michel, and Huggins (2016).

First, the supervisor and supervisee must use an encrypted videoconference program, where the supervisee calls his supervisor on the videoconference. Then the supervisee uses a "Share Screen" function to make his own screen appear on the supervisor's screen. The supervisee can then play a DVD on his computer or play a video file from an external hard drive that appears on the supervisor's screen. The two can now view the video at the same time, from different offices in the same building or in different parts of the world, and start and stop the video to capture key moments in the session and to offer precise supervision based on the data of the actual session.

Rather than transmit the video through videoconference, the supervisee may also send the file to a Health Insurance Portability and Accountability Act (HIPAA)–compliant file-sharing program from which the supervisor can download the file and play it on her laptop. Or the supervisee may use another encrypted website that is password protected, following which the supervisor can download the file for supervision. Of course, the supervisor must delete the files from her laptop following the session. With this model of supervision, both supervisor and supervisee can communicate via videoconference but view the videos on their respective devices without transmitting the videos through videoconference.

GROUP SUPERVISION

Group supervision can also be done via videoconference. Before initiating group supervision, it is wise to conduct a trial run to ensure that the software is running, the broadband connections are good enough, and the technical glitches have been worked through. Since group supervision often involves people communicating from several sites simultaneously, bandwidth can be a problem with transmission.

If there are problems with audiovisual transmission, have all participants turn off any other computer applications they may have running; also, have them turn off their cameras so that only the session video appears on the screen. Participants may also need to mute their audio input when listening, and turn it on only when speaking. If those changes do not resolve the problem, then you can try the following: (a) send files prior to supervision, rather than use the share screen option; (b) turn off the video and just listen to the audio; or (c) call over the phone or Internet.

Of course, supervision through videoconferencing software involves additional ethical issues. The videoconferencing software must be HIPAA compliant. If you downloaded a video for the supervision, erase it immediately after the conference. Members of the supervision group must agree not to copy other members' videos or view them outside of the supervision. Additionally, patients must give informed consent for the session videos to be viewed for the purpose of supervision.

REMOTE LIVE SUPERVISION

Live remote supervision is also possible via the Internet (Jakob, Weck, & Bohus, 2013; Rousmaniere & Frederickson, 2016; Yu, 2014). In live supervision, the supervisee makes the same arrangements as before to share screens. Then the supervisee attaches a video camera to the computer so that the image of the patient shows up on the therapist's screen. With "Share Screen," that image then appears on the supervisor's screen. Once the therapy begins and as it proceeds, the supervisor watches and can offer live supervision through brief written comments (which show up on the supervisee's screen and are visible only to the therapist). In this way, the supervisee receives moment-to-moment supervision, getting precise help exactly when she or he gets into trouble.

This kind of supervision leads to a much faster form of learning and mastery for the student. But it is most useful if the student has a good level of mastery of the approach. Otherwise, a therapist trying to learn a model while at the same time getting feedback will be overwhelmed in the moment by the supervisor's comments in real time. However, the client can benefit directly from the supervisor's involvement, leading to better outcomes and enhanced supervisee learning (Bernard & Goodyear, 2013; Moody, Kostohryz, & Vereen, 2014).

Live supervision has also been described as economical because trainees gain so much in so little time (Wong, 1997; p. 151). In fact, Bartle-Haring, Silverthorn, Meyer, and Toviessi (2009) found that a single session of live supervision improved supervisees' perceptions of patient progress. In this type of supervision, the supervisee is "naked." The supervisor can see the therapist's work and make comments in the moment. As a result, the trainee's anxiety can rise rapidly, leading to a learning misalliance. Thus, the supervisor must carefully monitor the supervisee's anxiety and responses to ensure that the relationship remains a good learning relationship.

One way to monitor the student's reactions is through a follow-up e-mail exchange during which the supervisor and supervisee can discuss what they learned and address any remaining questions (Bernard & Goodyear, 2013; Wong, 1997). In this way, both have extra time to process the learning and to assess any shifts in the learning alliance that need attention.

Of course, there are possible drawbacks to this model of supervision. As we just mentioned, it is inherently anxiety provoking for the trainee, which is why adequate competence in the model being learned is an important precondition. In addition, some practice role-plays may be useful in advance to reduce the student's anxiety (Wong, 1997). While some (Ford, 2008) have suggested that the presence of technology could distract the patient, leading to an adverse outcome, Rousmaniere and Frederickson (2016) found no evidence for this conclusion. Others have raised the concern that a supervisor might misuse remote live supervision for the purpose of showing off, encouraging student passivity or blind adherence to technique in the work (Bernard & Goodyear, 2013; Smith, Mead, & Kinsella, 1998). However, the narcissism of a supervisor does not require the existence of technology to show up in supervision (Epstein, 1986)!

Interestingly, one study of remote live supervision (Jakob et al., 2013) found that 96% of students found it useful, 88% found it not to be disruptive, and 88% found that it did not affect the therapeutic alliance negatively. So why do supervisors tend to resist this form of supervision? Rousmaniere and Frederickson (2016) hypothesized that supervisors resist this model because the supervisor is exposed; the cloak of anonymity is stripped away, and the student has the chance to see the supervisor's mistakes and model of learning from mistakes. Further research is necessary, but preliminary results show that this model of learning is one that deserves much more study and application.

Teaching

With the availability of Massive Online Open Courses (MOOCs), everyone knows how the Internet is changing the way education is done. Unfortunately, the premise of MOOCs is that teaching does not require a relationship between a teacher and a student, but rather education is a "download" of information. While this is a way to learn information, it is not a way to learn skills under the watchful eye of a master, which is the tradition of learning within crafts. Thus, when considering the impact of the Internet on the craft of teaching, we must look at several formats for psychotherapy teaching—what they can do and what they cannot do.

VIDEO LECTURES

Video lectures allow viewers to learn simple skills but, most important, learn information about psychotherapy. YouTube is the most popular format for this, with thousands of educational videos on psychotherapy topics available to the viewer. To establish a channel of YouTube videos, one can set up an account at YouTube, create a video, and then upload it to a file-sharing program. The teacher downloads the video to a personal channel and then labels the video and determines if it is to be viewed only by people who have the specific link or if it is viewable by the public.

Since there is so much competition on Youtube.com to get a video viewed, (a) the video should have good visual quality; (b) the message must be clear, simple, and understandable; and (c) the message should be under 5 minutes in length. In this age of short attention spans, long videos have a small viewership.

Some psychotherapists monetize their video lectures on formats other than YouTube. Vimeo is perhaps the most popular site for storing videos that are password protected. In this case, the teacher creates a video of a lecture, uploads it to a file-sharing program, and then downloads it to Vimeo. The teacher gives the video a label; and once on Vimeo, the video is given a password. No one can access the video without a password. Thus, when students pay for an online course, they receive a link to the video and a password that enables them to watch.

Students can register and pay for these courses on the teacher's personal website. Upon payment, attendees receive a code and a link. They click the link, enter the code, and access, for example, an hour-long lecture. When he or she finishes watching the video, the student can receive a test, which is scored automatically on the Internet, and then receive continuing education units, which are e-mailed. Only a few individual teachers have taken this final step, but several organizations have already set up online courses with these features. The Psychotherapy Networker is notable in this regard.

The most elaborate psychotherapy website for this kind of offering by an individual therapist is Dan Siegel's website (http://www.drdansiegel.com) with online courses and lecture series. Students can access numerous online courses he has recorded. If they take a certain grouping of those courses, they can receive a certification. Some people offer recordings of their lectures to audiences for a fee through Vimeo. Susan Warshow's DEFT Institute (http://www.deftinstitute.com) is a good example of this model of marketing lectures through the Internet.

Although recorded video lectures present information and allow people to get continuing education units today whenever they want, viewers can get only information. In effect, they are watching TV, and they cannot develop higher level clinical skills through interaction with a skilled teacher or supervisor through prerecorded videos.

Sadly, the use of lectures to convey information has become the norm for psychotherapy education, perhaps explaining why much psychotherapy supervision and teaching is not leading to increased skill acquisition and better outcome (Chow, Miller, Seidel, Kane, Thornton, & Andrews, 2015; Ellis et al., 2013). This reflects the hyperemphasis on theory and underemphasis on practice that currently characterize the field of psychotherapy.

LIVE VIDEOCONFERENCING

Live videoconferencing can be done through several formats, allowing teachers to give and students to attend a conference without having to travel. The advantage of live videoconferencing is that the students and the teacher can engage in live dialogue about the material without having to travel.

The teacher connects with each student's device through videoconference. The teacher shares their computer screen, and one student on the other end connects their laptop to a large screen and speakers so that a group can observe the lecture being given. If the teacher is teaching from a slide deck, the students can see the slides on the screen as well as the teacher's face. And they can ask questions just as they would if the teacher were in the room. In fact, depending upon the access to broadband, it is possible to offer a videoconference in up to two other sites at the same time. For example, one of the authors of this chapter (JF) gave an all-day presentation from his Washington, DC, office to a group of students in India! Likewise, if the teacher shows a video of a case on his laptop, he can show and teach with the video while the students view and study it with him. Using videoconference, and communicating to only one group with one screen, he could protect his patient's confidentiality, and the group can have a training they would not have had otherwise.

Although this is a way to offer a small conference, it is also a way to offer trainings and group supervisions at a distance. For example, a colleague and I (JF) are offering online training in intensive short-term dynamic psychotherapy to a group of trainees in India. Due to the burdens of travel and expense, we offer trainings using video-conference. The entire class gathers in one room with a very good broadband connection. They connect to videoconference through a large screen television hooked up to a computer. Then, following the instructions noted above, they can share the screen and we can watch their videotaped cases and supervise from across the world.

Although my coteacher and I were concerned at first about how to connect to the group as a whole when we were on opposite sides of the planet, we found that several things helped. We insisted that the students sit in front of the computer screen so we could see all of them at once and they could see us. Also, I take special care to ask more questions to keep them engaged. I tell less and ask more. I also take care to do "cold calls," asking questions of different members randomly, so no one knows who will be asked the next question. This keeps the entire group engaged and energized, knowing that at any moment they can be put on the spot—even when the instructor is thousands of miles away.

This speaks to the challenges of teaching via videoconferencing. Since the teacher is not in the room, it is easy for students to imagine the instructor does not see them. Thus, the teacher must be more active in asking the group questions to keep them actively involved in a dialogue with a virtual teacher. And the teacher must respond to nonverbal indications of distraction, dissatisfaction, or boredom. "Nitya, you seem far away. What is happening?" "Darshan, you had a response to what I said. Could you put that into words?" If a student is bored, then the teacher knows that the questions are not asked frequently enough or challengingly enough for the student, and the instructor responds accordingly. Although I always pay attention to such cues when present in the classroom, I pay even more attention when teaching virtually.

The teacher has to actively compensate for his physical absence. Otherwise, the group feels as if they are watching TV rather than talking to the instructor. This is an example of how the usual lecturing by a teacher in a virtual format can be more deadly than in an in-person classroom. It is easy to forget that when you are teaching online, the students are primed by their history to be watching TV passively, and will not necessarily engage with a teacher actively. The teacher must counter this priming through active questioning to remind students overtly and covertly that she or he can see them and is relating to them.

While videoconference works for small-group seminars and training groups, many websites have arisen to meet the demand for larger virtual conferences. Initially designed for far-flung corporations, these conference websites allow a presenter to give a lecture while attendees at multiple sites can "attend" virtually—either from personal laptops or from conference rooms at corporate sites around the country. In this way, hundreds or thousands of people can "attend" a presentation without the time and expense of travel.

Videoconferencing websites include Gotomeeting, Onstream meetings, Globalmeet, Adobe Connect, Click Meeting, Omnijoin, and Fuzemeeting. The teacher selects a level of service for a monthly fee. At the teacher's website, attendees register, pay their fee, and, in return, receive a code and time. At the designated time, they access the videoconferencing website, type in their code, and they are in the "conference room," where the teacher appears on schedule, prepared to give a talk live. Meanwhile, the "room" may very well be the teacher's office. Thus, from the privacy of the teacher's office, the teacher gives a presentation, and students from around the world can "attend." Some institutions purchase site licenses to offer remote classes, so if you are affiliated with an institution, make sure to check with your administrators before purchasing an individual package.

Now the challenge is how the teacher will handle questions from potentially hundreds of people. Since the back-and-forth of multiple questions from multiple sites would easily overwhelm bandwidth, videoconferencing websites have solutions for this. Sometimes people can type in questions, which show up on the teacher's page. Then the teacher can read the question and respond to it. But this can be burdensome for the teacher, who is trying to teach and at the same time read questions showing up on the screen.

Some videoconferencing websites recommend that the teacher have someone function as a monitor to whom participants can forward questions for review. Then the monitor, at an opportune moment, can interrupt the teacher to ask a student's question. Or, if the videoconferencing website allows it, the monitor can interrupt the teacher, press a button, and allow the attendee to ask a question. This allows the kind of back-and-forth interaction that can make for a lively presentation.

However, students often do not ask questions. Again, primed to be watching TV, they do not automatically feel like they are in the room with an instructor with whom they can interact. No one imagines they can talk to the TV set. So the instructor must repeatedly ask if there are any questions or comments to remind the viewers that this is a potential dialogue: Conversation is possible. It is probably best to think of this as a counter-projective maneuver. The instructor must counter viewers' implicit projection that they are watching an image when they could talk to the person who is on the screen.

On videoconferencing websites, the presenter will not see the audience on the screen, since attendees come from multiple places. Instead, the teacher will see the PowerPoint slide or lecture notes, and as the teacher goes through the PowerPoint slides, the audience will see them at the same time (due to the shared screen). But the audience also gets to see the teacher, even if the teacher cannot see them.

For the attendees, it's like attending a live lecture, since they see the instructor. However, for the instructor, the experience can be disorienting, since the teacher is speaking to an imaginary, invisible audience that never appears on the screen. In this case, since there are no visual cues, the instructor must take even greater care to assess audience response. Thus, when offering a videoconference without being able to see the audience, it is important for the instructor to ask lots of questions so that audience responses allow him or her to assess their understanding and also their level of anxiety.

Although teaching through videoconferencing websites has many advantages, it has one major disadvantage: It is impossible for the teacher to show videotapes of clinical work. Why? It is always possible for students to record the instructor's video onto their own device, even when they know that to do so is a breach of ethics. Until encryption strategies develop, this avenue of instruction through videoconferencing will not be possible. Thus, live videoconferencing through videoconferencing websites will continue to help students learn information but not develop skills.

Deliberate Practice

Increased emphasis on improving therapeutic outcome and recent research in expertise (Ericsson, Krampe, & Tesch-Römer, 1993) have led to an interest in deliberate practice (e.g., Chow et al., 2015; Miller, Hubble, Chow, & Seidel, 2013). That is, what skills do therapists need to become effective, and how can they be practiced to enhance skill acquisition? Recently, some therapists have been developing lists of skills and creating skill-building exercises for their acquisition. These skill-building exercises are made available in the form of downloadable audio files, which students can keep on their computers or cell phones and use to practice therapy skills just as they might practice learning a new language through Berlitz CDs. For instance, the following website offers such skill-building exercises for therapists: http://istdpinstitute.com/resources/skill-building-series-of-audio-courses/.

One online therapy training course puts together video lectures, video skill-building exercises, and live group supervision. Others offer directed practice to students using the skill-building exercises. A small group of students from different parts of the world can practice together with the instructor, developing their clinical skills. One clear advantage of this model is that by using various studies with students, the specific skills that are strong and the ones that require more practice can be quickly assessed. This provides students not only a quick and specific assessment of where they are weak but also a solution: practice specific skill-building exercises designed for those weaknesses.

Summary

Access to the Internet has expanded the availability of therapy and supervision. It has simultaneously expanded the options for training while offering new challenges for how teaching can be done in a virtual environment. The ongoing challenge for teaching is how to develop interactive models of instruction that will compensate for the passive withdrawal generally encouraged by video environments for learning.

References

Bartle-Haring, S., Silverthorn, B. C., Meyer, K., & Toviessi, P. (2009). Does live supervision make a difference? A multilevel analysis. *Journal of Marital and Family Therapy*, *35*, 406–414. http://dx.doi.org/10.1111/j.1752-0606.2009.00124.x

Bernard, J. M., & Goodyear, R. K. (2013). *Fundamentals of clinical supervision* (5th ed.). Needham Heights, MA: Pearson Education.

Chow, D. L., Miller, S. D., Seidel, J. A., Kane, R. T., Thornton, J. A., & Andrews, W. P. (2015). The role of deliberate practice in the development of highly effective psychotherapists. *Psychotherapy, 52,* 337–345. http://dx.doi.org/10.1037/pst0000015

Ellis, M. V., Berger, L., Hanus, A. E., Ayala, E. E., Swords, B. A., & Siembor, M. (2013). Inadequate and harmful clinical supervision: Testing a revised framework and assessing occurrence. *The Counseling Psychologist, 42,* 434–472. http://dx.doi.org/10.1177/0011000013508656

Epstein, L. (1986). Collusive selective inattention to the negative impact of the supervisory interaction. *Contemporary Psychoanalysis, 22,* 389–409. http://dx.doi.org/10.1080/00107530.1986.10746135

Ericsson, K. A., Krampe, R. T., & Tesch-Römer, C. (1993). The role of deliberate practice in the acquisition of expert performance. *Psychological Review, 100,* 363–406. http://dx.doi.org/10.1037/0033-295X.100.3.363

Ford, A. E. (2008). The effects of two-way mirrors, video cameras, and observation teams on clients' judgments of the therapeutic relationship. *Dissertation Abstracts International: B. The Sciences and Engineering, 69*(3), 1951.

Jakob, M., Weck, F., & Bohus, M. (2013). Live-Supervision: Vom einwegspiegel zur videobasierten [Live supervision: From the one-way mirror to video based online supervisions]. *Verhaltenstherapie, 23,* 170–180. http://dx.doi.org/10.1159/000354234

Miller, S. D., Hubble, M. A., Chow, D. L., & Seidel, J. A. (2013). The outcome of psychotherapy: Yesterday, today, and tomorrow. *Psychotherapy, 50,* 88–97. http://dx.doi.org/10.1037/a0031097

Moody, S., Kostohryz, K., & Vereen, L. (2014). Authentically engaged earning through live supervision: A phenomenological study. *Counselor Education and Supervision, 53,* 19–33. http://dx.doi.org/10.1002/j.1556-6978.2014.00046.x

Rousmaniere, T., & Frederickson, J. (2016). Remote live supervision: Videoconference for one-way-mirror supervision. In T. Rousmaniere & E. Renfro-Michel (Eds.), *Using technology to enhance clinical supervision* (pp. 157–173). Alexandria, VA: American Counseling Association.

Rousmaniere, T., Renfro-Michel, E., & Huggins, R. (2016). Regulatory and legal issues related to the use of technology in clinical supervision. In T. Rousmaniere & E. Renfro-Michel (Eds.), *Using technology to enhance clinical supervision* (pp. 19–30). Alexandria, VA: American Counseling Association.

Smith, R. C., Mead, D. E., & Kinsella, J. A. (1998). Direct supervision: Adding computer-assisted feedback and data capture to live supervision. *Journal of Marital and Family Therapy, 24,* 113–125. http://dx.doi.org/10.1111/j.1752-0606.1998.tb01066.x

Wong, Y.-L. S. (1997). Live supervision in family therapy: Trainee perspectives. *The Clinical Supervisor, 15,* 145–157. http://dx.doi.org/10.1300/J001v15n01_11

Yu, A. (2014, August). *iSupe live: There's an app for that.* Paper presented at the 122nd Annual Convention of the American Psychological Association, Washington, DC.

Steven A. Sobelman and Jeffrey J. Magnavita

Extending Your Mental Health Practice as an Entrepreneur

11

ental health professionals traditionally focus on face-to-face, "in the office" relationships. Our training requires that we take courses on diagnosing and treating mental, emotional, and behavioral disorders. After meeting the requirements of our program of study and completing our degree, we begin the process of studying for our licensing examination. And once we receive that coveted letter in the mail affirming that we passed the licensing exam, we are ready to commence our career as a practicing mental health professional. From there, we are committed to maintaining a high standard of care for our patients through an understanding of current professional and ethical standards, empirically validated intervention techniques, risk-managed business practices, and technological advances with the associated Health Insurance Portability and Accountability Act (HIPAA) and regulations.

For the most part, we adopt technologies that will augment those face-to-face interactions on which we build our practices. Some tools increase our efficiency with administrative tasks, so we can spend more time with human beings. Some tools help us learn more skills or sharpen our skills more quickly, so the quality of service we provide improves. And, as we've seen in this volume, still other tech tools completely transform the therapy process and/or the therapy experience. We gather and analyze data on these new treatments as they emerge, to test their effectiveness and safety against established standards.

http://dx.doi.org/10.1037/0000085-012
Using Technology in Mental Health Practice, J. J. Magnavita (Editor)

But technology is also allowing us, for the first time, to leave the confines of our offices and the constraints of traditional practice by opening up new frontiers in innovation and entrepreneurship. Canton (2015), looking to the future, predicted that "most jobs [will be] entrepreneurial and project based, working across borders and engaging deep, collaborative networks of people, companies, and technology" (p. 28).

Looking Beyond the Fee-for-Service Business Model

Primary to independent, group, or institutional practice is the need to maintain a business that is financially viable. Traditionally, our income is dependent on the formula of working for 1 hour for a specific market value. Some practitioners charge by their "product or service." In other words, if a psychologist provides a service for assessing a learning disability, she or he may charge for the assessment (generally based on how many hours it takes for an initial evaluation, testing procedure hours, report writing, and follow-up sessions). One limitation of the fee-for-service model, however, is that the only means of increasing our income once we fill our booking hours is to raise prices for clients, which is a difficult balancing act at best and, at worst, provides us with very little flexibility.

Mental health practitioners don't typically think of themselves as entrepreneurs, and one reason for this may be their reluctance to think beyond the fee-for-service model in a solo practice setting. I (Sobelman) once had a colleague ask me whether I'm a psychologist who practices the business of psychology, or a businessman who practices psychology. At the time, I had grown my private practice to be the largest mental health practice group in the Baltimore metropolitan area. The colleague was referencing both my private practice and my involvement in the dot.com world, since I was also the CEO of a company that was oriented toward web development and design, web hosting, data mining, and software development. These two businesses were forerunners of other entrepreneurial ventures that veered from the traditional formula of working an hour for a predetermined fee. Both authors of this chapter, who live and practice in different states, collaborated on several business ventures with the hope of providing passive income streams, while enjoying the challenge of innovation. We had many brainstorming meetings, either in-person or mostly through video-chat, that eventually resulted in creating products we believe to be useful for psychologists. Suffice it to say, our goal in this chapter is to encourage readers to think out of the box by showing them how they can use technology to create additional income streams beyond what their direct services alone can generate. We also hope that after reading this chapter, readers will consider ways to lend their professional expertise—whether in clinical work, research, or simply via thought leadership—to new technology developments that serve our health care sector.

This chapter, therefore, focuses on how technology has opened a new wave of possibilities for creative entrepreneurship and also provides an introduction to essential characteristics of entrepreneurs. Some of the trends that we believe are important for the future of psychology and mental health care are available now, while other trends are rapidly emerging. Regardless of your professional and personal goals, we believe that paying more attention to the ways technology can advance entrepreneurship by spawning and refining new developments is valuable to all of us and to the field of mental and behavioral health, in particular. In addition to keeping the field relevant, mental health professionals have a duty to prevent the science from being co-opted by less knowledgeable stakeholders.

Not everyone can or wishes to become an entrepreneur. Some readers may not be interested, others might be risk averse, and others may believe that they can hardly keep abreast of current professional demands and don't have the time or willingness to engage in the attitude shifts or changes that are necessary to become successful entrepreneurs. But our hope is that many who read this chapter may be inspired by the possibilities of entrepreneurship. We endeavor to help you proceed by providing a basic understanding of entrepreneurship, so that those who are interested might take advantage of technology to advance their practice. Many innovations have resulted from a partnership of two people, one who may be the inventor or creative force—*right brain*—and the other partner—*left brain*—who understands how to turn concepts into products and run a business (Issacson, 2014). Most mental health professionals have valuable ideas waiting to be developed, as well as other essential areas of expertise and skill sets. It is often when two people with these different strengths find something inspiring that great discoveries and advances in technology occur. Our hope is that you will find partners who share your dreams and interests, and who have skill sets that complement yours. This chapter will help you identify important characteristics of successful entrepreneurs so that, wherever you are in your professional or entrepreneurial journey, you will be open to possibilities for finding partners to help you develop your ideas and projects. Even if this is not something you aspire to, please keep reading, because regardless of your professional role (e.g., clinic administrator, director of a group practice, independent practitioner), there are always opportunities to use technology to create value.

What Opportunities Are Out There for Clinicians Who Want to Be Entrepreneurs?

In the past 20 years, digitalization has fundamentally changed the ways in which we communicate. "By 2025, the majority of the world's population will, in one generation, have gone from having virtually no access to unfiltered information to accessing all of the world's information through a device that fits in the palm of your hand" (Schmidt & Cohen, 2013, p. 4). "It is estimated that the doubling time of medical knowledge in 1950 was 50 years; in 1980, 7 years; and in 2010, 3.5 years. In 2020 it is projected to be 0.2 years—just 73 days" (Densen, 2011, p. 50). Breakthroughs that alter society and culture, and, more fundamentally, change our notions of being human, are taking place in multiple realms driven by advances in technology. Our society is witnessing self-driving cars (Google Cars), for example, and advances in robotics are reaching a point where they can interact with us in ways only imagined in science fiction. Developments in facial recognition, robotics, informatics, high-definition and 3D video cameras, and other areas are disrupting old formats and enhancing our ways of thinking and living. Cyborgs—a combination of human and machine—are on the horizon. We can access the world's information using search engines with the smartphones in our pockets, which are more advanced than the mainframe computer we used for our statistical analyses over 3 decades ago and that took up most of the room. We even have smartwatches, like the one Dick Tracy used, which seemed to be a fantastic but clearly futuristic design just a short time ago.

Cognitive and affective neurosciences are rapidly evolving with the assistance of new neuroscientific technologies, such as brain positron emission tomography scans, magnetic resonance imaging, and optigenetics. The latter refers to altering genes by making them produce florescent neuropathways, advancing our understanding of the cognitive, affective, and interpersonal domains that give rise to consciousness and being human (Siegel, 2017). These developments are creating new opportunities to develop novel approaches, incorporating technology, for the prevention and treatment of behavioral and mental health issues. "As global connectivity continues its unprecedented advance, many old institutions and hierarchies will have to adapt or risk becoming obsolete, irrelevant to society" (Schmidt & Cohen, 2013, p. 6). However, by and large, the field of behavioral and mental health has not capitalized on the rapid developments in technology that could advance the field.

Due in part to these rapid technological advances, the field of mental health is undergoing a highly disruptive paradigm shift, and as with any transformational event, this can provide abundant opportunities for those who can anticipate and influence these trends. Not only will clinical scientists and practitioners who wish to fully capitalize on technological advancements and become leaders in developing innovative approaches need to be knowledgeable about psychological science and tech generally, they will also need to appreciate the value of entrepreneurship and have a fundamental understanding of business. For example, if you are a behavioral health psychologist in a cancer center, it might be possible to develop stations where patients can easily access and use biofeedback, neurofeedback, or electrocranial stimulation to deal with the stress of treatment.

Is Psychology in Danger of Being Usurped?

From time to time the authors of this chapter are approached by businesspeople and investment bankers to assist in the development of a technology-based mental health start-up company. One such plan was to develop a business that would capitalize on efficiencies in the delivery of behavioral and mental health care. After a phase of consulting and due diligence, what was clear to us was that these individuals, while possessing extensive experience in technology, marketing, and the financial sector, lacked an understanding of mental health diagnoses, treatment, and research. Even though the business idea might have been financially viable, we felt its implementation would sacrifice standards of care. Thus, our decision not to participate was a fairly simple one. We withdrew from the project. That isn't to say that we weren't disappointed at leaving an opportunity on the table; rather, it was important to maintain a strong sense of integrity in the profession and the delivery of high-quality services. Finally, while valuing our potential partners' skill sets, we did not want to be part of a company that was not being led by those with deep knowledge of behavioral and mental health. What was clear from this experience is that there exists great opportunity to develop systems that will generate enormous profits for those who are able to creatively apply technology to the field of health care. If mental health professionals sit back and wait, others who are less knowledgeable about our field may co-opt our ideas and put them into action by creating new entities that are not controlled by mental health professionals. Although we applaud partnerships between mental health innovators and investors, we want to urge our colleagues not to play a passive role but, rather, to assume an innovative leadership position.

Advancing the field is going to require many diverse skill sets and participation from other disciplines and professionals, but the concern is that if psychology doesn't drive these advances, mental health professionals' knowledge and expertise will be packaged in ways that are not optimal for those in need but will primarily profit those with experience in business, whose primary allegiance is toward profit and not necessarily patient care and empirically vetted products. Part of the challenge the field faces is that it can be myopic in the pursuit of science and practice, and eschew the messiness, chaos, and uncertainty that come with innovation and entrepreneurship. Mental health professionals generally are exposed to very little, if any, curriculum in graduate school or beyond that deals with business, leadership, and entrepreneurship. Returning to the idea of cancer treatment stations mentioned earlier, let's say you came up with an idea for implementing the stations and you wanted to make a pitch to the cancer center's administrative board. Do you know how to make a pitch? Do you know how to identify funding sources or vendors to help bring your idea to fruition? If so, we are willing to bet you learned this after your formal education was over. This lack of business and leadership training can be a significant handicap to mental health professionals and researchers. However, without a grounding in the fundamentals of business, many learn the hard way, from trial and error, how to be successful. We believe that advances in technology have afforded many mental health practitioners new pathways toward meaningful and rewarding careers, as well as opportunities to push the frontier of clinical science and psychotherapeutics, while creating valuable assets and companies that will continue to thrive and produce income.

Another danger the field faces is the shaming of the entrepreneurial spirit among budding professionals who train under an outdated academic or purely service philosophy. When we began our careers in psychology over 3 decades ago, the zeitgeist was somewhat different from what we see now. In graduate school it was clear that our professors frowned on students whose goals included establishing private practices, which they believed had an avaricious "profit motive." We were being trained for "research and academic careers" or selflessly serving others, and those students who had other ideas were seen as unworthy. Obviously, during this era there was no training in how to run a successful practice, build a psychology-based business such as consulting, or launch a start-up company. Much has changed since our training days, but we have observed that a vestige of shaming remains. We believe it's time for the shame to end.

Characteristics of Entrepreneurs— Where Do You Fit?

Popular shows like *Shark Tank* have introduced many of us to the notion that perhaps ideas (and financial dreams) can be achieved through an innovative business venture or entrepreneurial effort. Outside the health professions, indeed, the idea seems mainstream now. Approximately 543,000 new businesses get started each month (Nazar, 2013)—joining the some 28 million that already exist. Small businesses generated 60% to 80% of net new jobs annually over the last decade.

Mental health professionals are generally good at understanding the personality characteristics that define or diagnose our patients. Practitioners use nomenclature from codified diagnostic systems and associated decision trees to arrive at the most accurate mental health diagnosis. Yet, mental health professionals have been less interested in learning about the characteristics that define entrepreneurs. This may be the result of being repulsed by those in the media who seem to be gross caricatures, falsely believing that entrepreneurship is based on the credo "Greed is good," like the character Gordon Gekko in the movie *Wall Street* or the *Wolf of Wall Street*'s villain played by Leonardo DiCaprio. Can mental health professionals learn from studying the characteristics that make for a successful entrepreneur? In the following section we provide a template that readers can use to assess whether they fit into specific entrepreneurial categories or profiles and to help them understand what characteristics are common. Hopefully readers will find the following helpful in self-assessment and when considering potential partners.

Bolton and Thompson (2000) defined an entrepreneur as "a person who habitually creates and innovates to build something of recognized value around perceived opportunities" (p. 5). An entrepreneur is someone who has a new idea and creates an organization to harvest the opportunity; the activity involved in that pursuit is called the *entrepreneurial life cycle*. The entrepreneurial life cycle is very much a series of fits, starts, and brainstorms. What makes an entrepreneur successful is the ability to navigate through uncharted waters and, when faced with a tough challenge, continue on. The economist Joseph Schumpeter (1991) wrote, "As the inventor produces ideas, the entrepreneur gets things done" (p. 143). Often innovations and advances in science and business are the result of collaboration between two individuals who have different skill sets and motivations.

Joseph Schumpeter, an Austrian American economist, was one of the first to study entrepreneurs and the impact of entrepreneurial capitalism on society. In 1934, when he wrote *The Theory of Economic Development*, he believed that innovation and creativity distinguished entrepreneurs from other businesspeople. He observed that innovation and entrepreneurship are closely interwoven and that the entrepreneur was at the center of all business activity. He noted that entrepreneurs create "clusters of innovations" that lead to business cycles because their actions create disruptive dislocations and arrive in huge waves. In fact, Schumpeter (1934) believed that entrepreneurs deserve credit for the industrial revolution. He introduced the term *creative destruction*, stating that the entrepreneur does not just invent things but also exploits in novel ways what has already been invented. He identified five types of entrepreneurial activity: (a) new product innovation or the introduction of a new service, (b) new process innovation or new methods of production, (c) market innovation or the opening of new markets, (d) input or resources innovation, and (e) organizational innovation (which is the complete restructuring of an entire industry or the breaking up of a monopoly).

In his 1934 definition, Schumpeter described tomorrow's entrepreneur as follows: one who is involved in the process of finding, leading, and coaching a close-knit group of talented people committed to pursuing an idea, as well as providing, marshaling, and allocating the resources needed to take advantage of a limited opportunity. That definition, from over a century ago, perhaps surprisingly, still works today. Carl Voigt (Moore, 2002) explained, "We sort of defined entrepreneurialism too narrowly as someone who wants to start their own business. But entrepreneurialism can also mean finding new business opportunities and expansion at existing companies." Here is where we believe opportunity for psychology in advancing mental health holds promise.

Broadly, an entrepreneur is someone who organizes a new venture, manages it, and assumes the associated risk. Within this definition, entrepreneurship can take different forms, which include small business or lifestyle entrepreneurs, high-growth potential entrepreneurs, professional or serial entrepreneurs, corporate entrepreneurs, and social entrepreneurs. What all of these have in common are the principal objectives of innovation, growth, and profit, and they will often employ formal strategic management practices to achieve them.

Drilling down more deeply into the common factors, Rampton (2014) asked the following questions regarding the traits and characteristics of an entrepreneur: (a) Is being born a prodigy the critical factor? (b) Is having a Type A personality the essential component for being an entrepreneur? and (c) Is being an extrovert who spends all their time tinkering around on projects the important feature? From the data he collected, Rampton found that entrepreneurs possess the following five common characteristics.

PASSION

Surprisingly, entrepreneurs are not motivated solely by financial incentives. Yes, Bill Gates and Steve Jobs were financially successful beyond imagination, yet the reality is that most entrepreneurs work tirelessly for little or nothing. To put it succinctly, they essentially want to solve a problem or find a solution to make life easier. They often enjoy the creative process and building viable products and companies. Throughout all the trials and tribulations, entrepreneurs reward themselves internally by realizing that they're on a mission for the greater good. No matter how bad it gets, it's their passion that motivates them between paydays and during all the times when everyone else tells them to quit.

RESILIENCE

Sir Winston Churchill once said, "Success is the ability to go from one failure to another with no loss of enthusiasm." As an entrepreneur, you're going to fail. That's just an unfortunate fact. Although something that drastic would be too much for most people to handle, an entrepreneur has the uncanny ability to get up, dust him- or herself off, and learn from failures. What went wrong? How can I succeed next time? These are the type of questions entrepreneurs will ask themselves. Entrepreneurs don't stay down when times get rough. They're resilient and thrive on challenges.

STRONG SENSE OF SELF

Any entrepreneur will tell you that there are always numerous problems to overcome. Whether it is securing enough funding, proving the naysayers wrong, or facing the competition head on, it's not easy being an entrepreneur. And being passionate and resilient can only go so far—which is why entrepreneurs also have an extremely strong sense of self. For example, being self-confident and self-motivated are key traits for most entrepreneurs. Entrepreneurs don't think that their idea could be good, they know it's good. And they're going to be motivated enough to illustrate to others that it's worth the time and money to go forward. Although they also understand that they can't do everything on their own, they realize that they are the only ones to make their idea a reality.

Just how confident are entrepreneurs? Campbell (2014) reported that a study by the Ewing Marion Kauffman Foundation, on behalf of *LegalZoom*, found that 91% of entrepreneurs are confident that their business will be more profitable in the next 12 months than it is at present.

FLEXIBILITY

Being able to adapt to changes and challenges is crucial for any business. In fact, most entrepreneurs will inform you that their idea or business plan is drastically different than when it began. An idea may be brilliant, but it isn't effective on its own. Entrepreneurs are flexible enough to make the adjustments to make that idea feasible. Furthermore, entrepreneurs are prepared and willing to modify their plan when new information arrives and circumstances change.

A great example of being flexible is the recent story behind Hyungsoo Kim and his company Eone, which is short for Everyone. Kim initially develop a wristwatch that featured braille, but he quickly discovered that people do not wish to draw attention to their disability. So, he discarded the original plan and came up with a watch that would not only be worn by the blind but also by people with sight. Now, the successful company sells the fashionable Bradley watch, which allows you to tell time by touch or sight.

VISION

Entrepreneurs see opportunity where others don't and are innovators who are always on the lookout to either develop a new idea or improve an existing product or service. Chances are that's the main reason they became an entrepreneur in the first place. At some point in their lives, they noticed something that needed improvement. But, instead of just saying that something could be better, they put a plan in motion. In other words, entrepreneurs can see the future before it happens.

Entrepreneurs are inspired by the idea of things that are yet to be discovered, and they have the vision to see ideas through. Jeff Bezos had a vision to tap into the new world of electronic retailing in 1994 and started "the world's most consumer-centric company." His little virtual bookstore was Amazon, which today is the model for all e-commerce businesses.

Bolton and Thompson (2003) offered another useful framework for characterizing the entrepreneur, based on six character themes that form the acronym *FACETS*, which stands for: (a) *focus*, (b) *advantage*, (c) *creativity*, (d) *ego*, (e) *team*, and (f) *social*. The character themes are described as follows:

- *Focus*. Successful entrepreneurs pursue the very best opportunities and avoid chasing after every option. Most successful entrepreneurs limit the number of projects they pursue, instead going after a tightly controlled portfolio of opportunities. In this regard, it is vital to develop a business plan.
- *Advantage*. People with an entrepreneurial mindset execute; in other words, they move forward and don't analyze things to death. They also exhibit the drive to pursue opportunities with enormous discipline.
- *Creativity*. A creative mind is the source of ideas and opportunities. Entrepreneurs passionately seek out new opportunities and are always looking for a way to profit from change and/or disruption in the way business is done.
- *Ego*. There are six components to ego, split into inner ego and outer ego. The inner ego embraces motivation (typically a desire to achieve, to make a difference, and maybe to "leave footprints"), self-assurance, and dedication. The outer ego is the entrepreneur's internal locus of control, a desire to be in charge of his or her own destiny. It includes responsibility and accountability and, especially significant, courage—an ability and willingness to deal with setbacks.
- *Team*. An entrepreneur should be able to find and select the right people and build them into an effective entrepreneur team. According to Bagchi (2006), an "A" team will be technically competent, have complementary skills, possess the ability to multitask, have a shared vision, enjoy personal integrity and mutual trust, be able to question each other and disagree, be resilient, and possess a sense of humor. Entrepreneurs should also know when and where help is required and have networking skills.

- *Social.* The social influences depend on the nature of the business or initiative, affecting the extent to which it has a community or environmental outlook. The social dimension also affects the culture and style of the organization and the way employees are treated.

Entrepreneurship isn't an all-or-nothing pursuit. It can be undertaken in stages or with different emphases. It is useful to consider different types of entrepreneurs and their goals. Smilor (2001) identified three types, as follows:

- *Aspiring entrepreneurs*—these entrepreneurs dream of starting a business. They hope for a chance to be their own boss, but have not yet left the security of their own employment to venture into the unknown world of a start-up.
- *Lifestyle entrepreneurs*—these entrepreneurs have developed a business that fits with their personal circumstances and way of life. Their central goal is to earn an income for themselves.
- *Growth entrepreneurs*—these entrepreneurs have the desire and ability to grow as fast and as large as possible. They are often referred to as gazelles and are key job creators.

These different types are likely more effective in particular situations. Having some knowledge of what type is called for in different endeavors will maximize outcome.

From the Entrepreneurial Person to the Process

In addition to the above characteristics, entrepreneurship involves a process that is also useful to articulate. Interested readers may take the Entrepreneur EDGE Scale (Pearman, Parks, Phillips, & King, 2013), which assesses four factors that are drivers of entrepreneur enterprise: (a) mind-set, (b) self-management, (c) dealing with others, and (d) business orientation.

There are several models that discuss the entrepreneurial process (Bhave, 1994; Bygrave, 2009). According to the Timmons model of entrepreneurship (see Figure 11.1), the three critical factors of a successful venture are opportunities, teams, and resources. The successful entrepreneur is someone who can balance these critical factors. Successful high-performance entrepreneurship does not happen by accident, although there is probably always some chaos—it is the nature of the systems, but controlled chaos succeeds.

The Timmons model is a useful way of explaining how the entrepreneurial process occurs. The entrepreneur searches for an opportunity, and on finding it, shapes the opportunity into a high-potential venture by drawing up a team and gathering the required resources to start a business that capitalizes on the opportunity. In the process of starting the business, the entrepreneur risks his or her career, personal cash flow, and net worth. The model is based on the premise that the entrepreneur earns rewards that are commensurate with the risk and effort involved in starting or financing the business.

FIGURE 11.1

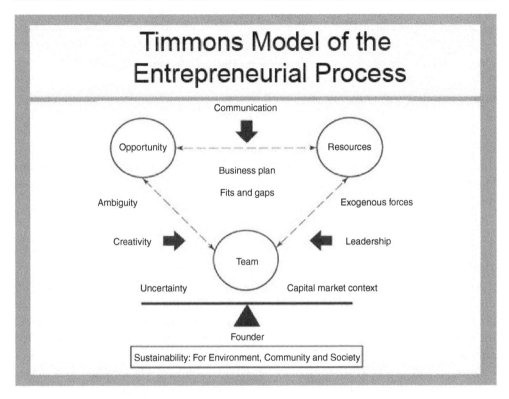

Timmons Model of the Entrepreneurial Process

From *New Venture Creation: Entrepreneurship for the 21st Century*
(8th ed., p. 110), by J. A. Timmons and S. Spinelli, Jr., 2009, New York, NY:
McGraw-Hill Irwin. Copyright 2009 by The McGraw-Hill Companies, Inc.
Reprinted with permission.

THE OPPORTUNITY FACTOR

The Timmons model states that entrepreneurship is opportunity driven, or that the market shapes the opportunity. A good idea is not necessarily a good business opportunity, and the underlying market demand determines the potential of the idea. An idea becomes viable only when it remains anchored in products or services that create or add value to customers, and remains attractive, durable, and timely. There are many such opportunities available in the mental health field to readers of this volume. Unlike conventional entrepreneurship models that start with a business plan and identify an opportunity, the Timmons model starts with a market opportunity. The business plan and the financing receive secondary importance and come only after identification of a viable opportunity. The model holds that a sound business opportunity would readily receive financing, so identifying the opportunity first makes the business plan failure-proof.

THE TEAM FACTOR

Once an entrepreneur identifies an opportunity, a team must be put together to start a business. The size and nature of the opportunity determine the size and shape of the team. The Timmons model places special importance on the team and considers a good team indispensable for success (a bad team can waste a great idea). Among all resources, only a good team can unlock a higher potential with any opportunity and manage the pressure related to growth. The two major roles of the team, relative to the other critical factors, are (a) removing the ambiguity and uncertainty of the opportunity by applying creativity, and (b) providing leadership to manage the available resources in the most effective manner by interacting with exogenous forces and the capital market context that keeps changing constantly. The ability to put together an effective team is a major factor of business success. Great teams, however, are scarce and the responsibility is on the entrepreneur to coach each team member to excel.

THE RESOURCES FACTOR

The Timmons model discounts the popular notion that extensive resources reduce the risk of starting a venture; instead, the model encourages bootstrapping or starting with the bare minimal requirements to attain competitive advantages. The advantages of bootstrapping include driving down market cost, instilling discipline and leanness in the organization, and encouraging creative resources to achieve more with the limited amount of money and other resources available. Some of the practical applications of bootstrapping include leasing instead of buying equipment, working out of a garage instead of rented space, and similar economy-driven choices. Like the formation of the team, the size and type of opportunity determine the level and extent of resources required. While good resources remain scarce, businesses with high potential and a good management team will have no problem attracting money and other resources. The entrepreneur works to "minimize and control" rather than "maximize and own." The role of the entrepreneur in managing resources includes building a good resource base to draw from when required and drawing up a business plan through a "fit and balance" method that balances the available resources with the opportunity and the potential of the team.

Reality Check Your Available Resources

Many entrepreneurs try to have all resources in place before starting a new venture. The Timmons model of entrepreneurship discounts this notion and holds only three factors as crucial: (a) a market-driven opportunity, (b) availability of a good team, and (c) adequate resources. These three critical factors of entrepreneurship remain interlinked, with any change in one factor having an impact on the other two. The reality is that opportunity, team, and resources seldom match. The Timmons model considers the major role of the entrepreneur to affect a match of the three critical factors of entrepreneurship at the correct time. Success of the business venture depends on the ability of the entrepreneur to ensure balance by applying creativity and leadership and by maintaining effective communications.

ASSESS YOUR TEAM

A key component of assessing your capacity for entrepreneurial ventures is to assess ourselves and others in terms of the role each person has in a team. We reviewed general characteristics of entrepreneurs above, but here we focus on roles each collaborator can take as part of a team. In assessing the capacity of your team, consider traits such as heart, smarts, guts, and luck (Tjan, Harrington, & Hsieh, 2012).

- If you are a HEART-driven entrepreneur, you bring purpose and passion to the business. As the founder, iconoclast, or visionary, you are consumed by a deep passion and driving hunger that you use to translate your purpose into reality. Starbucks CEO, Howard Schultz, is a great example of this style.
- If you are a SMARTS-driven entrepreneur, you are rational and focused on the facts. Your strength is steering a business by delegating and setting goals. You forge a system of accountability, articulate strategy, and emphasize performance. Your biggest strength is pattern recognition. Meg Whitman, the CEO of eBay, and Jeff Bezos are good examples of SMARTS-driven CEOs.
- If you've always been a risk-taker, then your predominant style is GUTS. GUTS-driven entrepreneurs can react quickly and conclusively at a time of crisis. These leaders aren't afraid to make changes for the betterment of the future. When you think of GUTS-driven leaders, think of Nelson Mandela or Richard Branson.
- Finally, if you are optimistic, intellectually curious, and humble, you might just be driven by LUCK. LUCK appears to be chaotic and unpredictable, but there have been lots of studies done to confirm the philosophy that luck favors the prepared. Tony Hseih, the founder of Zappos, is a good example of that profile in action.

Many believe entrepreneurs represent a different breed—they think, act, and live differently than the rest of society. By reviewing some of the characteristics mentioned here, we learn that the successful entrepreneurs seem to share a few of the same traits. Clearly, entrepreneurship is not for everyone. But how do you know whether it's for you? You should start by asking yourself what it takes to be a leader because, for the most part, you'll be doing a lot of the work up-front by yourself. If you can't lead yourself through start-up, chances are you won't likely be able to lead your business and future employees through growth and on to success.

CASE EXAMPLE: A TEAM IN ACTION

To illustrate how an entrepreneurial team can work, the authors offer the case example of their own efforts to build three tools: (a) a website—the Unified Psychotherapy Project (UPP), (b) an online publication—the *Journal of Unified Psychotherapy and Clinical Science*, and (c) a web-based compendium of techniques and methods of psychotherapy—*Psychotherapedia*.

As we developed all of these, we benefitted from many of the technological advances described throughout this volume. Before these developments the platform for these initiatives were not possible and would not have occurred. Referencing the partner profiles described above we identified ourselves as a *SMARTS*-driven partner (Sobelman) and a *HEART*-driven partner (Magnavita). With recognition of what talents each brought to their relationship, we first collaborated on a project that grew out of Magnavita's passion for developing a conceptual framework—the theory of unified clinical science and psychotherapeutics (Magnavita, 2005; Magnavita & Anchin, 2014). An expansion of this approach resulted in the website, the Unified Psychotherapy Project (UPP; http://www.unifiedpsychotherapyproject.org). The *Unified Psychotherapy Project* is a site where leading researchers, scholars, theorists, and clinicians who are devoted to advancing the field of clinical science and psychotherapeutics can contribute theoretical constructs, principles, empirical findings, as well as methods and techniques of contemporary psychotherapy. The team we built to make the site a reality was called the UPP Task Force. The task force is composed of an invited group of leading researchers, scholars, theorists, and clinicians who are devoted to advancing the field of clinical science and psychotherapeutics. The authors then developed *Psychotherapedia*, which is an Internet-based compendium of the techniques and methods of psychotherapy.

The authors continued the good energy of growing the UPP by developing *The Journal of Unified Psychotherapy and Clinical Science*, which seeks to bridge the interdisciplinary gaps among contemporary clinical sciences in order to advance a unified model of human behavior that will highlight theoretical and clinical knowledge, as well as provide empirical support for the component domains of the human personality and their interrelationships.

ASSESS YOUR PROJECT IDEA

In our experiences, we have learned that mental health professionals approach problems very differently than do businesspeople and entrepreneurs. We believe that many psychologists appear to be risk averse. In most cases, it isn't a matter of IQ points as much as it is the willingness to use what knowledge mental health professionals have gleaned from information and success that others who came before us have experienced. In reality, a need to reinvent the wheel isn't necessary. To illustrate how you might assess alignment of your project idea with a problem to be solved, we offer another case example from our own experience.

CASE EXAMPLE: DEVELOPING AN ELECTRONIC MEDICAL RECORD SYSTEM

One of the authors (Sobelman) moved outside traditional practice when he started a company that developed a proprietary software platform for the medical industry. The program streamlined office practice functionality by bundling record-keeping, archived records, and provided transcription services. The software solution allowed doctors a first true entry into the development of an electronic medical record (EMR) system.

Medical practices' back offices in 2006 continued to lag behind the technology curve of most industries. The majority of medical office staffs were still filing and retrieving records manually, in the same fashion as was done 50 years before. With the average patient file being 4 inches thick and filled with numerous transcribed patient encounters, the amount of time set aside to retrieve files, resend documents, and mail information represented 40% of the staffperson's business day. This high level of inefficiency and overhead cost structure was forcing medical practice owners to seek technological solutions, including EMRs.

The need to implement an EMR-type solution has been obvious. However, the main issue with such implementations to date has been the cost of current solutions, as well as converting their complicated formats into an industry standard. Our software was a solution that provided an efficient and cost-effective method that converted a hardcopy file into an EMR, while meeting budget requirements and addressing ease of use, implementation, and rapid file-retrieval needs.

Sobelman examined the EMR sector, which by some estimates was a $10 to $15 billion per year business in the medical practice automation segment of the medical records marketplace. Most of the companies that were establishing a market presence were relying on physicians to utilize handheld tablet computer processes in order to capture patient information. Our software process worked well not only for primary care practices but also for specialists, who must keep very detailed patient-encounter notes and, thus, must rely on transcription for medical record requirements.

Our software platform, which was HIPAA compliant, used web-based medical automation tools for medical document retrieval, transcription, and archiving. We offered virtually unlimited storage capacity with the idea of eliminating filing and refiling time by medical staff. There was no new hardware to purchase; our solution could be accessed from medical office legacy desktop computers, with, preferably, a broadband connection.

Here is what we learned from this experience about entrepreneurs that create a start-up company. First, we finished a business plan, which was approximately 80 pages long; we then extrapolated the information into a 5-page executive business summary. The executive business summary was used as part of their presentation to intended investors. The question then came up about financing the venture? We learned about angel investors, mezzanine investors, and venture capital, in addition to offering Series A and Series B stocks. Of course, there was always "bootstrapping," which means no funding at all. Since we determined that we needed approximately $1 million to support initial efforts, the bootstrapping financial strategy was not an option. We started with angel financing and raised our initial capital by making presentations to family and friends. The first 2 years saw a monthly burn rate of approximately $30,000 per month. We learned that legal costs, as well as engineering costs to develop the software product, were very expensive. The financial drain forced a second round of financing. However, at the end of 18 months, the new venture had some customers and a small income stream, which provided a better presentation to investors. At the end of 3 years, we had customers in nine states, a U.S. staff of 10 people, a transcription staff (India and Philippines) of approximately 100 people, and we began to become cash positive.

The new venture was an early entry into the EMR/EHR (electronic health record) world for small to medium medical groups. In other words, we were before the curve, and before the bigger explosion of mandatory EHR requirements and incentives by larger insurance companies. And we found out very quickly that our current competition had substantial financial resources. You may have heard of Cerner Corporation ($2.5 billion), Epic Systems ($1.5 billion), Allscripts, NextGen, and GE, all of whom dwarfed us as they began capturing the market share. As such, we began looking for someone to purchase their company; after an 8-month search, we were fortunate enough to find a buyer. An important note—during the preliminary plans, my partners and I envisioned mid-six to seven-figure salaries (sales + bonuses). For the first 3 years, we never took a salary and for the next 2 years, we took small draws, but nowhere near our initial projections.

This summarizes an almost 6-year journey. And in the end, I am still seeing patients in my private practice. The moral of the story? Sometimes we shouldn't leave our day job, but we can still dream, and perhaps even take a walk outside the box of our training. To prepare for the stressors of raising money and being responsible for your decision to pursue entrepreneurship, make sure you do your homework and get advice from those who have "been there before."

Conclusion

In the volume *Future Smart* James Canton (2015), wrote: "Innovation is the only competitive advantage" (p. 38). He predicted that the future will be defined by "accelerated change, fast innovation, smart technology, predictive systems, connected markets, digital everything, and mobile commerce" (p. 39). Connectivity and digitalization will be the hallmarks of this era. He described "future smart entrepreneurs" as "agile, adaptive, global, predictive, and innovative-savvy" (p. 25). He suggested that

> In the future everyone will be an entrepreneur or at least embrace the lessons we associate with an entrepreneur and more. Agility, embracing innovation, working across borders and with diverse teams, understanding technology futures—everyone must learn to understand how to develop, build, and manage a business. (p. 207)

If starting a new business seems intimidating, know that there are various low-risk pathways to gradually step into entrepreneurship. You can begin your journey and test the waters simply by providing thought leadership in the field (Blank, 2016). Depending on your areas of interest and expertise, thought leadership could look like any or a combination of the following:

- Publishing and sharing knowledge across many platforms, such as social networks (e.g., Twitter), podcasts, articles, and forums specific to one's discipline (e.g., APA monitorLIVE events; http://psyciq.apa.org/category/networking/monitorlive/).

▪ Contributing to policymaking efforts (e.g., by developing draft resolution language for a cause affecting public health or advising a county board of supervisors on an issue).

▪ Volunteering for leadership posts, mentoring opportunities, or career networks in your professional circles.

As thought leaders share their expertise, they learn by teaching. With increased social engagement, problems that might not have been apparent before may become clear. The thought leader can then begin to formulate innovative solutions before jumping in with both feet. Any information products one produces in the process of being a thought leader (e.g., ebooks, videos) can, of course, be monetized via download or subscription fees, thus creating, if not a sizeable income stream, then at least a low-risk trickle that can serve as inspiration for the next step.

Mental health professionals can study and emulate certain characteristics entrepreneurs display. Many of these characteristics were elaborated above and offer useful insight into what makes a successful entrepreneur. In order for the field of behavioral and mental health to advance, the coat of shame around money often worn by practitioners needs to be shed so that innovative and creative solutions to the challenges of providing services can be enhanced. As never before, technology offers us unprecedented opportunities to use digital connectivity to develop novel approaches and products for the delivery and optimization of mental health care.

References

Bagchi, S. (2006). *The high-performance entrepreneur: Golden rules for success in today's world*. New York, NY: Penguin Books.

Bhave, M. P. (1994). A process model of entrepreneurial venture creation. *Journal of Business Venturing, 9*, 223–242. http://dx.doi.org/10.1016/0883-9026(94)90031-0

Blank, A. (2016, September). You can be a thought leader—here's the first step. *Forbes*. Retrieved from https://www.forbes.com/sites/averyblank/2016/09/13/can-i-be-a-thought-leader-you-bet-and-heres-the-first-step/

Bolton, W. K., & Thompson, J. L. (2000). *Entrepreneurs: Talent, temperament, technique*. Oxford, England: Butterworth Heinemann.

Bolton, W. K., & Thompson, J. L. (2003). *The entrepreneur in focus: Achieve your potential*. London, England: Thomson Learning.

Bygrave, W. D. (2009). The entrepreneurial process. In W. D. Bygrave & A. Zacharakis (Eds.), *The portable MBA in entrepreneurship* (4th ed., pp. 1–26). Hoboken, NJ: John Wiley & Sons, Inc. http://dx.doi.org/10.1002/9781118256121

Campbell, A. (2014, February). The power of optimism: 91 percent of entrepreneurs confident. *Small Business Trends*. Retrieved from https://smallbiztrends.com/2014/02/power-of-optimism-91-percent-entrepreneurs-confident.html

Canton, J. (2015). *Future smart: Managing the game-changing trends that will transform your world*. Boston, MA: Da Capo Press.

Densen, P. (2011). Challenges and opportunities facing medical education. *Transactions of the American Clinical and Climatological Association, 122*, 48–58.

Issacson, W. (2014). *The innovators: How a group hackers, geniuses, and geeks created the digital revolution*. New York, NY: Simon & Schuster.

Magnavita, J. J. (2005). *Personality-guided relational psychotherapy: A unified approach*. Washington, DC: American Psychological Association. http://dx.doi.org/10.1037/10959-000

Magnavita, J. J., & Anchin, J. C. (2014). *Unifying psychotherapy: Principles, methods, and evidence from clinical science*. New York, NY: Springer.

Moore, B. (2002, March 27). Changing classes. *The Wall Street Journal*. Retrieved from http://www.wsj.com/articles/SB1016999863115842920

Nazar, J. (2013, September 9). 16 Surprising statistics about small businesses. *Forbes*. Retrieved from http://www.forbes.com/sites/jasonnazar/2013/09/09/16-surprising-statistics-about-small-businesses

Pearman, R. R., Parks, R. D., Phillips, B., & King, M. C. (2013). *Your entrepreneur edge: Your entrepreneur effectiveness guide*. Winston-Salem, NC: Leadership Performance Systems.

Rampton, J. (2014, April). 5 personality traits of an entrepreneur. *Forbes*. Retrieved from http://www.forbes.com/sites/johnrampton/2014/04/14/5-personality-traits-of-an-entrepreneur/#7b33fadf22f6

Schmidt, E., & Cohen, J. (2013). *The new digital age: Reshaping the future of people, nations and business*. New York, NY: Alfred A. Knopf.

Schumpeter, J. A. (1934). *The theory of economic development: An inquiry into profits, capital, credit, interest, and the business cycle* (Vol. 55). Cambridge, MA: Harvard University.

Schumpeter, J. A. (1991). *The economics and sociology of capitalism* (R. Swedberg, Ed.). Princeton, NJ: Princeton University Press.

Siegel, D. J. (2017). *Mind: A journey to the heart of being human*. New York, NY: W. W. Norton.

Smilor, R. W. (2001). *Daring visionaries: How entrepreneurs build companies, inspire allegiance, and create wealth*. Avon, MA: Adams Media Corporation.

Timmons, J. A., & Spinelli, S., Jr. (2009). *New venture creation: Entrepreneurship for the 21st century* (8th ed.). New York, NY: McGraw-Hill Irwin.

Tjan, A. K., Harrington, R. J., & Hsieh, T.-Y. (2012). *Heart, smarts, guts, luck: What it takes to be an entrepreneur and build a great business*. Boston, MA: Harvard Business School.

Jeffrey Zimmerman and Jeffrey J. Magnavita

Adopting New Technology for Your Practice
How to Assess Fit and Risks

12

In this final chapter, we summarize the various areas of technology already discussed and offer a glimpse at other important technological developments for our field. We then guide readers through the process of incorporating new technologies in a way that makes sense for their practice. As we have stated, the rapid advances in technology are altering the way mental and behavioral health is delivered. So it is vital that current practitioners educate themselves about these developments. With this information, you can make educated decisions about what is beneficial and necessary to incorporate into your practice. We hope that reading this volume and this final chapter will assist with this endeavor.

Promises and Challenges of Technology in Mental Health Care

In this volume, we have presented a few examples from the broad range of technological advances that are already available to help us improve access to mental health care, enhance treatment outcome, provide a wider range of treatment options, and sharpen our professional skills. In this chapter, we briefly review those advances and their associated challenges and address

http://dx.doi.org/10.1037/0000085-013
Using Technology in Mental Health Practice, J. J. Magnavita (Editor)

several other topics that are not covered in this volume but that provide valuable information for professionals.

Biometric Devices, Many Linked to Mobile Apps

Today, many biometric devices are available for a fraction of what they cost just a decade ago. When the authors first began practicing, for example, biofeedback systems were complicated and cost thousands of dollars, making this technology out of reach for most practitioners. Now there are many fairly inexpensive devices on the market that can be purchased by clinicians and also, if appropriate, used by patients at home. The most ubiquitous of these, of course, is the smartphone itself. With its built-in features, such as camera, microphone, GPS, step counter, and so on, user data can be collected and processed to reveal health-related insights. Heart-monitor connections and other biofeedback applications (apps) are now available for purchase and download on smartphones, making this technology readily accessible for many people. There are thousands of apps that have been developed for mental and behavioral health. Iozzio (2015) featured a few in an article titled, "The Doctor Is In (Your Phone)." One app, named PRIORI, was developed to discern speech patterns that are suggestive of a manic or depressive episode; if noted, the app sends an alert to the practitioner that intervention is needed. Sleep apnea is often an undiagnosed problem, which can cause both mental and physical disorders. ApneaApp was developed to detect variations in breathing to determine whether apnea is present. These apps and many others can expand the reach of the practitioner and afford us the opportunity to access vital data, such as sleep patterns, mood cycles, and anxiety states, and offer immediate strategies that can be used between office visits or for maintenance.

Additionally, portable biofeedback and neurofeedback machines can be used easily in clinical practice with minimal training. Portable electroencephalogram headsets can now be purchased and used with an array of apps as adjunctive treatment for many patients, and they provide a powerful research tool for those who want to explore new areas or want to create useful apps. Biometric devices to measure physiological states are also available to measure sleep patterns and levels of physiological activation to provide data about patients' emotional states.

The challenge with all of the above is integrating their use into professional care in a meaningful way that relates the biometric data and any changes tracked over time to the specific goals of therapy. Another huge challenge concerns the security of the user's individual data if it is uploaded and stored in the cloud. As noted in a report from American University (Montgomery, Chester, & Kopp, 2017),

> The degree to which users of wearable devices will be able to make informed privacy decisions—and thus exercise meaningful control over their personal data—will ultimately depend on the effectiveness of government and self-regulatory policies. In their current state, however, none of these systems provides adequate safeguards to patients or consumers in the Big-Data era. (p. 4)

Videoconferencing Technology for Telehealth

The development of high-quality video cameras, often embedded in computers, paired with high-bandwidth Internet capacity and secure video transmission programs, has opened a new frontier of telepsychotherapy, along with ethical and risk management challenges for practitioners. This technology is within the realm of most practitioners with Internet access and a suitable computer, and is being rapidly adopted by clinicians around the world. Telepsychology is a cost-effective and a reliable forum for conducting treatment in certain cases. It also affords a great deal of flexibility for practitioners who now can practice virtually. Especially in rural areas, telehealth offers access to specialized services that would not otherwise be available. Practitioners should be familiar with the licensing laws of the states or countries in which the patient is residing or visiting (http://www.apa.org/practice/guidelines/telepsychology.aspx) and obtain appropriate training and authorization where required, as described in Chapter 2.

Routine Outcome Monitoring

Many approaches have been developed to achieve positive treatment outcomes in mental and behavioral health status as efficiently and cost-effectively as possible. An important research-based technological advance in this regard is routine outcome monitoring (ROM), as introduced in Chapter 8. A number of ROM systems have been developed and been shown to enhance treatment outcome (Barkham, Mellor-Clark, & Stiles, 2015; Boswell, Kraus, Castonguay, & Youn, 2015; Brown, Simon, Cameron, & Minami, 2015; Duncan & Reese, 2015; Lambert, 2015). These systems can be incorporated in practice with minimal—and sometimes no—expense and are now available for independent practitioners, as well as clinics and hospitals. Patients can complete regular assessments using tablets in the office or on their own computers, providing direct feedback to clinicians to alert them to treatment disruptions or lack of response, so that they can be immediately addressed.

Professional Development

Supervision, training, consultation, and continuing education are now available regardless of the remoteness of one's location. Since the development of the Internet, digital video technology, and innovative online resources, practitioners can avail themselves of an array of opportunities to advance their professional skills and expertise, as described in Chapter 10.

Online Clinical Practice Guidelines

There has been a recent initiative by a number of organizations to develop practical guides for the latest in evidence-based treatment. Such guides are easily accessible on the Internet. Clinical Practice Guidelines (CPGs) are tools that help link research and practice (Bufka & Swedish, 2016). Three elements of effective clinical decision making are (a) clinical expertise, (b) patient values and characteristics, and (c) the best available research. The American Psychological Association has undertaken a major initiative in an effort to develop CPGs[1] (Bufka & Swedish, 2016; Hollon, 2016; Hollon et al., 2014). Although still in the early stages of development in North America, the United Kingdom has pioneered the development of the National Institute for Health and Care Excellence Clinical Guidelines, which can be accessed online in various formats. Those guidelines may not be generalizable to North America or other populations; however, they do provide meaningful evidence-based findings for clinicians. CPGs require sound judgment, without which they would represent a cookbook and be subject to artific application. Clinical expertise needs to be systematically developed with accurate feedback received and considered over time. The ROMs presented in this volume are one such feedback mechanism. An understanding of decision analytics aimed at reducing clinician biases is also important when dealing with CPGs (Magnavita & Lilienfeld, 2016).

Search Engines and Data Mining

The development of Internet search engines has led to remarkable improvements in access to information. In fact, some claim such search engines have fundamentally changed humans' social memories and transcended the limitations of human cognition (Wegner & Ward, 2013). Using search engines, such as Google, clinicians now have access to high-quality information never before so readily available. This can take the form of referral information, treatment programs, and other resources that clinicians can even look at with their patients in the clinic. Having a large monitor that is easily viewed by clients makes this an easy way to work collaboratively on behalf of the patient, couple, or family.

If one uses Boolean operators—search commands—to access relevant databases, clinical decision making can be enhanced with the stroke of a few keys (Norcross, Hogan, & Koocher, 2008). Clinical algorithms emerging from large data sets can be used to reduce bias in clinical decision making (Magnavita & Lilienfeld, 2016). Google searches can be mined for various research insights, such as tracking the geography of diseases (Yang et al., 2017).

Computerized Psychodiagnostic Assessment

Having access to high-quality psychometric information has never been as efficient. In the past, psychological testing required labor-intensive administration and hand scoring, making it impractical for the busy practitioner. Often, psychological testing had a long turnaround time, making this needed information less relevant. Advances

---

[1]Jeffrey J. Magnavita served on the Clinical Practice Guideline Steering Committee and, in his final year, as vice-chair of the committee.

in technology have dramatically improved this situation. Clinics, hospitals, residential treatment programs, and even independent practitioners can now offer cutting-edge psychodiagnostic services with rapid turnaround, providing relevant data for diagnosis, treatment planning, and progress monitoring.

Marketing and Social Media

The ability to thrive as a mental and behavioral health practitioner requires being able to attract patients who can benefit from one's services. One practitioner told a story about opening her practice, saying that her plan was to open an office, and when she did so, people would find her and request her services. Unfortunately, this approach did not lead to success. To have a successful practice, an individual, group, or clinic must be able to market their offerings to attract those that are in need of the services offered. When the authors first opened our respective practices, marketing primarily was done by contacting local physicians, giving talks in the community, and putting our names in the phone books. We have seen tectonic changes in the 3 decades in which we have been in practice. Technology has opened up the door for marketing services in ways that would never have been anticipated when we first started our practices.

One of the most effective technological tools available for marketing is a website. An appealing and up-to-date website allows your services to be easily found by anyone seeking help or those seeking to refer others to your services. There are many ways to develop a website. With basic computer skills, many will be able to use a site builder to develop an attractive website. Others who don't have the interest or expertise can easily find a website developer, who for a reasonable fee can help you represent yourself or your group in a professional and appealing manner. Chapter 11 lists a few resources for deciding whether and how professionals may also choose to present their thought leadership via social media platforms.

Regarding social media, some clinicians may wish to help their clients by sharing tips for managing their online identities, that is, their online social profiles. Questions to explore might be: How does the client present him- or herself online? Is this how they wish to be seen by others? How do the clients' good or poor communication habits and patterns of self-disclosure play out online? Is the client behaving like an online "troll" or bullying others? Is the client the victim of bullying or online stalking? What privacy restrictions on accounts or changes in social media use might be recommended as part of the behavioral or therapeutic plan?

Furthering the Field Through Scholarship and Professional Associations

The scientist–practitioner model for the profession of psychology instills the credo that psychological practice should be based on science. Even the most isolated practitioner has tools available to conduct research or be part of a collaborative research effort.

With the development of technology, clinician–researcher collaborative relationships are now possible in ways never imagined. Bridging the researcher–practitioner gap has been an initiative that seeks to allow clinicians to be part of ongoing research. Clinicians who are interested in conducting research have many resources available to them to facilitate this endeavor.

We are all responsible for advancing the field of mental health and clinical science. The practitioner–scholar is another model of professional psychology. Advances in technology afford all practitioners opportunities to advance the field through research, scholarship, and involvement in professional organizations devoted to clinical science and mental health treatment. Books, professional journals, podcasts, YouTube material, and just about all the information ever produced is accessible on the Internet right in our offices. Never before has it been so convenient for mental health professionals to keep abreast of developments in the field and the societal trends that affect the mental health of society. This information can offer innovative and creative therapeutic opportunities.

Investing in Technology for Your Practice

The purchase of technology is often not a trivial expense. These costs go directly against one's bottom line; paying them off may take years, and during that time what was brand new technology often become obsolete. So it is essential to think about that expense carefully before making a purchase.

Looking at technology purchases from the standpoint of an outside investor who seeks a needs assessment can be quite helpful in determining whether the technology is an appropriate purchase. Imagine you are the financial backer of a business and the manager is asking you for the same technology. It would be useful to know the following before you authorize the expenditure of funds—your funds:

- What specific practical need is the technology filling?
- How is this need aligned with the goals of the business?
- What other ways are there to address the needs?
- What are the various competitive products or services to the specific one being proposed or considered?
- How much time will it take to learn how to effectively use the technology?
- How will the technology help the business's bottom line?
- How much will the maintenance of the technology cost?
- What is the timeline for generating enough revenue and depreciation (if pertinent) for the technology to pay for itself?

These questions can all be applied to the top contender options such that, rather than being influenced by the marketing or sales pitch, you can make a more informed business decision. The authors have seen many instances of these major financial decisions being made in the impulse of the moment, which is craftily manipulated by an expert salesperson or impacted by other pressures.

ESSENTIAL PURCHASE: ADMINISTRATIVE SYSTEMS

Vital to any successful mental and behavioral health practice, whether in an independent, clinic, hospital, or group practice setting, are the administrative systems, which when working properly allow practitioners to function efficiently and effectively. Mental health training requires a major commitment of resources. For doctoral-trained mental health professionals, the cost of education, the time missed earning a salary by delaying the start of an income-earning career, and the sacrifice required are significant. Many doctoral-level providers begin their careers in significant debt that will require decades to repay. Starting salaries for mental health practitioners are generally not commensurate with the level of responsibility, commitment, and extended period of costly education and training. As discussed in Chapter 11, there is often an implicit or explicit shaming that occurs if one is interested in private practice or entrepreneurship. The message is often that mental health clinicians are supposed to be selfless and not concerned with financial gain. We hope that if you hold this type of dysfunctional belief, you are reconsidering it.

Much effort goes into training mental health practitioners to provide effective treatment and compassionate care, but for most the administrative side of the practice or organization is left to someone else. Psychologists and other mental health professionals are not trained in the fundamentals of business or the technology they will need to be successful in independent practice. Those who do not receive an education in business and technology can become demoralized and unduly stressed, often questioning the commitment they made to their profession. These stressors on the clinician can certainly impact the care that is being provided. This is a sad state of affairs, as there is a need for qualified mental health providers to serve the mental health needs of the communities in which they practice. Many are choosing not to follow the calling to mental health practice because of these challenges. Many of the best and the brightest are attracted to other careers that promise financial security and advancement. In our experience (both authors have been running successful practices for a combined period of over 60 years), attending to the administrative side of practice is vital to success. Any practice or institutional system should aim to support the clinician in doing what she or he is trained for—providing the highest quality behavioral and mental health services to those in need. Some of this support relates to the essential aspects of office administration. These include accurate billing for services, scheduling, accounting, managing intake and other "onboarding" procedures, routine correspondence, and gathering and safely maintaining the confidential information necessary for billing and medical records.

In practice, without the ability to accurately keep track of services rendered, submit completed health care insurance forms to the appropriate insurance companies, and keep track of patient payments, your practice or institution is in immediate danger of not surviving. It is also at greater exposure from the standpoint of regulatory compliance and risk management (Barnett, Zimmerman, & Walfish, 2014). With the development of desktop computers and specialized programs, practitioners have been able to efficiently document and track patient services and generate completed insurance forms that can, in many cases, be submitted electronically. These developments in computers and software have been remarkable in that they have allowed practitioners to keep track of services with a minimal of time and effort. Computer billing software is offered by a number of companies, and each clinician and institution should determine what company offers them the best product. Many of these programs also combine scheduling with medical documentation. Zimmerman and Libby (2015) discussed the importance of not only tracking billing but looking at a "dashboard" of metrics related to the business of running the practice (e.g., productivity, referral patterns, and accounts receivable).

EXAMPLE OF A "MAYBE PURCHASE": VIDEO EQUIPMENT

Practitioners who strive to have a technology-based practice should consider the advantages and the technical aspects of audiovisual cameras, digitally storing any videos made, and, if appropriate, a method for allowing patients to view their session. One thing that I (JJM) have found to be extremely valuable is having a large monitor on the wall that serves many purposes. Considered to be the microscope of psychotherapy, audiovisual cameras allow for videotaping and reviewing sessions. A relatively inexpensive investment, this technology affords us the opportunity to closely examine our work and get feedback from others to increase our effectiveness. With a large wall-mounted monitor, patients are able to clearly view various types of biofeedback without having to strain to see. When appropriate, it is also helpful to be able to share online resources that can be viewed together to highlight an issue or as psychoeducation. For example, when working with individuals with attachment issues of certain types, I (JJM) often find it useful to show a videoclip to demonstrate or bring home a point. One that has been standard in my practice is Edward Tronick's Still Face Video (https://www.youtube.com/watch?v=apzXGEbZht0).

APPLYING THE NEEDS ASSESSMENT APPROACH

Suppose a practice was looking to invest in a billing system. There might immediately be three options to explore. They could use a do-it-yourself (DIY) approach, with a spreadsheet to track each client account and send out bills. Alternatively, they could use an online service. Or they could hire a billing service. Each of these options has a different profile of costs, functionality, and risk.

The DIY model might involve setup time and training of a staffperson, if the owner is not going to input data. Backup systems need to be in place and, of course, Health Insurance Portability and Affordability Act (HIPAA) considerations need to be taken into account, as do procedural methodologies to make sure postings are correct. The practice also needs to anticipate system failures, such as hard drive problems or a broken laptop. Each of these has a cost.

The online system may seem much simpler to cost out, as there may only be a monthly fee to consider. However, one needs to look more carefully. What are the learning curve costs? How many people in the practice need to be trained in this system? This is a crucial decision to ensure that the owner is not left in the lurch if the billing person who uploads information has consistently been making errors which are not immediately discovered, or if the person leaves the practice or is out ill for a considerable length of time. How do current data get uploaded into the new system? What are the costs associated with uploading current data, or is there a need to run two systems (the old and the new) concurrently until current patients have left the practice? Compatibility with your current configuration of hardware also needs to be considered. Logistical considerations need to be thought through, as internal procedures and forms might need to change to yield efficiency in data entry with the new system. Perhaps of key importance is the ability to have frequent backups of the data. By this we mean that the files need to be able to be read by an alternative system if the online source ceases to be in operation or if at some point you want to change to a different service. These are part of your assessment, as they all have costs such as money, time, and lost opportunity.

A billing service might require the same type of consideration around setup of the online system. Similarly, the costs of reconfiguring the data and entering it into another system should also be computed (e.g., if you should decide to change vendors).

With each of these options it is also crucial to map out the implementation phase of the new system. This is true with any technological investment. Training costs, peripheral equipment, and even the costs of breaking down an old system and converting data need to be computed.

Last, the fit of the decision with your practice's needs and culture should be part of the analysis. Investing in a system that is not going to be usable or embraced by the users is akin to getting no return on the investment of time, energy, and money that will occur. Fit can often be at least partially assessed by testing the system and having various users or potential users also test it.

As one weighs the direct and indirect costs mentioned here, a decision can emerge that makes sense and is less likely to be based on the emotions of the moment (e.g., fear, excitement, frustration) or on ego.

Developing a Technology Integration Plan

Buying or leasing the technology is just the first step. There also needs to be a plan for its on-boarding or integration with the rest of the practice. While training is essential, it is also important to calculate setup time and the time to convert and upload basic data that may need to go into the system. Many practice owners underestimate this timeline, hence inflating the amount they expect to earn from the technology and deflating the costs of getting the system operational.

Such an integration plan should also include the time it will take to run multiple sets of tests to make sure the system is doing what you intend it to do under different conditions and with various users. The testing should try to "break" the system, leading to a fault of sorts that will help you determine what might go wrong when the system is live. Do not assume the users will always use the technology correctly. What happens if Plug A gets put into Socket B? What happens if someone hits the wrong set of keys? Do you lose your data? How easy is it to sabotage the system (e.g., by a disgruntled staffperson who is leaving the practice) or for you to get "locked out"? You should also in this phase be running tests of reports that might be generated by the system to be sure they are set up correctly and producing the results you think they are producing. To do this, enter and compute values by hand and match them with the reports the system generates to make sure you get the data you need. Sometimes variables and labels need to be set up in ways that are counterintuitive in order for the output to be usable. This, for example, can easily occur with accounting (as contrasted with billing) software.

The integration plan needs to contemplate the following:

- In what areas will technology be integrated?
- What is the time frame?
- Will technology installation interrupt patient care?
- What data security and recovery strategies need to be implemented?
- Will the technology be completely integrated at once or phased in via a step-wise approach?
- How will you be sure to have usable data when this technology integration is obsolete?

Signing a Contract for Leasing or Buying Technology

Many significant purchases of technology require the signing of a contract. This is not something to be taken lightly, even if presented as such by the salesperson, billing service, or computer consultant. Contracts are usually presented in ways that favor the person who wrote the first draft. They may be presented as a formality and nonnegotiable, but generally this is not ultimately the case. The contracts are legal agreements—you need to read them, understand them, and agree with them, or ask that they be modified.

Many people will seek attorney consultation for very complex contracts. Although this is a good idea, we also believe it is important to seek consultation from another mental health professional who is experienced in negotiating such contracts. They can look at the contract from practical and compliance/ethical (not legal) perspectives and help you attend to factors that your attorney may not consider in terms of implementation and the dismantling of the technology. This last point is very important to consider but is often neglected. Most technology will be dismantled at some point. When this occurs, the specifications in the contract (if present) will become far more relevant than they were thought to be when you were excited to be getting the technology in the first place.

Picking a Technology Consultant

In addition to your attorney and mental health practice management consultant, it is important to have an accessible technology consultant(s). For Internet technologies, you may not need this person to be local. They may be able to help from afar with things such as website design, search engine optimization, and security. For certain types of hardware, such as your basic computer, you may be able to buy a service contract at the time of purchase. However, for other technologies (e.g., billing software; biofeedback equipment; assessment equipment; other specialized software and peripheral equipment, such as scanners, backup devices, printers), it is important to have a technology expert who can help you with installation and troubleshooting. You may need someone who can configure your own server or deal with a hard drive that stopped functioning. This person can be crucial when called upon in an emergency, so that you are not "out of business" for days or weeks trying to solve a problem yourself. They may also help you avoid problems in the first place, as this type of consultant can help you evaluate systems you are considering purchasing and assess the components, configuration, and the suitability of a particular system.

When picking a technology consultant consider doing the following:

- First, get recommendations from people you trust so that you are interviewing people who have a proven track record.
- Interview the consultant as you would any other person you would hire. Do they seem like a good fit? Do they understand your core values and the way you run your practice?
- Assess their installation, routine and emergency fee structure, and cost increases.
- Do not assume that the consultant who charges more is necessarily better. Do a cost/benefit analysis. Do you need everything they are promising? Are you paying for a large infrastructure (i.e., their business or company)? Do they charge for all services provided or do they sometimes provide a value-added consultation and answer small routine questions without charging you a fee? Do they provide written detailed descriptions of all services rendered so that you know exactly what they have done and when (especially if a problem is not ultimately resolved when you thought it was)?

Ongoing Evaluation of Needs

Adding technology to your practice is not a "set it and forget it" proposition. It is an ongoing process of evaluation and change. In fact, this occurs across multiple technologies, as you may have various systems in your practice that all need to be routinely assessed. Whether it is making sure they comply with HIPAA, are operated safely, or are state-of-the-art, it is important to routinely look at the technologies in your office to ensure that they are up to standards and are helping you run your practice and provide the best clinical services possible.

Conclusion

In this final chapter of this volume, we addressed the rapid technological changes that have taken place with regard to health care in general and, more specifically, in the provision of mental health services. We discussed how technology can complement excellence in clinical care and even help enhance the care that is being delivered. We addressed the need for thoughtful planning around the integration of technology in the development of an entrepreneurially sophisticated practice that is dedicated to the provision of high-quality services. When technology is successfully incorporated in clinical practice, it is possible to build an environment that is sustainable and one in which the clinician(s) can achieve both clinical and financial rewards.

References

Barkham, M., Mellor-Clark, J., & Stiles, W. B. (2015). A CORE approach to progress monitoring and feedback: Enhancing evidence and improving practice. *Psychotherapy*, *52*, 402–411. http://dx.doi.org/10.1037/pst0000030

Barnett, J. E., Zimmerman, J., & Walfish, S. (2014). *The ethics of private practice: A practical guide for mental health clinicians*. New York, NY: Oxford University Press.

Boswell, J. F., Kraus, D. R., Castonguay, L. G., & Youn, S. J. (2015). Treatment outcome package: Measuring and facilitating multidimensional change. *Psychotherapy*, *52*, 422–431. http://dx.doi.org/10.1037/pst0000028

Brown, G. S., Simon, A., Cameron, J., & Minami, T. (2015). A collaborative outcome resource network (ACORN): Tools for increasing the value of psychotherapy. *Psychotherapy*, *52*, 412–421. http://dx.doi.org/10.1037/pst0000033

Bufka, L. F., & Swedish, E. F. (2016). Clinical practice guideline development and decision making. In J. J. Magnavita (Ed.), *Clinical decision making in mental health practice* (pp. 105–123). Washington, DC: American Psychological Association. http://dx.doi.org/10.1037/14711-004

Duncan, B. L., & Reese, R. J. (2015). The partners for change outcome management system (PCOMS) revisiting the client's frame of reference. *Psychotherapy*, *52*, 391–401. http://dx.doi.org/10.1037/pst0000026

Hollon, S. D. (2016). Developing clinical practice guidelines to enhance clinical decision making. In J. J. Magnavita (Ed.), *Clinical decision making in mental health practice* (pp. 125–146). Washington, DC: American Psychological Association. http://dx.doi.org/10.1037/14711-005

Hollon, S. D., Areán, P. A., Craske, M. G., Crawford, K. A., Kivlahan, D. R., Magnavita, J. J., . . . Kurtzman, H. (2014). Development of clinical practice guidelines. *Annual Review of Clinical Psychology*, *10*, 213–241. http://dx.doi.org/10.1146/annurev-clinpsy-050212-185529

Iozzio, C. (2015). Advances: Mobile technology—The doctor is in (your phone). *Scientific American*, *313*(2), 18. http://dx.doi.org/10.1038/scientificamerican0815-18

Lambert, J. M. (2015). Progress feedback and the OQ-system: The past and the future. *Psychotherapy*, *52*, 381–390. https://doi.org/10.1037/pst0000027

Magnavita, J. J., & Lilienfeld, S. O. (2016). Clinical expertise and decision making: An overview of bias in clinical practice. In J. J. Magnavita (Ed.), *Clinical decision making in mental health practice* (pp. 23–60). Washington, DC: American Psychological Association. http://dx.doi.org/10.1037/14711-002

Montgomery, K. C., Chester, J., & Kopp, K. (2017). *Health wearable devices in the Big Data era: Ensuring privacy, security, and consumer protection.* Washington, DC: American University Center for Digital Democracy. https://www.democraticmedia.org/sites/default/files/field/public/2016/aucdd_wearablesreport_final121516.pdf

Norcross, J. C., Hogan, T. P., & Koocher, G. P. (2008). *Clinician's guide to evidence-based practices: Mental health and the addictions.* New York, NY: Oxford University Press.

Wegner, D. M., & Ward, A. F. (2013). How Google is changing your brain. *Scientific American, 309*(6), 58–61. http://dx.doi.org/10.1038/scientificamerican1213-58

Yang, S., Kou, S. C., Lu, F., Brownstein, J. S., Brooke, N., & Santillana, M. (2017). Advances in using internet searches to track dengue. *PLoS Computational Biology, 13,* e1005607. http://dx.doi.org/10.1371/journal.pcbi.1005607

Zimmerman, J., & Libby, D. (2015). *Financial management for your mental health practice: Key concepts made simple.* Camp Hill, PA: TPI Press.

Index

About the Editor

Jeffrey J. Magnavita, PhD, ABPP, is a licensed psychologist who has been in full-time practice for over 30 years. He is nationally recognized for his innovative work and scholarship in psychotherapeutics, personality theory, unified psychotherapy, technology-based approaches, and clinical decision making. For over a decade, he led a supervisory group of colleagues, focused on reviewing videotapes of various approaches to psychotherapy in order to better understand both process and technical aspects. He is one of the leading figures in the Unified Psychotherapy Movement (UPM), he cofounded the Unified Psychotherapy Project (UPP), and is the editor-in-chief of the *Journal of Unified Psychotherapy and Clinical Science*. He has authored and edited 10 volumes, many of which have received high acclaim, and he has published extensively in peer-reviewed journals. He is considered a master psychotherapist and was featured in two American Psychological Association (APA) psychotherapy videotapes. Dr. Magnavita presents his work at conferences and seminars internationally. He served on the *APA Clinical Practice Guidelines Advisory Steering Committee* and is the past president of the Society for the Advancement of Psychotherapy (2010). He was the developer of *Psychotherapists-Face-to-Face*, which features eminent psychotherapists. His interest in improving the delivery of mental health care has led him to launch a new technology-based company called Strategic Psychotherapeutics, LLC, of which he serves as CEO. He is a lecturer in psychiatry at Yale University and was an affiliate professor in clinical psychology at the University of Hartford. Dr. Magnavita has been recognized for his work by numerous awards, including APA's Award for

Distinguished Professional Contribution to Independent Practice in the Private Sector (2006), Distinguished Psychologist of the Year Award from the Community of Psychologists in Independent Practice (2010), and Distinguished Psychologist of the Year Award (2016) from the Society for the Advancement of Psychotherapy. His most recent books are *Unifying Psychotherapy: Principles, Methods, and Evidence From Clinical Science* with Jack C. Anchin (2014) and *Clinical Decision Making in Mental Health Practice* (2016).